SLAVERY AND SECESSION IN ARKANSAS

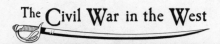

The Civil War in the West

Series Editors: T. Michael Parrish
and Daniel E. Sutherland

Slavery and Secession in Arkansas

A DOCUMENTARY HISTORY

EDITED BY
JAMES J. GIGANTINO II

University of Arkansas Press
Fayetteville
2015

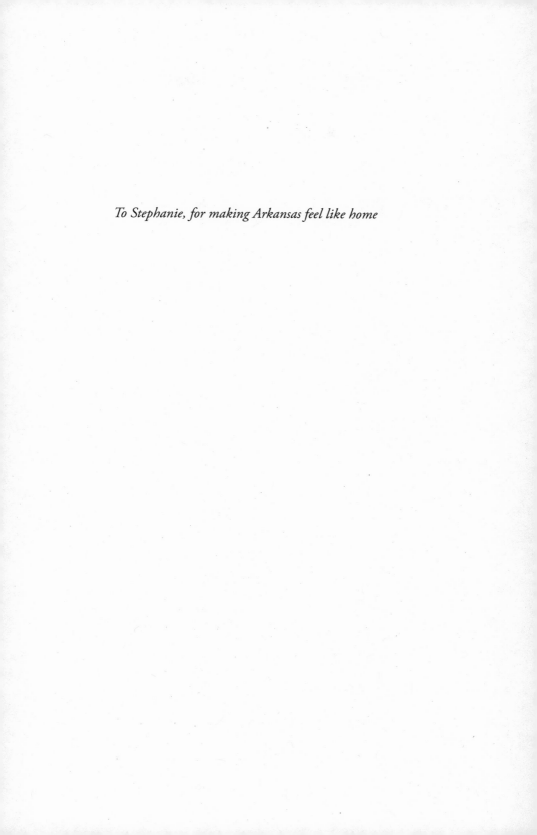

To Stephanie, for making Arkansas feel like home

Contents

SERIES EDITORS' PREFACE

The Civil War in the West series has a single goal: to promote historical writing about the American Civil War in the western states and territories. It focuses most particularly on the trans-Mississippi theater, which consisted of Missouri, Arkansas, Kansas, Texas, most of Louisiana (west of the Mississippi River), Indian Territory (modern-day Oklahoma), and Arizona Territory (two-fifths of modern-day Arizona and New Mexico) but also encompassed the adjacent states of Tennessee and Mississippi, which directly influenced events in the trans-Mississippi. It is a wide swath, to be sure, but one too often ignored by historians and, consequently, too little understood and appreciated.

Topically, the series embraces all aspects of the wartime story. Military history in its many guises, from the strategies of generals to the daily lives of common soldiers, forms an important part of that story, but so, too, do the numerous and complex political, economic, social, and diplomatic dimensions of the war. The series also provides a variety of perspectives on these topics. Most importantly, it offers the best in modern scholarship, with thoughtful, challenging monographs. Secondly, it presents new editions of important books that have gone out of print. And thirdly, it premieres expertly edited correspondence, diaries, reminiscences, and other writings by participants in the war.

It is a formidable challenge, but by focusing on some of the least familiar dimensions of the conflict, The Civil War in the West significantly broadens our understanding of the nation's most pivotal and dramatic story.

No event provides a better example of how the trans-Mississippi West encapsulates the broader war than does the region's response to the election of Abraham Lincoln and southern secession. Two of four trans-Mississippi states, Louisiana and Texas, joined the first wave of secession and helped to create the Confederate States of America. The Indian Territory could not technically secede from the Union, but the majority of its tribes sided with the Confederacy in the summer of 1861. The two remaining states, Arkansas and Missouri, rejected secession during the first suspenseful months following Lincoln's election, but then Arkansas became one of four southern states to reverse course and join the Confederacy after the attack on Fort Sumter and Lincoln's call for troops to put down the rebellion.

The absorbing collection of documents presented in this volume traces Arkansas's torturous road to secession and war. Drawn from contemporary pamphlets, broadsides, legislative debates, public addresses, newspapers, and private correspondence, it follows the intricate twists and turns of the political drama in Arkansas between early 1859 and the summer of 1861. From an early warning of what Republican political dominance would mean for the South, through the initial rejection of secession, to Arkansas's final abandonment of the Union, readers, even while knowing the eventual outcome, will find the journey both suspenseful and revealing.

James J. Gigantino II, who teaches history at the University of Arkansas, is the perfect editor for this collection. As an expert on the national clash between pro-slavery and anti-slavery advocates in the eighteenth and nineteenth centuries, he has selected documents that reveal both the unique features of the secession story in Arkansas and those features that Arkansas shared with much of the rest of the South. By focusing on one of the last states to secede (only North Carolina and Tennessee delayed longer), Gigantino is also able to take the long view of the secession crisis, and so illustrate the thinking of politicians and citizens in a state that reacted not in hot haste to the crisis but, instead, weighed carefully the benefits and dangers of disrupting the Union. With the nation's sesquicentennial observance of the conflict recently concluded, it seems fitting to reexamine those benefits and dangers and to consider how and why the Civil War erupted.

DANIEL E. SUTHERLAND
T. MICHAEL PARRISH

ACKNOWLEDGMENTS

As a historian of slavery but not of Arkansas, this project charted some new waters for me, and I owe substantial thanks to the many people who have helped me navigate them. Dan Sutherland, Larry Malley, and Mike Bieker all took an early interest in this project and helped give it a home, for which I am especially grateful. Patrick Williams and Jeannie Whayne, two of the most distinguished historians in the Arkansas community, read and commented on the entire manuscript. Their comments strengthened it immensely, and I am thankful for their time and enthusiasm in supporting me and the project. Finally, a special thanks to Misti Harper and Sarah Riva, who provided research assistance that sped this volume to completion.

Even though I have lived in Arkansas for over five years, it never really felt like home until I met Stephanie. Her love, support, and laughter, along with many hours of playing with Bosco, our four-legged friend, have enriched life beyond my wildest expectations. I am excited to continue to build our home in Arkansas together. I dedicate this volume to her.

INTRODUCTION

"What caused the Civil War?" has been one of the most debated historical questions in the last fifty years, especially among the general public. As historian Charles Dew noted, even the Immigration and Naturalization Service had a hard time coming up with a clear answer, recognizing both "slavery" and "state's rights" as correct responses for those taking the US citizenship exam.[1] The debate, however, is not merely about history. Instead, it is very much wrapped up in questions of identity and resonates for many today.

In Arkansas, as in the rest of the South, debates over the cause and conduct of the Civil War still rage, most notably in various local chapters of the Sons of Confederate Veterans (SCV), though the uncertainty of the war's cause continues to exist even in Arkansas public schools. Like the INS citizenship exam, Arkansas's 2007 "Social Studies Curriculum Framework" for kindergarten through eighth grade noted that, in grade four, students should "identify events that led to Arkansas's involvement in the Civil War," events that included "excise taxes, state's rights, and slavery."[2] At the same time, the Civil War sesquicentennial commemoration, beginning in 2011, allowed SCV chapters to reflect on the war's causes. The Seven Generals Chapter of Helena did just that on its website, The Arkansas Toothpick, when in January 2011 they promised not only to keep readers updated on "the goings-on in Arkansas 150 years ago" but also to "quell any myths as to the original causes of the War for Southern Independence."[3] A little over two weeks later, the chapter elaborated on the meaning of the earlier post, claiming, "Sadly, a lot of the people who are commemorating have that attitude . . . that the Civil War was a war fought over slavery." Instead, "as a majority of us know, the history books and lessons used to teach about the civil war in schools across the nation do not tell of the factual events of the war. They make it out to be about slavery only," even though Lincoln argued incessantly that it was not in the war's early years. More importantly, though, these history books "do not tell of the illegal tax and tariffs the Northern states were trying to impose on the southern states, which is what really led up to the rebellion and succession [secession] of the Confederate States."[4]

Like most things, the origins of the Civil War and the conduct of its leaders are quite a bit more complicated than many participants in these debates would admit. Southerners supported secession for a variety of reasons, which varied on individual experiences and relationships with the federal government and the institution of slavery. Most importantly, from Lincoln's election in November 1860 to Arkansas's secession in May 1861, opinions were not stagnant; they constantly changed based on events happening across the nation. Yet, in the words of those involved in the secession debates, slavery was spoken of often. Participants in these debates across the South in 1860 and 1861 openly discussed their ideas on slavery and fears of slave rebellion, of black equality, of amalgamation, and of the dangers inherent in abolition. It is their words, collected and reproduced in this book, that allow students of history to compare and contrast the different arguments for and against secession in Arkansas. Most speak to concerns over the future of slavery explicitly, while others raise concerns over issues that were stand-ins for larger concerns over the institution's future. Still others provide a larger context for the world that Arkansans lived in during this pivotal period, discussing events that influenced their decisions apart from slavery. Through an examination of these historical actors' real words, we can better understand why the Civil War began, the role that slavery played in the founding of the Confederate States of America, and why so many white Arkansans felt that secession was the only viable option left to them in May 1861.[5]

Slavery was the most important economic system and most valuable form of property-holding in the United States in 1860 and had been integral to the development of the nation from its very inception—historian Adam Rothman appropriately claims that the United States was founded as a "slave country."[6] The institution was, of course, not merely a southern one. Northerners held slaves, participated in both the Atlantic and interstate slave trade, and grew rich alongside southerners from the agricultural products slaves produced. At its very core, slavery pervaded all walks of American life for slaveholders and non-slaveholders alike.[7]

In Arkansas, like in the rest of the South, slavery was important economically and fueled the nineteenth-century growth of this frontier state. Even though Quapaw, Osage, Frenchmen, Spaniards, Englishmen, and Americans had lived in Arkansas for many years, Arkansas at mid-century remained more underdeveloped than most of the South.

The state had only achieved statehood in 1836, and its small population and desperate financial condition, due to a series of banking scandals, left it without many internal improvements. However, it did have fertile ground that sped migration to the state, especially in the 1840s and 1850s. Slavery was key to this growth as the number of slaves increased by 335 percent from 1830 to 1840 and by another 136 percent from 1840 to 1850. Cotton production similarly increased, from 6 million pounds in 1840 to 26 million pounds in 1850, as did the value of Arkansas farms, from $15 million in 1850 to $91 million in 1860. The 1850s heralded an economic boom that helped transform Arkansas into not only a strong agricultural power but a commercial center. The Arkansas River, flowing to the Mississippi near Memphis from the border with the Indian Territory near Fort Smith, linked the growing state to St. Louis, New Orleans, Cincinnati, and dozens of other cities along the Mississippi, Missouri, and Ohio Rivers.[8]

The meteoric economic growth seen in the 1850s, however, exposed regional tensions within the state. Plantations filled with slaves predominated in eastern and southern Arkansas while mountainous northern and western Arkansas had few slaves and far more small yeoman farmers. By 1860, almost 82 percent of the state's slaves lived in southern and eastern Arkansas, where slaves in some counties, like Chicot, made up 81.4 percent of the population. In comparison, slaves in Newton County in northern Arkansas made up only 0.7 percent of the population.[9] In the 1850s, however, average white Arkansans were less interested in the debates over slavery that had predominated national politics than in pushing for internal improvements, education, and economic development. For example, in 1860, the state had less than fifty miles of railroad and had only just been linked into the national telegraph system that year. What little Arkansas had accomplished with respect to education and infrastructure had come from federal lands and funds. The need for internal improvements led Arkansans toward the Union in greater numbers than in other parts of the South where fire-eaters, or radical proslavery advocates, had taken hold. Many Arkansans knew the state was not only too weak to stand against the federal government but needed it for railroads, telegraphs, and the recently federally financed swampland reclamation program that had reclaimed nearly one-tenth of the state's land. Equally important, those in western Arkansas were keenly aware

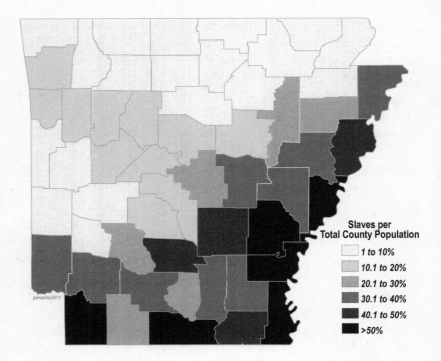

Slaves per
Total County Population

	1 to 10%
	10.1 to 20%
	20.1 to 30%
	30.1 to 40%
	40.1 to 50%
	>50%

paradise2014

of their dependence on the federal dollars spent to support army units stationed along the border with the newly created Indian Territory.[10]

Much of the resistance to fire-eating came from the domination of the state's political system by the "Family" or "Dynasty." Members of the Conway, Sevier, and Johnson families and their allies had largely controlled state politics since the late territorial period and had served as a level-headed political machine concerned more about preserving their power than becoming demagogues. By the 1850s, some of the Dynasty's newest members, including Robert Ward Johnson, elected to US House of Representatives in 1846, spoke vigorously against the perceived aggressions of the North, but the state's noisiest fire-eater actually made his career in opposition to the Family. Thomas C. Hindman, originally allied with the Family and awarded a seat in Congress for his support, broke with them in 1858 when he founded his own newspaper, the *Old Line Democrat,* to support his candidacy for the state's open US Senate seat. At war with the establishment, Hindman mobilized dissident Democrats, former Whigs, and the legions of Arkansans who had just recently arrived and lacked Dynastic loyalty in support of both himself and anti-Family candidate Henry Rector in the 1860 governor's election. However, amidst this violent factionalism, there was little disagreement over slavery. Both the Family and Hindman supported slavery's westward expansion and the quick return of fugitive slaves. Hindman, however, tended to be more of a political firebrand than the establishment, as can be seen through his speeches in chapter 1. He not only supported southern property rights and the return of fugitive slaves from the North but also advocated the reopening of the Atlantic slave trade in order for more slaves to flow into Arkansas and thereby depress their prices and allow greater economic development. Even though Arkansans clearly supported slavery's continuation in the nation, only Hindman exerted much energy on national battles over it.[11]

The four-way presidential contest in 1860 was likewise tame in comparison to those in other states. The Republican Party, which opposed slavery's expansion in the western territories, had no infrastructure in Arkansas, and few Arkansans were likely inclined to cast their votes for Lincoln. Since both the Hindman and Family sects of the Democratic Party distrusted Illinois senator Stephen Douglas, the nominee of the Northern Democratic Party, his idea of popular sovereignty—that residents in western territories should decide for themselves on the slavery question—failed to attract many votes. Instead, they threw their support to John C. Breckenridge, the Southern Democratic Party candidate who staunchly supported slavery's expansion and protection. Former Whigs and Know-Nothings, largely an anti-Family party since Arkansas had few immigrants or Catholics to attack, propped up John Bell and the Constitutional Union Party, which opposed secession and hoped to form a unity government to mediate the differences between the North and South. They helped give Bell a strong showing, but the majority of Arkansas's voters supported Breckenridge.[12]

Lincoln's election in November 1860 spurred on much debate over Arkansas's place in the nation and the continued importance of protecting slavery. Across the South, critics of Lincoln claimed that he and other "Black Republicans," the moniker southerners gave Republicans whom they felt supported black equality and civil rights, would encourage abolitionism, halt slavery's expansion into western territories, and further slow the return of fugitive slaves from the North. Fear was a powerful motivator among southerners scared of Republican domination; many in the South latched onto three key threats that they believed Republicans represented: the danger of racial equality, the possibility of race war, and the intermarriage or amalgamation of the races.[13] Many of these fears came from a misunderstanding of Republican sensibilities. Few were abolitionists and fewer still actually believed in black equality. Instead, most supported a free soil ideology, one that hoped to keep slave labor out of western territories, and some, including Lincoln, would rather have seen blacks relocated to Liberia by the American Colonization Society than compete with these newly freed workers on an even footing. Despite these realities, Arkansans and other southerners feared what they believed to be abolitionist and anti-democratic policies of the wholly northern Republican Party and said so repeatedly after Lincoln's election and during the debate over secession.[14] One of their main complaints, that the northern states had violated their constitutional responsibility to return fugitive slaves, had some truth to it. Numerous speeches and resolutions written by Arkansans in 1860 and 1861 and reproduced in this volume cite northern failures in returning fugitive slaves as one of the main reasons why the North could not be trusted to participate any longer in the federal compact. The protection of slave property lost through the lack of northern cooperation in fugitive recoveries was so great that many southerners believed it a primary reason to leave the Union. Indeed, the issue had been critical in the creation of the 1850 Fugitive Slave Law, part of the Compromise of 1850 that quelled sectional dissention after California's admission as a free state. Many northern states had, in the 1840s and 1850s, placed restrictions, called personal liberty laws, that impeded fugitive returns. They claimed that southerners had violated northern state's rights to protect those within their borders from unwarranted seizure. These laws infuriated slave-holders as they purported to defend northern state's rights against the rights of southerners to reclaim their constitutionally protected property. Slaveholders therefore argued forcefully for federal guarantees of protection from northern personal liberty laws. As historian Stanley Harrold has illustrated, this tension-ridden relationship over fugitive slaves precipitated a border war in the 1850s that created violent clashes, such as Bleeding Kansas, all along the border between North and South.[15]

In November 1860, Arkansans were faced with a difficult decision.

Those who had supported John Bell and the Constitutional Union Party, especially planters in eastern Arkansas, gradually allied with the two wings of the Democratic Party that had backed Breckinridge. Led by US congressman Thomas Hindman and his press, many in eastern and southern Arkansas pushed for secession to protect property rights in slaves. Chapter 2 reproduces numerous petitions, speeches, and debates from within the legislature, chronicling this debate during the early winter of 1860–61. These debates illustrate a growing gulf between western, northwestern, and northern Arkansas and the rest of the state, as upcountry yeoman, non-slaveholders, and those economically dependent on federal troops in western Arkansas opposed secession. Many of these Breckinridge voters, feeling abandoned by their former political allies, believed Lincoln's mere election did not necessitate such a bold move. Some even felt that the pro-secession Delta planters were plotting to further their own political power at their expense. Therefore, in general, support for secession was directly related to the percentage of a county's enslaved population. By early December 1860, few likely believed that Arkansas's secession was inevitable, as the state lay geographically divided over secessionism and slavery. Yet anti-secession's strength in Arkansas relative to other southern states does not mean that slavery played any smaller role in the debates over secession. On the contrary, discussions over the future of slavery in Arkansas and the nation at large remained vital to how Arkansans understood the benefits of leaving the Union.[16]

On January 15, 1861, after South Carolina, Mississippi, Florida, and Alabama had already seceded, the state senate agreed to call a state convention in March 1861 to discuss secession. Voters would, on February 18, vote on whether a state convention should be held and simultaneously vote for delegates to represent their county at the convention if one were approved. Four weeks of campaigning before the election, chronicled in chapter 3, set off debates across Arkansas both in favor of remaining in the Union and in favor of joining the Deep South in rebellion. The secessionist cause was helped when Albert Pike, a longtime opponent of the Family, wrote a stirring pamphlet distributed across the state that called for disunion. He believed that Arkansas needed to join the South in defending its property rights against northern incursion. Pike had, before the election of 1860, opposed Douglas's popular sovereignty concept and instead supported the unrestricted access of slavery to the territories in the same vein as the Supreme Court's Dred Scott decision, alleging that the Union could be dissolved if an individual state felt that its rights had not been protected by the federal government.[17] Likewise, most in northwestern and western Arkansas rallied around the idea that they were *cooperationists*, believing that although slavery needed to be defended, it was too early to consider leaving the Union. Instead, Arkansas could not secede on her own but needed to cooperate with the slave states of the upper South, especially its most important neighbor, Tennessee, in deciding how to handle the crisis. The vast majority of Arkansas Unionists would have classified themselves as cooperationists and hoped that a compromise over the issue of slavery could be reached in the Union.[18]

Before the election, however, the state was rocked by fears that the federal government had attempted to reinforce the federal arsenal in Little Rock. In November, federal troops under Captain James Totten had been transferred to the arsenal under routine orders. Pro-secession forces in the Delta, especially around Helena, spread rumors that federal forces would soon arrive to support Totten's troops. Hundreds of "volunteers" arrived from the Delta and pledged themselves to defend Arkansas against this federal incursion and seize the arsenal to prevent its reinforcement. Little Rock natives, unhappy with the increasing numbers of Delta firebrands arriving daily in their city, were angered when Governor Rector negotiated with Totten to surrender the arsenal on February 8. The arsenal crisis, though it ended peacefully, revealed the determination of pro-secession forces and further accentuated the divisions between Unionists and secessionists.[19]

The election on February 18 affirmed the need for a convention, with a vote of 27,412 to 15,826. Unlike other states, which returned larger numbers of pro-secession delegates to their conventions, Arkansas's Unionist/cooperationist contingent was stronger and returned five more seats than secessionists did. The majority of these Unionists/cooperationists came from northern, western, and northwestern Arkansas, while secessionist delegates came from eastern and southern Arkansas. When the convention assembled on March 4, 1861, the Unionist/cooperationist majority helped elect David Walker of Fayetteville as convention president. Chapter 4 details the discussions within the first meeting of the convention, which lasted from March 4 to March 21, and includes numerous calls for secession based on a defense of slavery and the rights of southern slaveholders. Likewise, resolutions that supported the Union as well as remembrances of the convention from delegates in the early twentieth century are also reproduced. During these roughly two weeks, the seventy-seven delegates heatedly debated secession, with Unionists/cooperationists seeking a mediated solution with support from other slaves states that had not yet left the Union, while the secessionists believed further negotiation would be unproductive. The majority of these men were either farmers or lawyers (73 percent) and almost two-thirds were slaveholders. In total, the delegates held 881 slaves, with the average holding among slaveholders at 18.7; and 17 of the 77 were planters, holding more than 20 slaves, while 30 held no slaves. Of the slaveholders, most supported secession, while Unionists/cooperationists held few or no slaves. The main difference between the delegates, however, was in their relative wealth. Those who supported secession had a median real property holding of $13,170 while those who opposed secession only had a $2,500 median.[20]

While the convention met in Little Rock, the state's newspapers continued the debate, noting national developments as well as raising fears of black equality and amalgamation just as their representatives did in the convention. As in other slaveholding states that had not yet left the Union, commissioners sent from the seceded states attempted to convince convention delegates to support the newly formed Confederate States of America. Arkansas was geographically important to a future Confederacy because of its border with the Mississippi River and its proximity to Missouri, whose secession was even more uncertain. Delegates from Alabama and Texas arrived in Little Rock to support secession, including Texan Williamson Oldham, a former Arkansas politician who now represented the Confederate government. Although Oldham likely did little to change delegate's minds, his words tell much about how politicians in the Deep South understood the importance of slavery in their decision to secede from the Union and why Arkansas should join them. A motion to secede from the Union failed and delegates instead voted to send representatives to a border state convention and work diplomatically with the federal government and other states to head off the looming crisis. The Unionist/cooperationist majority, however, made clear that it did not oppose war nor did it disagree with the grievances that pro-secessionists raised over federal treatment of slavery. Instead, the Unionists/cooperationists believed the nation needed more time to find a solution. The convention adjourned, able to be called back into session, if developments warranted, while citizens prepared for a vote on secession in August.[21]

In the aftermath of the convention, Arkansans continued to follow the national crisis and communicate with each other about the secession movement, especially as the state prepared for an August vote. However, the April 12, 1861, bombardment of Fort Sumter in Charleston harbor turned most Arkansans to support secession. As shown in chapter 5, tensions over secession exploded, especially when Lincoln called for 75,000 volunteers to suppress the southern rebellion. Indeed, Governor Rector rejected Lincoln's effort to enlist 780 Arkansans into the Federal army, claiming, "The people of this commonwealth are freemen, not slaves, and will defend to the last extremity their honor, lives, and property against Northern mendacity and usurpation." Leaders from other states, including Governor Joseph Brown of Georgia, tried to convince Arkansans to leave the Union in Fort Sumter's aftermath. In Brown's letter, he carefully teased out for Rector the unity that Georgia and Arkansas had, especially over their slaveholding, and how the federal government had repeatedly injured their constitutional rights to hold slaves. The immediate threat to slavery that Lincoln's call for troops presented, combined with their opposition to fighting fellow southerners, encouraged Arkansas's cooperationists to abandon Unionism. Even though many of the Unionists/cooperationists had always believed that Lincoln's government had threatened the institution of slavery, only Fort Sumter had convinced them that cooperation was no longer a viable option. Therefore, in chapter 5, fewer documents specifically mentioned slavery but instead declared that the time for compromise and cooperation was over. On May 6, 1861, the convention reassembled in Little Rock and debated secession yet again. Only five delegates now opposed it, with four of them changing their vote in an attempt to create unity as the fate of Arkansas was sealed. Arkansas joined the Confederacy in fighting the Union.[22]

In the end, the documents in this collection illustrate how Arkansans debated their place in the nation and, specifically, how slavery fit into their decision to leave the Union and fight alongside much of the South for four bloody years of civil war. Despite not having enough secession-ist support to leave the Union before Fort Sumter, the debates over the question heavily centered on slavery and its defense against a perceived aggressor. In this sense, the political leaders in the state held similar opinions to those in almost every other southern state. The only difference in Arkansas is that cooperationists held their ground against secessionism far longer, only faltering when the federal government asked them to not only endanger their property rights in slaves but also fight against other southerners. However, just because slavery encouraged the state's political leaders to leave the Union does not mean that the average Arkansan who fought the war believed the same thing. Men enlisted for dozens of reasons: for money, because they were forced to, either by law or by fear of retribution from their community, for adventure, or to defend their homes. In any case, the political leadership that started the war was likely far more invested in defending slavery than the average Arkansan fighting in the war—a truism that likely applies for most soldiers from any southern state.[23]

Editor's Note

Most of the sources included in this volume have been edited for both readability and space. All attempts were made to maintain formatting, grammar, and syntax from the original sources, though, in some cases, some spelling and grammar were changed to improve readability.

Notes

1. Charles Dew, *Apostles of Disunion: Southern Secession Commissioners and the Causes of the Civil War* (Charlottesville: University of Virginia Press, 2001), 4.

2. "Arkansas Social Studies Curriculum Framework," Grades K–8, revised 2006, amended November 2007, http://www.arkansased.org/public/userfiles/Learning_Services/Curriculum%20and%20Instruction/Frameworks/Social%20Studies/soc_studies_k_8_051308.pdf, accessed September 18, 2014.

3. "Toothpick Update (January, 2011)," *Arkansas Toothpick*, January 2, 2011, http://arkansastoothpick.com/2011/01/toothpick-update-january-2011/, accessed September 2, 2014.

4. "Editorial Regarding Recent Attacks in Pine Bluff Newspaper Website," *Arkansas Toothpick*, January 17, 2011, http://arkansastoothpick.com/2011/01/editorial-regarding-recent-attacks-in-pine-bluff-newspaper-website/, accessed September 2, 2014. For other Toothpick articles that have similar sentiments, see entries dated December 26, 2010, January 2, 2011, May 6, 2011, May 21, 2011, September 27, 2011, and February 17, 2012.

5. Dew, *Apostles of Disunion*, 10—12.

6. Adam Rothman, *Slave Country: American Expansion and Origins of the Deep South* (Cambridge: Harvard University Press, 2007).

7. Anne Farrow, Joel Lang, and Jennifer Frank, *Complicity: How the North Promoted, Prolonged, and Profited from Slavery.* (New York: Ballantine, 2005); James J. Gigantino II, *The Ragged Road to Abolition: Slavery and Freedom in New Jersey, 1775–1865* (Philadelphia: University of Pennsylvania Press, 2014), 3.

8. Thomas DeBlack, *With Fire and Sword, Arkansas, 1861–1874* (Fayetteville: University of Arkansas Press, 2003), 1–4; James Woods, *Rebellion and Realignment: Arkansas's Road to Secession* (Fayetteville: University of Arkansas Press, 1987), 6–7; Michael Dougan, *Confederate Arkansas: The People and Politics of a Frontier State in Wartime* (Tuscaloosa: University of Alabama Press, 1976), 1–3.

9. Woods, *Rebellion and Realignment*, 26; DeBlack, *With Fire and Sword*, 4–5; Historical Census Browser, 1860 Census, http://mapserver.lib.virginia.edu, accessed October 2, 2014.

10. DeBlack, *With Fire and Sword*, 4–7; Woods, *Rebellion and Realignment*, 45–49; Dougan, *Confederate Arkansas*, 3, 9–12.

11. DeBlack, *With Fire and Sword*, 8–15; Woods, *Rebellion and Realignment*, 70–87, 97–98; Dougan, *Confederate Arkansas*, 12–21, 23–24.

12. Dougan, *Confederate Arkansas*, 27–34; DeBlack, *With Fire and Sword*, 16–17.

13. Dew, *Apostles of Disunion,* 77–79.

14. For free soil and Lincoln, see Eric Foner, *Free Soil, Free Labor, Free Men: The Ideology of the Republican Party before the Civil War* (New York: Oxford University Press, 1970); and Eric Foner, *The Fiery Trial: Abraham Lincoln and American Slavery* (New York: Norton, 2011). For general overview of this period, see James McPherson, *Battle Cry of Freedom: The Civil War Era* (New York: Oxford, 1988), 202–75.

15. Stanley Harrold, *Border War: Fighting over Slavery before the Civil War* (Chapel Hill: University of North Carolina Press, 2010).

16. Woods, *Rebellion and Realignment*, 116–26; DeBlack, *With Fire and Sword*, 19–20; Dougan, *Confederate Arkansas*, 113–16; William Freehling and Craig Simpson, eds., *Secession Debated: Georgia's Showdown in 1860* (New York: Oxford, 1992), vii–xi.

17. Dred Scott v. Sandford, 60 U.S. 393 (1857).

18. Dougan, *Confederate Arkansas*, 39–41, 44; DeBlack, *With Fire and Sword*, 17, 20–21; Woods, *Rebellion and Realignment*, 125–26; Walter Lee Brown, *Life of Albert Pike* (Fayetteville: University of Arkansas Press, 1997), 349–51.

19. DeBlack, *With Fire and Sword*, 21–22. Also see Woods, *Rebellion and Realignment*, 127–29; Carl Moneyhon, "1861: The Die Is Cast," in *Rugged and Sublime: The Civil War in Arkansas*, ed. Mark Christ (Fayetteville: University of Arkansas Press, 1994), 4–5; Dougan, *Confederate Arkansas*, 41–43.

20. Ralph Wooster, *The Secession Conventions of the South* (Westport, CT: Greenwood Press, 1962), 158–60, 168–69; Woods, *Rebellion and Realignment*, 145.

21. Woods, *Rebellion and Realignment*, 141; DeBlack, *With Fire and Sword*, 25–26; Dougan, *Confederate Arkansas*, 54–58; Michael Dougan, "Secession Convention," *Encyclopedia of Arkansas History and Culture,* http://www.encyclopediaofarkansas.net/encyclopedia/entry-detail.aspx?entryID=6304, accessed July 1, 2014; Michael Dougan, "'An External Chitter Chatter Kept Up in the Galleries': The Arkansas Secession

Convention in Action, March–June, 1861," in *The Die Is Cast: Arkansas Goes to War, 1861,* ed. Mark Christ (Little Rock, AR: Butler Center, 2010), 20.

22. Henry Rector, quoted in Moneyhon, "1861: The Die Is Cast," 6–7; Dougan, *Confederate Arkansas,* 59–61; DeBlack, *With Fire and Sword,* 27–28; Woods, *Rebellion and Realignment,* 155–63.

23. Carl Moneyhon, "Why They Fought: Arkansans Go to War, 1861," in *The Die Is Cast,* ed. Christ, 53–74. Also see James McPherson, *What They Fought for, 1861–1865* (Baton Rouge: Louisiana State University Press, 1994).

CHAPTER 1

Approaching the Election of 1860

In the 1850s, Arkansas had seen massive economic growth, which had vastly increased the number of Arkansans with a direct stake in slavery, strengthened the power of planters in Eastern and Southern Arkansas, and further entrenched slavery into the economic life of the state. Even though slavery had become increasingly more important in the two decades after statehood, Arkansans took little interest in pursuing national issues related to slavery. Congressman T. C. Hindman, the first politician to actively use a pro-state's rights platform in Arkansas, would eventually come to the forefront of the secession movement and is indicative of the growing power of slaveholding newcomers in Arkansas. This chapter contains two of Hindman's speeches from 1859 and 1860 both of which challenge northern abolitionism and the Republican Party's accession to national power.

DOCUMENT I

Thomas C. Hindman on Federal and Arkansas Politics

Source: Thomas C. Hindman, *Federal and State Politics: Speech at Little Rock, February 15, 1859* (Little Rock: James Butter, 1859), 3–17.

In this speech, Hindman provides a historical context for how he understood his role as a states' rights Democrat.

He indicates that the debate over the rights of the states
and the centralization of the Federal government had as
"its most formidable development . . . the agitation of the
slavery question."

FELLOW-CITIZENS: As a freeman, born and bred in our southern land of independence, and as a State-Rights Democrat, without fear
and disdaining concealments, I have not felt at liberty to decline the
invitation to address you here to-night. I have had no wish to decline.
On the contrary, gratified by the compliment of the original request
and at its endorsement by such an audience as this, I rejoice that I am
enabled, under such auspices, to proclaim boldly, in this metropolitan
heart of Arkansas, whose pulsations are reputed to reach the uttermost
borders of the State, words of truth and honest counsel to the people—
words of warning and brotherly entreaty to the Democracy—words of
rebuke and stern defiance to the enemies of both. . . .

FEDERAL POLITICS—CENTRALISM AND STATE RIGHTS.

In the consideration of federal politics, I shall leave out of view those
questions which, however great in their consequences, are but secondary
in their nature, and will go beyond them to the principles from which
they emanate and which underlie the system. Every government is the
seat of a conflict, lasting during its life-time, based on the efforts made
to enlarge its powers and the struggles to confine it to its appropriate
functions. The pages of history are one unbroken record of these con-
tests, which are as continuous and implacable as the moral war between
good and evil. . . . The history of our own country affords evidence
enough, and that evidence is the only elucidation of our politics. It is
therefore proper, and I trust will not be tedious, for me to discuss some
of its leading facts.

After the war of the revolution, its blood-dyed "articles of confederation" were laid aside, like a dismantled battle-ship, on the score of
non-adaptation to the needs of the constituent States. The parties to
that league had made the government resulting from it their agent, giving it such powers as the "articles" expressed. When those powers were
resumed by the principals, the agency ceased and the agent died. That
resumption of powers was a separate act of each State, as an independent

sovereign, and, on the part of each State, amounted to what is termed "secession"—a right then deemed clear and unquestionable, but since vehemently denied. Simultaneously with the demise of the old confederation, a new compact, called the "Union," was formed, with the "constitution of the United States" for its organic law. It still exists, holding its lease of life and all its powers by the same tenure its predecessor did—the consent of each sovereign State whose agent it is.

The men of that generation, who were eye-witnesses to this summary destruction of one government and creation of another, by separate State action, could not reasonably question the right of a State to imitate that precedent in the future. They would naturally incline, one would think, to respect the creative power as first in dignity and importance, and to regard the creature as subordinate and dependent. The Union had been too recently made to be exalted above its makers. The facts within their own personal knowledge established, as the true theory, the doctrine that each State is a star of the first magnitude, and the Union the satellite of them all. Had this wholesome teaching been universally concurred in and carried out—had it been made the touchstone of every act and question—the shibboleth for all parties and politicians—comparatively few of the internal troubles that have been the bane of the confederacy would have been known. The same fraternal love that bound the States together in their early struggle for freedom would still unite them with its strands of gold. There would be no geographical parties—no sectional enmities and dissensions—no alienation of the North and South. As one harmonious band of brothers—animated by like impulses of patriotism—protected equally, in all our rights, by a just and well administered government—we would now be marching on, irresistibly, to unbounded greatness and prosperity.

But, unhappily, this was not to be. That same fierce thirst for power that had displayed itself elsewhere was destined to exert its baleful influence here. By an error of education, of temperament, or of the items, many leading spirits of the revolution honestly doubted the capacity of the masses for self-government. It was this sentiment, at the close of the war of independence, that seized on accidental discontents in the army and shaped them into a movement for the erection of a monarchy, with Washington for king—which movement the "father of his country" annihilated by a frown. The same sentiment magnified the defects of the old confederation and contributed largely to its displacement—chiefly because of the jealous strictness with which its articles guarded State Rights. The same sentiment, in the convention of 1787, proposed a monarchical plan, in lieu of the system adopted by the convention and acceded to by the States. The same sentiment, when the Union had been established, induced those entertaining it to desire the absorption by that agent of all the sovereignty of its principals, as the only preventative of anarchy and a relapse under European control. The part these men had taken in the revolutionary contest was dictated by a sincere hatred of tyranny, and they were as true to the cause as the most faithful soldiers of liberty; but they had no enmity towards the British form of government, administered according to its usages, customs and laws, denominated the "British constitution." With very slight changes, they wished to assimilate our government as nearly as possible to that. Central strength, in the hands of the favored few, was their ruling idea; State Rights and popular self-government their aversion.

Of this class, John Adams and Alexander Hamilton were types and leaders. Their deserved reputations as patriots and their abilities as statesmen gave them a commanding influence. The friendship of the great Washington covered them also with his mantle of power, and, before the close of his last administration, they built up a political party, controlling the government. The whole firmament then became tinged with the color of Centralism. Office holders and office-hunters made haste to profess the faith in public, and thereby the entire weight of the federal system was brought to bear in favor of centralization. The most heterodox notions were the off-shoots of this tendency of things. It was insisted, in gross violation of all the facts of history, that the Union was formed, not by compact between the several States, but by the people of all the States, en masse and as one people; that the constitution should be construed favorably towards governmental assumptions of power; and that the government was the sole judge of the extent of its powers. These heresies led to others, and one excess in error followed on the heels of another. Very soon, the sense of responsibility to the people was reduced to a shadow—the idea of accounting to them for official conduct was derided as demagogical, or as the wild vagary of a lunatic.

Thus, without the consent of the States, and without asking their consent, the character of the government was effectually changed and the constitution virtually nullified. But one short step was lacking, in order to substitute the kingly scepter for the republican liberty-pole. The once humble satellite blazed with a radiance so brilliant and dazzling that its creative stars were eclipsed by its lustre. To the eyes of the rulers, those stars were at best dim moons, shedding a borrowed and murky light, and revolving obsequiously around their magnificent, vitalizing sun—the Union.

Such was Centralism, and such were its effects under the teaching and practice of the old Federal party. Had it been made lastingly pre-dominant, how vainly would the blood of our fore-fathers have been poured out on the colonial battle-fields! To prove this, let me refer you to a chapter in the history of those days—whose incidents are often flippantly styled threadbare, yet had then, and have yet, and must con-tinue to have an influence on the rights of the states and the liberties of their people second only, if at all, to that of the secession of the thirteen colonies from Great Britain.

The French revolution, with its saturnalia of blood, burst on the nations like some frightful comet, filling the minds of men with horror. Monarchists in the old world, and their kindred Centralists in the new, gloated over its excesses, as proof that the masses could not govern them-selves. This was the prevalent sentiment, though were those who thought and said that much might be pardoned to the spirit of liberty, frenzied by the wrongs of grey centuries and reeling under the intoxication of tyranny's overthrow. Republican France, beleaguered by the armies of the kings of Europe, called on her American sister for a return of the aid given by Lafayette and his sovereign. To have acceded to this request would have been madness, and it was refused. But there was many a sympathetic response, as well from native-born citizens, as from French refugees then in the United States. The fervor of those responses irritated the Centralists in power, who resolved to stifle them by legal pains and penalties. In pursuance of that determination, they passed, in June 1798, "an act concerning aliens." The constitution at the time guaranteed the right of jury-trial in all criminal prosecutions, but this act nullified that guaranty by empowering the President, by his mere order, to drive into exile any alien obnoxious to him. With the same view, they passed, in July, 1798, an act usually called the "sedition law." The constitution prohibited Congress from making "any laws abridging the freedom of speech or of the press," but this law set aside those provisions, and made it an offence for any person to be concerned in "writing, printing, uttering or publishing" words calculated to bright either house of Congress or the President into disrepute.

Arrests were made and punishment inflicted under these alien and sedition laws. There was no grim and fearful Bastile in America, like that then just demolished in France, yet many a victim of Central tyranny groaned despairingly in the poisonous jails of the country. There was no remorseless Jeffereys, to enforce a despot's behests with hand and heart of iron, yet that English butcher had his imitators in our vaunted "asylum of the oppressed." There was no anointed king, exercising sovereignty in his own right, yet, by the predominance of Centralism, the elected President of the Union and his judicial appointees, were vested with authority over the free people of the States, almost equal to that of the Russian Czar over his serfs.

Patriots were justly alarmed at these rapid strides toward absolutism and tremendous assumptions of powers not delegated. At this juncture, Thomas Jefferson, the canonized "Apostle of Liberty," appeared as the Savior of State Rights and the Restorer of Freedom in America. Exerting all the enthusiasm of his warm nature, the force of his great intellect, and the influence of his world-wide reputation, he caused to be passed, by the Legislatures of Virginia and Kentucky, the immortal resolutions of 1798.

The Virginia resolutions were drafted by James Madison. I quote from them as follows:

> "That this assembly doth explicitly and peremptorily declare, that it views the powers of the federal government as resulting from the compact to which the State are parties—as limited by the plain sense and intention of the instrument constituting that compact —as no farther valid than they are authorized by the grants enumerated in that compact; and that, in case of a deliberate, palpable and dangerous exercise of other powers, not granted by the said compact, the States have the right, and are in duty bound to impose, for arresting the progress of the evil and for maintaining, within their respective limits, the authorities, rights and liberties, appertaining to them. . . ."

These are the words of Jefferson himself,—they were written by the same hand that wrote the Declaration of Independence, and are entitled to as high a place even as that renowned and sacred manifesto in the affections of the people. As it embodied an affirmation of the unalienable rights of freemen, and paved the way to their maintenance, so they embody, in terms that prove themselves, an assertion of the sovereign rights of the States, without which individual rights would have no protection.

On the issues thus made up, the great Presidential contest of 1800 was fought,—between Centralism, represented by Adams and the Federal party, and State Rights, represented by Jefferson and the Democracy. The enemies of State Rights then initiated a mode of warfare to which their descendants have since closely adhered. It was to prefer the unfounded charge of hostility to the Union against every man who insisted that the States ought to resist infractions of the constitution. Their persistent and false clamor of "disunionist," "ultra," "traitor," and the like, had then— as it has had in later times and is designed to have in the future—the effect to embitter many good citizen against the only doctrine really preservative of the Union as formed. But Jefferson maintained himself against these aspersions. He demonstrated that the true State-rights-man is the only friend of a constitutional Union . . . however boisterous may be his professions of devotion to it. The intelligence of the people was equal to the emergency. The Federal party was defeated and Centralism repudiated,—State Rights principles were endorsed and Democratic supremacy firmly established. Another somewhat more distant result, was the dissolution of the old Federal organization and the abandonment of that party-name forever.

But, though that first champion of Centralism has long been sepulchred in the golgotha of heresies, yet Centralism itself, still lives and grasps as greedily as of yore at the rights of the States and at the rights of the people. Its most formidable development has been in the agitation of the slavery question, and the right arm of its present strength is that mighty anti-slavery party of the North, called "Black Republican." Should that party obtain control of the government, and administer it according to the declarations of its authoritative platforms and recognized leaders, what would be the consequences? In the first place, the immense lever of official patronage would be wielded directly against slavery in the States,—every federal appointee, from the highest to the lowest, would be selected because of his hostility to slavery—Black

Republicans would be imported, fresh from Yankee-land, if necessary—and the means would thus be provided for implanting, fostering and strengthening anti-slavery sentiment in the midst of slaveholding communities. In the second place, the inter-State slave trade and slavery in the District of Columbia would be prohibited. In the third place, slavery would be forbidden in the territories, and no new slave State would be admitted into the Union.

The idea that the agent may rightfully commit such acts of war on its principals, or any one of them, is preposterous. The claim of right must rest on an utter denial of agency—on denial of a compact between the States—on the bold and dangerous assumption that the powers of the general government come to it directly from the whole people of the Union, as one consolidated nation. This is the doctrine of the Black Republican party. It is Centralism, in its most unmitigated form.

If admitted, the power is thereby conceded to the federal government, not only to overthrow slavery, but also to abrogate any other domestic institution, and to destroy any other property right whatsoever. It annuls the constitution—substitutes mobocracy for its saving checks and balances—and makes the will of an unbridled majority the arbiter of all State and private interests. This may account for the fanatical furor with which the agrarian masses of the so-called "free States" have embraced it; and the land-owners, the "merchant-princes," the "solid men" of the North may yet rue the day when they warmed this adder into life. It may sting them as venomously as it now stings the South.

Against Centralism, thus resurrected, but one party offers opposition. It is the same that Jefferson founded, and has now, as in 1800, his doctrine of State Rights for its corner-stone and main support. Between these parties, in 1860, a battle will be fought, as portentous and fearful as any combat of the bloodiest war. Compare with it, the Revolution, which established, and the contest of 1800, which restored our liberties, will lose their grand proportions and be dwarfed almost to mediocrity. It will be the life-and-death grapple of the constitution with its foes—the Armageddon, in this government, of Centralism and State Rights. If Black Republicanism triumphs, its shout of victory will be the dirge of the Union. The Southern States have been so often driven to the wall by the ferocious, brute force of the North, and have so begirt themselves with solemn pledges and recorded vows to resist this crowning outrage, that they will scarcely humiliate themselves by further retraxits and surrenders. If not, "the die is cast."

DOCUMENT 2

"That Black Republican Bible—The Helper Book," T. C. Hindman in the House of Representatives, January 19 and 20, 1860

Source: *Congressional Globe,* 36th Congress, 1st session (1860), appendix, 81–88.

Almost a year after his above speech, Thomas C. Hindman delivered this address while representing Arkansas's First Congressional District, which included his hometown of Helena in Phillips County. Phillips County, on the Mississippi River, was the second largest Arkansas county by population in 1860 and had the most slaves (8,941), 60 percent of its total population. The "Helper Book" that Hindman refers to, entitled *The Impending Crisis of the South*, was published in 1857 by Hinton Helper of North Carolina. The book criticized slavery as economically inefficient and against the interests of non-slaveholding southerners.

Hindman delivered this speech as part of the ongoing debate over the election of the Speaker of the House. John Sherman (R-Ohio), whom Hindman discusses at length, was the leading Republican candidate whom Democrats vigorously opposed. After multiple ballots, no candidate was able to gain a majority. Hindman accuses Sherman of being an abolitionist and discusses the important issue of fugitive slaves at length. The speech also refers to John Brown's October 1859 raid on the federal arsenal in Harpers Ferry, Virginia, which he believed had been orchestrated by the Republican Party. The speech uses a popular trope that southerners deployed against northerners, contrasting how northerners treated free laborers with how southerners treated slaves. In many instances, this was a strategy to counter abolitionist critics by purporting that the North's free labor system abused its workers far more than slavery ever did. Finally, the speech illustrates the belligerence for which Hindman was widely known.

. . . At the opening of the session, a formidable political organization, from the northern States exclusively, claimed control of all the offices to be filled. Its entire vote, lacking but three or four of a majority of the whole number, was concentrated upon a single candidate for Speaker—Mr. SHERMAN, of Ohio. If the principles and policy of that party had been at all national; if the antecedents of its candidate had been in the least degree conservative, there would, perhaps, have been no sufficient excuse for prolonged and unrelenting opposition on our part. After such resistance as would have saved our honor as a party, we might have made a virtue of necessity, and gracefully acquiesced in its success.

But in the present case the most conscientious convictions of duty allowed us no such alternative. The party opposed to us was, and is, that known as Republican—a title synonymous, in our estimation, with sectionalism, with hostility to State rights, with disloyalty to the Constitution, with treason to the Government, and with civil war, bloodshed, murder, and rapine.

That it is a sectional party is shown by the fact that it has no representative here except from the northern States, and that it sprang to life out of the festering prejudices of northern anti-slavery malignity, and is kept alive by appeals to those prejudices only.

That it is hostile to State rights, and disloyal to the Constitution, is shown by its openly avowed intention to keep the leading property interest of the South out of the common Territories, by congressional prohibition of slavery there, which the Supreme Court of the Union has solemnly adjudged to be unconstitutional.

That it is a treasonable party is shown by its nullification of the fugitive slave law, in at least eight northern States, and its persistent refusal to comply with the Federal compact for the delivering up of fugitive slaves. Not only is this done in that number of States, but constant efforts are made to add to the black list of recreant and dishonored sovereignties.

In the great State of New York, an appeal and petition have been circulated for signatures, requesting the Legislature to accomplish there also the nullification of the fugitive slave law, and the nullification of the Federal compact, by passing one of these shameful "personal liberty bills. . . . "

It may, perhaps, be not inappropriate in me now to digress a little from the lien of my argument, for the purpose of exposing, by fact of recent occurrence, that degree of blindness with which fanatics habitually look abroad in quest of imaginary evils—not seeing, or caring to see, real and terrible wrongs at their own door. I have seen, within a few hours past, certain proceedings of the Pemberton Mills operatives, in Massachusetts, published in the New York Herald of yesterday, which I ask to be read as a portion of my remarks.

The Clerk read, as follows:

Proceedings of the Pemberton Spinning Operatives and Strikers.

1. *Resolved,* That we, the spinners of the frame or ring spinning on the Pemberton Mill Corporation, have long enough endured the low prices for our hard labor—wages which are too low to live by, as we cannot meet our bills for the necessities of life with such a contemptible compensation for our labor as has been paid us for the past year.

2. *Resolved,* That we respectfully solicit a public investigation of the facts of the case, and a public exposure of the oppression and tyranny, abuse and obscenity, which have been perpetrated upon the female department of the Pemberton spinning room, from time to time, by cringing tools of a monopolist corporation.

3. *Resolved,* That such language, and such obscene behavior, such malicious abuse, as we have endured from time to time, perpetrated upon us by the menials and slave drivers in high and low places, placed over us to drive and hunt us down in our labor, from early morning until late at night, is more appropriate to the barbarous or dark ages than the enlightened age of the nineteenth century; yes, more appropriate to the slave-drivers of the negroes of the South than to the tyrannical monopolists of an enlightened community, who seek to make the condition of the white laborers at the North worse than that of the slaves of the South.

4. * * * * * * * * *

5. *Resolved,* That such abuses, such vile and oppressive means as have been resorted to, to still persist in crushing our every right and

just demand into a perfect annihilation, are too much for a brute creation to withstand, and much more for a white and intelligent community.

6. *Resolved*, That it is these wrongs, and this vile, tyrannical oppression, combined with incompetency of government, and wages so low that negro slavery is far preferable, and death sweet, rather than continued durance vile.

7. *Resolved*, That we believe a generous and just public will sympathize and investigate our affairs and our condition; and, also, after such investigation, every candid and unprejudiced individual, black, yes, even the despised negroes of an abolition community, as well as the white Anglo-Saxon, both high and low, will render the verdict, namely: that such abuse, and such oppression and wrongs, such mean, contemptible, tyranny over us, in the shape of sneaking, cringing tools to the meanest tyrannical dynasty that exists in the manufacturing world at large, having driven us to this revolt or strike for our rights and for justice at this inclement season of the year.

8. *Resolved*, That unless a different state of affairs exists in the future, both in regard to wages and in the mode of government over us, we will die on our strike rather than submit to such heinous and outrageous injustice from the Pemberton tyrants.

9. *Resolved*, That in the language of a noted anti-slavery agitator, in regard to the perpetuation of the Federal Union, we also say, that under these circumstances that now exist, and have existed between us and our employers, let the former Union and the present slide forever, *before they shall any longer enslave and abuse us.*

10. * * *

11. *Resolved*, That the above resolutions are the unanimous sentiments of the Pemberton frame spinning operatives; also, that the same are authorized by us to be printed in one or more or the public presses in this city.

LAWRENCE, *February* 14, 1859.

Mr. HINDMAN. From the paper just read, let the civilized world judge between the slaveholders of the South, who hold the negro in that subordination for which nature and nature's God intended him, and the false philanthropists of the North, who inflict, or consent to the infliction, on white men and women, of such intolerable outrages and grievances as are there set forth.

Mr. GOOCH.[1] Where do these resolutions come from?

Mr. HINDMAN. I get them from the New York Herald of yesterday. . . . In order to make their origin clear, I request the Clerk to read the letter that precedes them.

The Clerk read, as follows:

FARMINGTON, NEW HAMPSHIRE, *January* 16, 1860.

As I was reading the Boston Journal a few days since, the printed extracts here inclosed interested me very much, as they relate to the late Pemberton Mills, of Lawrence, Massachusetts. It so happens that it is not quite one year since I was employed there, in charge of a section of one of the rooms. I was removed from that berth on the charge of daring to sympathize with the poor operatives who were then out of the mill on a strike for justice and living wages. But the inclosed resolutions, which the spinners, in a body, passed, without a single dissenting voice, explain their feelings much better than I can at the present time.

The poor slaves were not successful in their strike. They were told if they would not submit to their present wages and situation, the owners would stop the whole mill, as they could not afford to pay any more for their labor. By this threat the most of the operatives were driven to submit; but a few of the most useful never returned to work, and still remain alive as witnesses of the tyranny and abuse of the masters placed over them.

I now see it stated in the papers that this Pemberton corporation has been doing a very successful business the past year, (which includes the time the poor operatives struck for living wages,) having made $150,000 for the owners. The above speaks for itself, and need not be commented upon by me. That the labor cost the owners less than the same amount of slave-labor would at the South, is without a doubt in my mind. Your statement that the northern operatives experienced not the commonest feelings of humanity from their masters, I fully indorse. And to prove it here,

---

1. Daniel Gooch (Republican-Massachusetts) served from 1858 through 1865.

I will relate an instance that actually occurred in the Pemberton Mills less than four months ago.

A woman went to her master and told him that she wished to be relieved from work, as she was sick. The master replied, "Go to your work, a woman can play sick at any time." The next morning that woman gave birth to a child. As your paper extract suits my ideas, though I saw it in the Boston Journal, I wish you to send me a copy at once—put my name down for one year's subscription. Send me the next issue and your bill, and I will cash it on the return of mail. Publish in your paper all I have written, with the resolutions, and let the Journal snap and snarl over his pets, for I have more to write in future, to give the corporation their just due.

HIRAM G. GOVE.
To the Editor of the New York Herald.

Mr. GOOCH. It strikes me that this matter is precisely as I understood it. That letter comes from Farmington, New Hampshire, from a man who had been dismissed from the employ of the company. He certainly is not in such a position, with regard to that corporation, as that his testimony should be entitled to a very high degree of credit anywhere.

Now, one thing further in regard to this matter. I cannot state precisely the amount which these spinners earn in the mills; but my impression is that they earn from one and a half to two dollars per day, working ten hours.

Mr. HINDMAN. What I said is true. The resolutions do purport to come from Lawrence, Massachusetts. The letter just read comes from New Hampshire. I shall not go into a discussion with the gentleman from Massachusetts upon the authenticity of that document, or upon the credibility of the person whose name appears as vouching for the statement.

It seems, however, that he is inclined to discredit and disbelieve whatever may emanate from one of these oppressed white laborers of his northern factories; but whether, if the same utterances had come from runaway negroes from the South, the testimony would not have been ample and sufficient, even for his satisfaction, is a matter of which this House can judge.

Mr. GOOCH. If the gentleman will pardon me a moment, I will say that, so far as I entertain opinions concerning slavery, they are not founded upon the statements of runaway slaves. They rest upon different testimony.

Mr. HINDMAN. As I do not propose filing a bill of discovery for the purpose of ascertaining the grounds of the gentleman's belief, I beg that he will not take up more of my time.

Mr. GOOCH. Go on.

Mr. HINDMAN. I said that the tenets and practices of the Republican party lead to civil war, to bloodshed, to murder, and to rapine. That is shown by John Brown's invasion of Virginia, and slaughter of her peaceable citizens. The Republican members here may now disclaim all sympathy with that old traitor; they may say again and again that they contributed nothing to his enterprise, either in men, money, arms, or favorable wishes; but until they shall have abandoned Republicanism, and repented their connection with it, a discerning and intelligent public will deride and spurn all such protestations.

These innocent lambs that now bleat so gently, under fear of popular condemnation, are the same men who wrought up the northern mind to that pitch of frenzy out of which John Brown's blood raid proceeded. By their maddening and furious abuse of slavery and slaveholders, they set on fire the brain of that old fanatic. Had there been no Republican party, there would have been no invasion of Harper's Ferry. John Brown was the tool of Republicanism, doing its work, and now, that work is done, Republican politicians cannot skulk the responsibility. The country will hold them to it, and will gibbet them for it, as effectually as if the hemp that strangled John Brown and his confederates had also strangled these his instigators, from SEWARD,[2] the author of the infamous irrepressible-conflict doctrine, down to his last made convert and disciple, the member from Pennsylvania. [Laughter on the Democratic side.] I refer to that member from Pennsylvania [Mr. HICKMAN][3] who has, on this floor, twice threatened to apply the teachings of SEWARD, and to reenact the conduct of John Brown, by mustering and marching

---

2. William Seward was a Republican senator from New York.

3. John Hickman was an anti-Lecompton Democrat, though in the election of 1860 he switched to the Republican Party and favored war after the southern states began to secede from the Union.

eighteen million northern men against the South, to whip her into submission to the higher law.

When that invasion is made, the price of hemp will go up, for our
whole crop will be needed to hang the Abolition soldiery; [laughter from
Democrats and the galleries;] but the price of arms will go down, for
we will take from our invaders arms enough to equip our whole population. [Applause from Democratic benches and the galleries.] . . . That,
sir, will be the fate of the invaders of southern soil. In the language of a
prominent Republican member of this House, "we will welcome them,
with bloody hands, to hospitable graves." [Applause in the galleries.]

This traitorous, sectional, and bloody Republican party is the one
that met us at the threshold of this House, on the first day of the session,
demanding the Speakership. Not content to rely upon its abominable
record, to which I have thus briefly adverted, it presented a candidate
with a still more abominable record of his own; thus adding to our sense
of injury the galling consciousness of intended insult. That candidate
has repeatedly referred us and the country to his congressional record
here, as the index to his opinions on the great question of the day, and
announces his willingness to be judged by that test. It is not my purpose
now to make a recital, in detail, of all his votes and expressions relative
to slavery, during his four years' service on this floor; but I have given
them particular examination, and the knowledge I have of them justifies the statement that he stands in the very front rank of Republican
ultraism. On one occasion, he insists upon the exclusion of slavery from
certain territory by congressional legislation; and then he declares that
new slaveholding States shall not be admitted into the Confederacy. At
one time he brands the fugitive slave act as "a savage and inhuman law";
then he stigmatizes slavery as "an injury to the master and a crime against
the slave." And, finally, giving full scope and vent to his abolition zeal,
he becomes a practical encourager of negro-stealing, and an assistant of
the underground railroad.

That this declaration may be distinctly understood, I refer members
to the proceedings of this House on February 28, 1856, as set forth in the
Congressional Globe:

"Mr. GREENWOOD[4] offered the following resolution:

---

4. Alfred Greenwood (Democrat-Arkansas).

Resolved, That the Committee on the Judiciary be instructed to inquire into the propriety of providing by law for the indictment and punishment of persons for the stealing of slaves in the Indian territory."

Mr. SHERMAN.[5] I object.

[Mr. HINDMAN.] Now, Mr. Clerk, the object of that resolution is defined by its own terms. It was to prevent interference, by professional slave-stealers of the North, with property in slaves in the Indian territory. That such legislation was necessary, that it was proper, there could be no question; that it ought to have been granted is clear to the mind of every one conversant with the facts. What was the course of the member from Ohio upon that subject? Did he, like a loyal man, like one willing to do justice to the property interests of every section of the Confederacy, come forward and help to accomplish that object? No; the very moment the proposition was made, he obtruded an objection to its consideration, thrust his enmity to it upon the House. Is there any excuse—any palliation for that action of his? I am aware of the fact that ordinarily a mere objection to the consideration of a resolution of this character does not commit the objector either to or against the matter objected to; but in this case that general rule is set aside by the subsequent facts. There is a particular reason given for the objection, and that reason is not left to inference alone. It is set forth plainly, distinctly, so as not to be misunderstood or mistaken.

Mr. GREENWOOD. If the gentleman who objected to the resolution will allow me, I will state the grounds for the necessity of it. The reason is, that under the law as it now exists, and under the decision of the courts, persons on the borders of the Indian territory can go into such territory and steal slaves therefrom and take them into the *southern States,* and there *sell them* with impunity.

Mr. SHERMAN. Being satisfied with the explanation of the gentleman, I withdraw my objection.

[Mr. HINDMAN.] Mr. Clerk, the character of the resolution of my predecessor; the fact that objection was made by the present Republican candidate for Speaker to its consideration, unanimous consent being

---

5. John Sherman (Ohio) was the leading Republican candidate for Speaker in 1860.

necessary; the peculiar nature of the explanation given; and the prompt withdrawal of the objection; all these circumstances point conclusively, as I think, to this, as the attitude held by Mr. SHERMAN on the subject of negro stealing. For the punishment of that crime, pure and simple, he would give no aid. The agents of the underground railroad might ply their trade and go scot free, so far as he was concerned. Stealing slaves and taking them abolitionward was, in his view, a philanthropic enterprise, not only not to be punished, but to be shielded by non-legislation and sheltered by well-put parliamentary objections. But when it appears that the thieves have strong pro-slavery proclivities; that they are "sound on the nigger question," and carry their spoils, not North, but South; that they put them in southern cotton fields, instead of transporting them to the mock freedom of non-slaveholding States; then the position of the member from Ohio changes; his action is reversed, and his objection is withdrawn. A pro-slavery negro thief must be punished by all means. To that there is no objection. Oh! no, sir; but an anti-slavery negro thief must not be molested. This is one of the beauties of the record on which the Republican candidate so complacently plumes himself.

It is not surprising, Mr. Clerk, that such opinions and sentiments as those which he is thus proved to have entertained and expressed, should lead him into other excesses. It is not at all strange or inconsistent, but perfectly natural and in character, that JOHN SHERMAN should cordially indorse Mr. Hinton Rowan Helper. He might have written the Helper book with his own hand and pen, and published it to the world over his name, without creating the slightest astonishment or inducing the least surprise in the mind of any man familiar with his antecedents. No wonder, then, that he so obstinately refuses to disavow the Helper doctrines. If he should disown them, he would repudiate the very pith and marrow of his own teachings. Sewardism, Helperism, and Shermanism are identical. The black mantle of Republicanism covers them all. It and they are one and the same. That they lead to violence and bloodshed, to revolution and anarchy, is shown not only by what I have referred to, but by the declarations of the archapostle of the faith. In his speech, made in the Senate Chamber, on the 3d March, 1858, Senator SEWARD used this language:

"Free labor has, at last, apprehended its rights, its interests, its power, and its destiny, and is organizing itself to assume the Government of the Republic. It will, henceforth, meet you boldly and resolutely here; it will meet you everywhere, in the Territories or out of them, where ever you may go to extend slavery. It has driven you back in California and Kansas, *it will invade you soon in Delaware, Maryland, Virginia, Missouri, and Texas*. It will meet you in Arizona, in Central America, and even in Cuba. The invasion will be not merely harmless, but beneficent, *if you will yield seasonably to its just demands*.

"It proved so in New York, New Jersey, Pennsylvania, and other slave States, which have already yielded in that way to its advances. You may, indeed, get a start, under or near the tropics, and seem safe for a time—but it will be only for a short time. Even there you will found States only for free labor to maintain and occupy. The interest of the white race demands the ultimate emancipation of all men. Whether that emancipation shall be allowed to take effect with needful and wise precautions against sudden change and disaster, *or be hurried on by violence*, IS ALL THAT REMAINS FOR YOU TO DECIDE."

Now, sir, if any proof could be brought forward that would afford a clearer conception of the aims and purposes of the Black Republican party than the extract which has just been read, it will be found in the "crystallized platform," as my friend from Ohio [Mr. Cox] would express it, contained in that Black Republican bible, the Helper book. Here it is:

The banner to stand or die by

Inscribed on the banner which we herewith unfurl to the world, with the full and fixed determination to stand by it or die by it, unless one of more virtuous efficacy shall be presented, are the mottoes which, in substance, embody the principles, as we conceive, that should govern us in our patriotic warfare against the most subtle and insidious foe that ever menaced the inalienable rights and liberties and dearest interest of America:

1. Thorough organization and independent political action on the part of the non-slaveholding whites at the South.

2. Ineligibility of the pro-slavery slaveholders; never another vote to

any one who advocates the retention and perpetuation of human slavery.

3. No cooperation with pro-slavery politicians; no fellowship with them in religion; no affiliation with them in society.

4. No patronage to pro-slavery merchants; no guest-ship in slave-waiting hotels; no fees to pro-slavery lawyers; no employment of pro-slavery physicians; no audience to pro-slavery parsons.

5. No more hiring of slaves by non-slaveholders.

6. Abrupt discontinuance of subscriptions to pro-slavery newspapers.

7. The greatest possible encouragement to free white labor.

It has been intimated that the brutal and bloody character of the Helper book has been exaggerated in some degree by gentleman from the South in this discussion. In order to remove any such impression, and show conclusively that we have been right in our interpretation, I read from the *Compendium of the Impending Crisis in the South*, by Hinton Rowan Helper, showing why Helper himself did not cause his book to be published in the southern States. It will be seen that he confesses that the failure to publish it there was *because he knew it to be insurrectionary and incendiary in its character.* . . .

This, then, is the platform of the Republican candidate for Speaker. No man holding such positions directly or indirectly, or refusing to disavow them, is fit to preside over this House; and no man who indorses him ought to preside over it. It is an outrage upon the South to propose it, and an insult to the conservative sentiment of the whole country to insist upon it. If these vaunted Union meetings of the latter days in the northern States are not all empty, hollow, and delusive—if they indicate the existence of any genuine Union-loving sentiment there—why is it that the tens of thousands of voters taking part in them are not now thundering against this Black Republican phalanx, which is trampling the spirit of Unionism under foot by striving to force such a man upon us as our presiding officer? Why do they not proclaim their indignation against Sewardism, Helperism, Shermanism, Republicanism, and instruct out of their seats the members who adhere to either of them? That would be some practical evidence of a returning sense of justice and renewed devotion to the Union. Until such evidence shall be given, southern men must not only be pardoned in doubting the sincerity of these Union demonstrations, but the facts will demand that they shall hold them in contempt, as hypocritical and treacherous.

The responsibility for the failure to organize, with all the consequences of injury to the Government and disaster to private citizens, rests chiefly on the Republican party. Had it not been a sectional, aggressive, and unconstitutional party; had not its candidate for Speaker been an indorser of treason and incendiarism, and a preacher of servile war and murder, no such delay could have taken place. The House would long ago have been organized. . . . [T]he further cost of [the Republican Party] continuing to live shall be the destruction of the Union itself.

FRIDAY, *January* 20, 1860.

. . . Mr. SHERMAN. . . . Mr. Clerk. I said, when I rose the other day, that my public opinions were on record. I say so now. Gentlemen upon the other side have said that they have examined that record to ascertain what my political opinions were. They will look in vain for anything tending to excite insurrection, to disturb the peace, to invade the rights of the States, to alienate the North and South from each other, or to loosen the ties of fraternal fellowship by which our people have been, and should be, bound together. I am for the Union and the Constitution, with all the compromises under which it was formed, and all the obligations which it imposes. This has always been my position; and these opinions have been avowed by me on this floor, and stand now upon your records. . . .

It is true that the other day one gentleman did say I objected to the introduction of a bill. So I did; but, when the gentleman who introduced the bill made what I conceived to be a satisfactory explanation, I withdrew it. That was all I could do, and that it was proper for me to do. And, sir, the country will take notice that that is the only accusation made against me while I have been a candidate for Speaker before this House. If there be any others, bring them forward.

Mr. HINDMAN. As I am the Democrat referred to by the member from Ohio, will he permit me to refresh his recollection as to some other points which I made in regard to his record? I charged the gentleman with having previously advocated upon this floor the exclusion of slavery, by congressional legislation, from certain Territories. I charged him with having avowed his intention to oppose the admission of new slaveholding States into this Confederacy. I charged him with having branded the fugitive slave law, an act based upon the Constitution of his country, as a savage and inhuman law. I charged him with having stigmatized a domestic institution of the southern States of this Union as an injury to the master and a crime against the slave. Those matters are yet to be met by the gentleman, and I call his attention to them.

Mr. SHERMAN. In other words, I am charged with being a Republican. That is my offense; none other. I have never sought to invade the rights of the southern States. I have never sought to trample upon the rights of citizens of the southern States. I have my ideas about slavery in the Territories; and at the proper time and in the proper way I am willing to discuss the question. I never made but one speech on the subject of slavery, and that was in reference to what I regarded as an improper remark made by President Pierce, in 1856. I then spread upon the record my opinions on that subject; and I have found no man to call them into question. They are the opinions of the body of the Republicans. They are the opinions which I now entertain. Gentlemen are at liberty to discuss these questions as much as they choose, and I will bear my share of the responsibility for entertaining these opinions. . . .

Mr. HINDMAN. I desire not to call the attention of the House back to the explanation of the gentleman from Ohio, in reference to one of the charges I made against him yesterday, based upon his congressional record. . . .

It appears, then, that in the first place, the resolution of my predecessor was, on the face of it, leveled against negro stealing simply—a crime perpetrated for the most part by men of northern birth and residence. The member from Ohio stood in his place here, objecting to any action, under the evident impression that it was aimed at some of his northern compatriots. Then my predecessor explained that the resolution was not directed against abolition negro thieves only—the region of the country occupied by the slaveholding Indians being too far remote for their depredations—but that its object was to punish pro-slavery negro thieves; to punish men who stole negroes, carried them South, and sold them into slavery. Then it was that the gentleman from Ohio found the explanation satisfactory and withdrew his objection. Why was the objection made in the first instance? Why was it withdrawn? Do not all these record facts sustain the charge I have made? He said here, just now, that as to the other charges I preferred against him, based on his congressional record, they amounted to nothing more than the assertion that he was a Republican; and as to this latter charge of favoring negro thieving, that it was of no consequence. Now, I put it to him, I put it to the country, to say whether or not it is an unimportant matter that a member of the Federal Congress, a man recognized as the congressional leader of a political party, great in numbers, if great in nothing else, should consider it a matter of small moment that his record here practically commits him in favor of the plunder and theft of southern slave property?

What is his explanation? He says that when the resolution, as first introduced, was satisfactorily explained, he withdrew his objection. Will the gentleman state why the explanation satisfied him? Why did he first object, and subsequently withdraw his objection? What was there in the explanation made by my predecessor that was satisfactory to his mind? What was there in that explanation that induced him to cease his opposition to the consideration of the resolution? Can there by any other implication—can there be any other inference, whatever—than that, in his own heart of hearts, he looked with favor on the practices of those northern men who try to sap the foundations of the institution of slavery by constantly robbing us of our property? What other explanation can there be of that act, than that—regarding slavery, as he had before said, as not only an injury to the master, but a crime against the slave—he considered it also a crime to punish those men who strike at the foundation of the institution, by robbing our people of their negroes? If he occupied any other position than that, let him now make an explanation before the country.

He declines doing so. Then what is there to delay the pronouncing of judgment here against him, as guilty of encouraging negro-stealing? He says that when I charged him with having declared that slavery should be excluded by congressional legislation from the Territories of the Union, and when I said he had declared himself opposed to the admission of new slave States, I simply alleged, in effect, that he was a Republican. I ask him now to answer here this question: Is it the position of the Republican party, that when the people of any of the Territories, claiming and exercising the right to form and regulate their own domestic institutions in their own way, shall present a State constitution establishing slavery in that proposed new State—is it, I ask the gentleman, and I ask his colleagues of the Republican party, the position of that party, that such new State shall not be admitted into the Union, and that the people of a Territory shall not be permitted to have slavery, even if they desire it? . . .

MR. SHERMAN. I refer the gentleman to the platform of my party on which I stand. The gentleman knows where to find it. If he finds the Philadelphia platform, he will find my doctrines. . . .

Mr. HINDMAN. I believe the gentleman is one of the Representatives from the State of Ohio. What is your position upon the subject of the admission of new slaveholding States into this Confederacy? Will you vote for it?

Mr. EDGERTON. The gentleman asks me a question. I will say to him that, when the proper time comes, I will answer his question. . . . I will say further, that the Representatives from the State of Ohio do not admit the right of the Representative from the State of Arkansas to put them upon the witness stand. . . .

Mr. COX.[6] The gentleman will find the resolutions of the Republican Legislature, "joint resolutions in relation to slavery and the extension thereof," published in the General Laws of Ohio, page 298.

Mr. EDGERTON.[7] What date?

Mr. COX. The 17th day of April, 1857—a Republican Legislature. The third resolution reads:

> *Resolved,* That our Senators and Representatives in Congress are hereby requested to vote against the admission of any State into the Union, unless slavery or involuntary servitude, except for crime, be excluded from the constitution thereof. . . .

Mr. CAREY.[8] I am from Ohio, and I am the oldest man in Congress from that State. I have no delicacy or hesitation in saying to the House and to the world, that I adopt fully that resolution.

Mr. HINDMAN. I thank you, sir, for that confession; and now I ask the other members of the Ohio delegation to evince equal nerve and

---

6. Representative Samuel Cox (Democrat-Ohio).
7. Representative Sidney Edgerton (Republican-Ohio).
8. Representative John Carey (Republican-Ohio).

manliness, and say what position they occupy. I appeal to the candidate of the Republican party to follow this example, and to say whether he, in like manner with his colleague, will obey the instructions of the Legislature of Ohio? What position does he occupy on that subject?

Mr. EDGERTON sought the floor.

Mr. HINDMAN. Wait for one moment, until this gentleman answers.

Mr. SHERMAN, (in his seat.) I decline to answer.

Mr. EDGERTON. While I do not admit the right—

Mr. HINDMAN. Wait one moment. I simply desire to make a note of the fact, that the Republican candidate for Speaker refuses, positively, to respond to the inquiry I addressed to him.

Mr. EDGERTON. While I do not admit the right of Arkansas to interrogate the great State of Ohio, yet I have no hesitation in giving my opinion. I will read my opinion. It is already in language.

Mr. HINDMAN. I intend to act justly by the gentleman. I intend to act fairly by him. He must act fairly with me. I ask him to give his own opinion, and not to interpolate a long document into my remarks. [Cries from the Republican benches, "Read!"]

Mr. EDGERTON. My opinion is expressed here.

Mr. HINDMAN. I ask you for your intention. What do you intend to do? Will you obey the request of your State Legislature? Answer yes or no, if you are disposed to give an answer. To do that I will yield; but otherwise I will not.

Mr. EDGERTON. If I answer at all, I will say to the gentleman from Arkansas, I must answer in my own way and in my own language, and not under the gentleman's dictation.

Mr. HINDMAN. If the gentleman declines to answer, he cannot have the floor.

Mr. THEAKER.[9] I for one, sir, say that I object to being interrogated, and then have an attempt made to put words in my mouth as to how I shall make my answer. I am one of the Representatives of Ohio upon this floor, and at the proper time, and in a proper manner, I will tell the gentleman and the House all of the opinions I entertain on this

---

9. Representative Thomas Theaker (Republican-Ohio)

vexed question of slavery; but I want that side of the House to understand that I am not to be interrogated, and then have words put into my mouth as to how I am to answer.

Mr. McKEAN.[10] I move that the delegation upon this floor from the great state of Ohio be committed for contempt, for not answering all the questions the gentleman from Arkansas can ask them. [Great laughter and applause on the floor and in the galleries.] It ought not to be tolerated that they should dare do such a thing.

Mr. HINDMAN. I second the motion that they be committed, not for contempt of myself, but for a contempt of the country and of the Constitution they are bound to support. [Applause and hisses upon the floor, and in the galleries.] And, sir, I call upon their Black Republican compeers to sustain the motion.

Mr. GROW.[11] I rise to a point of order.

> [There was much confusion in the Hall; members had crowded into the area and the main aisle, and just previously, members upon the Democratic benches, and the galleries, had broken out into cheers of applause on Mr. HINDMAN's seconding Mr. McKEAN's motion. When members had returned to their seats, and order was restored,]

. . . Mr. HINDMAN. . . . Now, Mr. Clerk, it has been show here today that the candidate of the Republican party for Speaker stands committed by his record in Congress to oppose the admission into this Union of any new slaveholding State, even if its people, with perfect unanimity, desire to have the institution of slavery among them.

It appears, also, that he has further strengthened that committal, announced by himself in a congressional speech, by refusing now to say whether or not he would comply with the resolutions of the Ohio Legislature. What, then, is the position he occupies?

The Constitution of the Union most clearly and distinctly provides for the admission of new States into the Confederacy, upon one condition only. What is that? That their constitutions shall be republican in form. . . .

---

10. Representative James McKean (Republican–New York).
11. Representative Galusha Grow (Republican-Pennsylvania).

What I want to call attention to is the fact that the Republican party propose to add a new test, a new condition, to the Constitution on the subject. They propose to put upon new States a disability, additional to the one imposed by the Federal compact. In so doing, they at once destroy the rights which the people of the States, who may be residents in the Territories, may have in the premises. They make the admission of new States merely dependent upon partisan feeling and anti-slavery prejudice. They declare that where the people of a new State shall themselves unanimously desire to have a certain domestic institution among them, they shall not have that institution; or, if they will have it in any event, then they shall not be admitted into this sisterhood of States, but shall remain outside, isolated, outlawed, degraded, and put under the ban of inferiority. That is the position of the Republican party, and that is the position to which the candidate of that party, by his past record, and his present ominous silence, is most distinctly committed. If such demands had been made by anti-slavery men in the Convention of 1787, the Union never would have been formed; for at that time all the States but one, I believe, were slaveholding. It is not to be supposed that they would have consented to a compact that would have precluded their citizens from determining domestic matters of this sort according to their wish, when forming new States. No, sir, not for a single instant. This Republican dogma of excluding new States, for such a cause, is a departure from the spirit of the Constitution, if not a violation of its letter. . . .

The onus of explanation is upon the member from Ohio. He owes it not only to himself, but to us upon this floor, of whatever party, and to the country, to get up at once and show that he is a man of brave impulses and patriotic feelings, by repudiating and spitting upon that foul and infamous book of Helper.

[CHAPTER 2]

From Election to Call for Convention

NOVEMBER 1860–JANUARY 1861

Abraham Lincoln's election in 1860 spurred debate in both Arkansas and the rest of the South concerning the Republican Party's plans to deal with slavery. From his election until mid-January, Arkansans debated the merits of secession and saw South Carolina leave the Union in December. By January 15, 1861, Arkansas called for a vote on a secession convention to debate the matter in more depth.

This chapter contains speeches, resolutions, and petitions concerning secession in the roughly two months leading up to the call for the convention election. Especially in the petitions from citizens across the state, the fears and desires of pro-Union and pro-secession sentiment can be seen. Fears that Lincoln and the Republican Party would end slavery, limit the return of fugitive slaves, and upset the racial order dominate these discussions for secessionists, while Unionists/cooperationists, especially in Northwest Arkansas, tempered that hysteria by arguing that Lincoln's election was not a tipping point and secessionists should not mistake a few abolitionist voices in the North as indicative of how Lincoln would act.

DOCUMENT 3

Governor Rector's Inaugural Address, November 15, 1860

Sources: *Arkansas State Gazette*, November 24, 1860; and
*Journal of the House of Representatives: The Thirteenth
Session of the General Assembly of the State of Arkansas*
(Little Rock: Johnson & Yerkes, Public Printers, 1861),
103–5.

Nine days after Abraham Lincoln was elected president,
Arkansas governor Henry Rector, in his first address
to the legislature, asked lawmakers to act on a series of
issues. Most dealt with the state's banking system, the
building of railroads and schools, and swamp land reclamation. Extracted here is the section where Rector asked
the legislature to examine the state's militia code, citing
the real possibility that slaveholding states might soon be
engaged in "unprovoked and diabolical warfare" waged by
non-slaveholding states. In what historian James Woods
calls "the most misconstrued speech in Arkansas history,"
Rector's address discussed perceived violations of the federal fugitive slave law by northern states but fell short of a
general call for secession, as earlier historians had depicted
it. Instead, Rector argued that Arkansas's interests were
aligned with the other southern states and that if any
seceded from the Union, Arkansas might be better suited
to join them, especially if the federal government took
coercive measures to reintegrate them into the Union.

MILITIA—I invite your most rigid scrutiny of the militia code,
which having, until recently been a dead letter upon the statute book,
practical enforcement has not, thus far, to my mind, displayed a necessity for amendatory statutes. Should any suggest themselves to you, as
important to the immediate and thorough organization of the militia,
it is well, perhaps, that they should be passed at an early period in the
session. For life and liberty may soon, in each slaveholding state, find
protection only behind the breastworks of the citizen soldiery.

It would be scarcely prudence, but more of cowardice in me, to disguise from you and our common constituency, what my convictions and sentiments are, touching the present threatening and perilous condition of our common country.

A most unprovoked and diabolical warfare, marked by ingratitude, malice and ignorance, is now being waged by the people of the non-slaveholding states, against the peace, dignity and independence of all those recognizing that institution. The "irrepressible conflict" is, and still will be going on.

The fanaticism of the North has well-nigh reached its culminating point; and the states stand trembling upon the verge of dissolution. Its march has been steady and onward, and its footprints marked by blood and treason; and it seems as unalterable as destiny, that sooner or later dissolution must come. . . .

What portion of the confederacy will be so infatuated as not to prepare for the coming of this sad event? What magistrate of the law will lull his people into fancied security, by promises of peace and safety, when an enemy is at their door?

God forbid that I should be an alarmist; that I should be insensible of the wide-spread desolation that would fix itself, like a pall, upon the American people, should disruption ensue. But I am not, nor will I content myself with anything less than a faithful exposition of my views upon this subject.

Eleven of the northern states, by solemn legislative enactments, have nullified, revoked and trampled upon the federal constitution . . . [and have] prohibited their officials and citizens, from aiding in the execution of the "fugitive slave law." By their action, the federal compact has been broken! *They have revolutionized* the government, and have left every other state absolved from its federal allegiance, and free, as an independent and sovereign government, to seek its own destiny.

But the question is asked, whether or not these offences, coupled with the election of a chief executive avowedly hostile to an extension of slavery, is cause, justifying, as a matter of policy, immediate secession.

To my mind, no farther *local* justification is necessary. Still, if the Union was severed to-day, leaving the slave states standing as they originally stood, sovereign and independent governments, [then] reconciliation and compromise might, nevertheless, be induced by moderation, and a free interchange of sentiment evolved by authority through conventions assembled by the northern and southern portions of the Union, respectively.

In view, then, of the bare possibility that the North may still be induced to retrace her steps, and award to the southern states the rights guaranteed to them by the constitution, I cannot counsel precipitate or hasty action, having for its object a final separation of the States, and breaking up of the Union.

Should any one of the southern states, however, prompted by a spirit of just resentment towards the North, deem it necessary to declare her independence, and assert a separate nationality, Arkansas, having like grievances and a common purpose to subserve, ought not to withhold her sympathies and active support, if coercive measures be adopted by the general government.

Under such an exigency, I should regard it as an imperative duty to convene the General Assembly, that the matter might be referred to the people for their primary action and advice.

DOCUMENT 4

Proposed General Assembly Resolution on the Election of 1860, November 19, 1860

Source: *Journal of the Senate for the Thirteenth Session of the General Assembly of the State of Arkansas* (Little Rock: Johnson & Yerkes, Public Printers, 1861), 116.

This resolution was offered soon after and in response to the election of 1860, citing the "aggressive fanaticism" of the North against the South. The resolution proposed the creation of a committee on federal relations that would be the first stop for many resolutions dealing with the sectional crisis.

Be it resolved by the General Assembly of the State of Arkansas, That we view with sorrow and regret, the result of the last presidential election, as it plainly manifests a spirit of aggressive fanaticism, which if not speedily checked will override the constitution and destroy the equality of the states.

Resolved, That we do not regard the election of Abraham Lincoln alone as a breach of our federal rights, but the spirit which prompted it, is cause for just alarm, and too plainly indicates that laws and compacts are of no force when opposed by the general spirit of fanaticism, which seems to pervade the northern mind.

Resolved, That we will defer to our older southern sisters, that if they choose to submit, we will abide their decision. But if they or any of them deem it wise and prudent to withdraw, we will regard it as our sacred duty to follow, and let the consequences rest upon those whose constant spirit of aggression induces the necessity of this step and evinces a desire to trample under foot the rights of states and individuals, and destroy alike our country and its constitution.

Resolved, That a committee of five shall be appointed by the President of the Senate, to be called the committee on "federal relations," whose duty it shall be to take this subject into consideration and report by bill or otherwise, at some early period of the present legislature.

DOCUMENTS 5–7

Newspaper Reports in the Aftermath of Lincoln's Election, November 17 and 24, 1860

Sources: *Fayetteville Arkansian,* November 24, 1860; and *Arkansas State Gazette,* November 17, 1860.

Arkansans followed the unfolding sectional crisis and debate in the state's various newspapers whose articles illustrated how average Arkansans were told of the dangers of Abraham Lincoln and the Republican Party. Familiar refrains such as concern over personal liberty laws and the perceived abolitionist leanings of the Republicans were present. The *Arkansas State Gazette,* hostile to both the Dynasty and Hindman/Rector wings of the Democratic Party, hoped that various factions might join together and form a Union Party to save the Union from its impending destruction. The *Fayetteville Arkansian,* aligned with the Dynasty, took a more strident tone.

Arkansas State Gazette, November 17, 1860

The election is over and Lincoln, the representative of the Black Republicans, is elected. The first announcement of this fact struck horror into many bold hearts, for the same wires that brought it, brought also the intelligence that South Carolina had seceded from the Union. That report, however, has been contradicted, and it is now hoped that the President elect will govern the whole people for the time for which he has been constitutionally chosen to serve.

In this emergency it is proper that our people should act upon wise and discreet counsels, and do nothing rashly or inconsiderately. Lincoln is elected in the manner prescribed by law, and by the majority required by the Constitution. Let him be inaugurated and let no steps be taken against his administration until he has committed an overt act which cannot be remedied by legal and Constitutional means. Then the people have the remedy in their own hands, for revolution is a second and an inherent right in all.

The main feature in the Republican platform to which Southerners object, and resistance to which has been advocated by Southern leaders even to a dissolution of the Union, is the declaration of opposition to the extension of slavery into the Territories. Upon this one idea the republicans fought the late Presidential battle and upon the converse of the proposition the Breckinridge democracy fought the same battle. It was wrong in the republicans thus to open the contest, and it was wrong in the Southern democracy to meet it as they did, for already in the minority even with their whole forces united they went into this contest as a divided house and their defeat was a forgone conclusion. . . .

The democratic party which is now defeated and no more, has, under one name or another, ruled the country, except at a few short intervals, for sixty years. Its members claimed that it was a "time-honored" party and that it was always the peculiar friend of the interests and the institutions of the South. The democratic party embraces the elements of disunionism at the South and this disunion element prides itself upon its party consistency. Then, if the Republican administration do no worse for the South than has been done by democratic administrations whatever we, of the opposition, may say, it will not be in the mouths of these democratic endorsers of the "time-honored" usages and practices of their party to condemn or oppose it.

Let us see what has been done by the "time-honored" democracy upon the subject of slavery in the Territories:

Mr. Jefferson, one of the founders of the party, and the author of the celebrated resolutions of 1798–9, was the author of the ordinance abolishing slavery in the Northwestern Territory.

As admitting the power of Congress to abolish slavery in the Territories, the States of North Carolina and Georgia, in ceding the Territories of Tennessee and Mississippi to the United States, made an express stipulation that Congress should not abolish slavery within their Territorial limits.

Mr. Monroe, one of the Presidents who was contemporary with the Constitution, approved the Missouri Compromise, which abolished slavery in all that part of Louisiana Territory North of 36° 30'.

Mr. Polk, a Southern democratic President, approved the Oregon Territorial bill which contained the Wilmot Proviso.

Mr. Pierce approved the Kansas bill, which, though it repealed the Missouri compromise, yet contained the Badger Proviso, prohibiting the revival, by that repeal, of the local laws of Louisiana Territory protecting slavery.

With these facts before them, the "time-honored" democracy would be inconsistent (a deadly sin in their party) by rebelling against an act of Congress abolishing slavery in the Territories: And the chances of dis-unionism are small if that be the only cause; for the doctrine as applied to the Territories of the United States, would be of no practical effect— the merest abstraction.

All parties have had sins to answer for in their day; and General Joseph Lane, late democratic candidate for the Vice Presidency, holds the democratic party responsible for the evils which are at present upon the country, saying that they *dodged their duty, dodged the Constitution, and dodged the truth!* For years we have believed and persisted in saying that the democratic party, with its two faced platforms made to catch the votes of extreme sectionalists both North and South, was dividing the country against itself, and that when the line come to be drawn the North being the stronger section would prevail. Few intelligent and candid men will deny that the democratic party made the republican party by its persistent agitation of the slavery question. All know that the republican party is not the controlling one of the country. . . .

The hope of the country is now in the Union party. With the history of other parties before it let its leaders avoid the shoals and quicksands upon which they have stranded. The Republican party is a party of onesides. It must fall to pieces of its own weight. The democratic party is already disintegrated. All elements of conservatism must unite and form the great opposition party to the republicans in order to save the country. We think the Union party is nucleus around which this great conservative element must gather. If so, its future is big with the destiny of the country.

Arkansas State Gazette, November 17, 1860

For the first time in the history of our Government we have a President elected exclusively by a sectional vote, and by the agency of a party organized geographically. The consequence of this departure from the chart of Washington and from the spirit of the Federal Constitution remains to be seen. We deplore—deeply deplore it—and yet as good citizens, it is our duty to make the best of it, and to acquiesce in it, as under the forms of, if not in the spirit and intent of the Constitution.

What our Southern countrymen may do, remains to be seen; but we hope their apprehensions will be soothed, if not assuaged by the fact that the House of Representatives as well as the Senate are to be conservative and cannot be wielded for destructive principles against the States of the South. We are well aware, however, that the apprehensions of the South come not from Congress but from the Northern States themselves—their Personal Liberty Bills—their Underground Railroads—their incendiary publications—their Judicial Decisions, as in the Lemmon case, and from that general feeling of hostility which the States of the north manifest against the States of the South, and which, as the South fears, must end in the revolution of the Federal Judiciary and thus in the overthrow of the Judicial, as well as the Constitutional protection these States have had since the foundation of the Government, and of the old Confederation. We hope and trust the newly elected President will avail himself of the earliest opportunity to cut himself loose from the passions and prejudices that have elected him, and so give a pledge to the now fermenting Southern States, a pledge that he himself means nothing, whatever his party or partizans may mean by the election.

Fayetteville Arkansian, November 24, 1860:
Black Republican Conservatism

The black republican journals which have been engaged during the canvass in soothing the South into a belief that Lincoln's administration will be scrupulously watchful of her constitutional rights, now assert broadly and positively that Abraham Lincoln is elected, and that the South will find that he will respect all her rights.

The Constitution of the United States as authoritatively expounded, not as black republican "higher law" men "understand" it, contains a provisions that "no person held to service or labor in one State, under the laws thereof, escaping into another, shall in consequence of any law or regulation therein, be discharged from such service or labor; but shall be delivered up on claim of the party to whom such service of labor may be due."

The Congress of the United States has passed laws, which are now in full legal force, to carry out and give effect to the foregoing mandate of the Supreme Law, and thus "respect the rights of the South," but, in the face of the Constitution and defiance of the law, nine Northern States where Mr. Lincoln's party is largely in the ascendant, and which gave overwhelming Lincoln majorities, have passed laws imposing heavy pecuniary fines and inflicting long terms of imprisonment upon anybody who may ask for the rendition of his fugitive slave, or invoke the Constitution and the laws of Congress for his protection against spoliation.

The recent action of the governments of Wisconsin and Ohio in the case of the rendition of fugitives from labor leave[s] no doubt as to how they "respect the rights of the South," and we have yet to learn that a single republican leader, editor, or speaker, has rebuked or disapproved their flagrant violation of the Constitution and the enactments of the National Legislature. We have also to learn that any one of the nine States whose statute books nullify the laws, has evinced the slightest desire to wipe out its resistance of the Constitution, and we have further yet to learn, where in the Northern States which have elected Mr. Lincoln, republican public sentiment has been expressed openly and authoritatively in favor of "respecting" the right of the Southern master to reclaim and recover his fugitive slave.

What meaning is there, then, in the bald assurance that, under the

Administration of a man whose election is the emphatic expression of the strongest antislavery sentiment—of the sentiment embodied in the unconstitutional laws to which we have referred "all the rights of the South will be respected?" Does it mean that Mr. Lincoln will do everything in his power to force the governor of Ohio, the judiciary of Wisconsin, and the legislatures of New Hampshire, Maine, Vermont, &c, to retrace their steps, and abandon the course of insulting aggression and robbery which they have pursued with impunity against the "rights of the South," under the cover of their official power, and under the express sanction of immense majorities of their people? Does it mean that Mr. Lincoln has led these nullifiers to believe that he shared their sentiments and approved their action in order to get their votes; but that now that he is elected, he will repudiate them, condemn their conduct, and use the power which they have given him in order to force them "to respect all the rights of the South?" Or does it mean that Mr. Lincoln will respect only such rights of the South as he and Sumner and Giddings and Lovejoy believe that he possesses? Is it the Constitution, as Mr. Lincoln and Mr. Seward and Mr. Sumner "understand" it, that the President elect will respect and enforce; or is it the Constitution as expended by the judges of the Supreme Court of the United States?

The South is not disposed now to be jolled by honeyed words or soothing promises. She wants clear, explicit, and unquestionable proof that "all her constitutional rights will be respected." She has trusted to promises long enough. She has kept her faith with a steadfastness which must excite wonder when we consider the amount and gravity of the wrongs done to her. She has never asked for anything more than the constitutional rights to which the only authorized expounders of the Constitution have declared that she is entitled, and we trust that she will never be content until those rights are not only respected but guaranteed. . . .

When public sentiment at the North progresses in favor of "all her rights," when the negro thief is treated and punished as the horse thief, when we cease to hear Southern men who own slaves vilified as "negro-drivers" and as the embodiment of all crime against society, humanity, and religion, when the Southern man ceases to be told that he has no right to the share of the public property which his blood helped to conquer or his money helped to purchase, unless he abandons his property and accepts the Massachusetts standard . . . when clerical firebrands cease to disgrace Southern men as mere lepers and Southern institutions as crimes against God . . . then . . . will have ground to believe that "all rights will be respected." . . .

DOCUMENT 8

William H. Faulkner to Sandford Faulkner Jr., November 22, 1860

Source: Faulkner Family Collection, Center for Arkansas History and Culture, Little Rock, Arkansas.

William and Sandford Jr., sons of Sandford Faulkner Sr., who wrote the story that accompanied the famous song "The Arkansas Traveler," corresponded after the election of 1860 while Sandford Jr. was in California. William Faulkner provides a good look at the general demeanor in Little Rock in November of 1860 and reports on not only the secession crisis but also other important personal issues, like Sandford's sweetheart, that remained prevalent in Arkansans' minds.

Dear Brother,

I suppose by this time you are in San Francisco if you have had good luck. I should have written to you before now, but I have been about half sick ever since you left, and in the last two or three weeks we have been in a perfect whirl of excitement here. The Presidential Election is over and Lincoln is President of the Northern States, the Union is as good as dissolved. South Carolina has gone out. All of her Congressman and Federal Officers have resigned. Senator Toombs of Georgia and Wigfall of Texas have both sent in their resignation to the President. Georgia, Alabama, Mississippi, and Texas are all holding conventions preparing to go out. The rest of the Southern States will follow.

The excitement here in Arkansas is great, and the cry is for a Southern Confederacy from all excepting some northern loving milk-sops there has been some pretty sharp words passed on the streets in Little Rock which came very near two or three times ending in a fight. I saw one Gentleman one Sunday evening offer to cut another ones Throat because he said he would be willing to shoulder his musket to force South Carolina back into the Union. Another man came near being lynched because he said he was willing to serve under Lincoln. It was Moody that told Dr. Young he would be the first man to cut his throat if he made a motion towards shouldering his musket for the Purpose of forcing any state back under Lincoln Administration. The other case was a man a lawyer by the name of Piney. He remarked that he was willing to serve under Lincoln and came near getting himself into trouble by it. The excitement has quieted down here some and it is a settled fact that the Southern states are not going to be governed by Mr. Lincoln.

All of the States South are arming. The Governor of Virginia has ordered the troops there to hold themselves in readiness for any emergency. The blue Cockade and minutemen are all the go now through the South. This State goes for Breckinridge by 10,000 majority over all other candidates. All the other Southern States have gone excepting (three doubtful) for him also. Missouri has gone for Douglass they think have not heard for certain. It is very close between him and Bell, in Kentucky and Tennessee the other two doubtful ones; it is very close between Breckenridge and Bell. The last accounts the Back Counties were rolling up big majorities for Breckenridge. He was some little ahead.

Now for local matters: our legislature are in session and the capitol has been quite gay with different kind of amusements. Agricultural Fairs, parties, and the Governor's inauguration also military parades. We had a tournament the last day of the fair. There were 17 knights entered (I among the number but did not get the Ring but once). Bob Stevenson carried it off four times (we had five Rides at it distance one hundred and twenty-five yards). Cozzens carried it off three times as Steverson was a married man he gave the crown to Cozzens, he crowned Mattie[1] Queen of Love and Beauty. All the Young Ladies are well and some ask about you every time I see them. I have seen your sweet heart Miss Ann Merrick two or three times since you left. She gets prettier every day and seems as if she could run you down into your boots at one look from them soft black eyes. A thing of beauty is a joy forever, "one look

---

1. Mattie was their younger sister.

from them eyes" ("What would you give to see them"). Tis better than a dream of Joy.

She sends her love to you, don't think that I am any way taken in that direction, she talks of you whenever I meet her. I'll tell her that you sent her a Kiss. Then I'll get ahead of you. Will you be jealous, but more anon. . . .

What are you and Major Brown doing? What kind of trip did you have over the Plains, and do you think you will like the job, if the Union is dissolved, I don't think there will be any need of the Major doing his work for he would not get any pay. He knows best though I suppose. You have had a rough time, have you now since you left home. Write to me and give an account of every thing and how you like the undertaking so far.

DOCUMENTS 9–12

Legislative Petitions, November 27, 1860

Sources: *Journal of the House of Representatives for the Thirteenth Session of the General Assembly of the State of Arkansas* (Little Rock: Johnson & Yerkes, Public Printers, 1861), 230–36 and *Journal of the Senate for the Thirteenth Session of the General Assembly of the State of Arkansas* (Little Rock: Johnson & Yerkes, Public Printers, 1861), 189–90.

Arkansans sent petitions to the legislature that concerned both the election of Abraham Lincoln as well as the secession preparations in South Carolina, which called a convention of its leaders on November 10, 1860 (to meet on December 17) and voted to leave the Union on December 20. Leaders of Phillips and Chicot Counties, the largest slaveholding counties, filed two resolutions encouraging legislators to oppose Lincoln's election and join with the other southern states in defense of "constitutional rights." The subsequent two resolutions filed on the same day indicate which rights were most important to legislators in Little Rock. The first, offered by D. L. Kilgore of Columbia County, where slaves made up almost 30 percent of the population, took a much more aggressive tone against perceived injustices done by the North to the South and indicted Lincoln for his hostility toward slaveholding. The second, offered by John Loudon of Sebastian County, where slaves made up 7 percent of the population, advocated a much calmer approach. Though it expressed discontent with perceived constitutional violations, Loudon's resolution represented the opinions of many conditional Unionists who did not believe Lincoln's election alone necessitated secession.

Resolutions of Meetings of Citizens of Phillips and Chicot County

INASMUCH as in the present threatening aspect of public affairs, common sense as well as patriotism dictate that every community in the south should speak out their views:

We, the people of Phillips county, in mass meeting assembled, entertaining the hope that our rights in the Union may yet be maintained, and believing that in any event the time is now upon us when a good understanding and united action among all the southern states can and ought to be brought about, resolved as follows, viz:

Resolved, That it is our deliberate conviction, that the legislature of Arkansas, now in session, ought to take prompt action toward bringing about the proposed southern convention, and should, forthwith, pass the legislation necessary to have Arkansas faithfully represented therein.

Resolved, That our legislature ought, forthwith, to take some official action to induce South Carolina, and the more hasty of our southeastern sister states, to join in with, and abide the well-considered action of a southern convention.

Resolved, That as a basis to such united action, and as an inducement thereto, our representatives should go to such convention, instructed to demand for each and every southern state, all her constitutional rights in the Union, or, failing in this, an independent Southern Confederacy out of it. . . .

At a meeting of the citizens of Columbia, Arkansas, and vicinity, held on the 14th day of November, 1860 . . . unanimously adopted

WHEREAS, Notwithstanding we are loyal people, and have ever

advocated the Union of our fathers, as guaranteed to us by the constitution, we do sincerely believe, from the recent election, that the rights of the South, and her institutions, will no longer be respected by the states of the North; therefore,

Resolved, That we, the citizens of Chicot county, do, without party distinctions, unite in the following resolutions:

Resolved, That the election of Lincoln and [Hannibal] Hamlin [to] the Presidency and Vice Presidency of the United States, is detrimental to our institutions, and ought not to be submitted to; and that we request our legislature to communicate these resolutions, at their earliest convenience, to our senators and representatives in Congress, and co-operate with our governor in calling a convention of the people of this state, to determine a mode of redress.

Resolved, That we recommend the legislature to pass such laws as will be likely to prevent any embarrassment of the commercial interest of the state that our political emergency may require.

Resolved, That we respectfully request that the legislature will, as soon as possible, organize and arm the force of the state. . . .

Resolution Passed in the House of Representatives

WHEREAS, The people of the northern or free states of this confederacy, have elected Abraham Lincoln President of the United States, *solely* upon the ground of his hostility and opposition to the institutions of the southern, or slaveholding states; thereby fully confirming the determination, heretofore evinced on their part, to no longer regard our rights, or their constitutional obligations.

And whereas, We have suffered much injury, unjustly, at the hands of the people of the northern states, inasmuch as they have robbed us, to the amount of many millions of dollars in value, of our property; and, urged on by a spirit of blind, suicidal fanaticism, continue to despoil us of our property at every opportunity, by every means in their power, not even hesitating to resort, in numberless instances, to the low, mean crime of theft; and, inasmuch as they have disregarded, violated and trampled upon the Constitution of the United States; by passing laws, in nearly all of their states, virtually annulling the law of Congress, known as the "fugitive slave law," and perpetrated against us many other acts of insult, wrong and injustice, such as denying us the right of passing through their states with our property; and denying us our rights in the territories purchased by our common blood and treasure; sending their emissaries amongst us to steal and destroy our property, murder our citizens, and incite our slaves to insurrection; while we have uncomplainingly borne the burden of the government by paying seven-tenths of the revenue, and they have reaped most of its benefits;

And whereas, In view of all these facts, and of his avowed sentiments, the election of Lincoln is an insult and a degration to the South, too grievous to be borne, and conclusively proves that if we submit to his administration, and the domination of the misguided party by which he was elected, our equality in the Union is forever lost; therefore,

Be it resolved by the General Assembly of the State of Arkansas, 1st, That our senators are hereby instructed, and our representatives in Congress requested, to refuse to take their seats in the Congress of the United States during the administration of the said Abraham Lincoln; *Provided,* That the other members of Congress from the southern states, or a sufficient number of them to reduce that body below a quorum, will do likewise.

2d. Resolved, That in order to submit this matter, and all questions pertaining thereto, directly to the people, this General Assembly deems it necessary to call a state convention, and authorize, by law, the election of delegates to the same.

3d. Resolved, That we favor the holding of a national convention, for the purpose of making a last effort to adjust the difficulties between the northern and southern states; and that a convention of the southern states is hereby recommended, and advised to take place at as early a day as practicable; and that the state convention, when assembled, shall be empowered to appoint delegates to said convention.

4th. Resolved, That strict commercial non-intercourse with the northern states is earnestly recommended to the people of this state, as it is now evident that we must, in self-protection, rely upon other sources, and upon ourselves; the sooner we adopt this course, the better for our ultimate welfare and prosperity.

5th. Resolved, That the State of Arkansas, by this General Assembly, pledges herself, in this alarming crisis of our country's history, to share the fortunes, and stand by her sister southern states in defence of their constitutional rights, "at all hazards, and to the last extremity;" she will not falter or hesitate in the plain path marked out by stern duty; she would say to an insulted and outraged South, be calm, be prudent, but firm and determined, let us demand nothing more than our rights, and, with the help of Almighty God, no longer submit to anything less.

6th. Resolved, That the secretary of state is hereby required to furnish the governors of the several southern states a copy of the foregoing preamble and resolutions, with a request that they lay them before their respective legislatures when convened.

Passed, 43–23

Resolutions Referred to the Committee on Federal Relations

Resolved, That although we regard the election of Abraham Lincoln to the presidency, by the sectional black republican party, as a great national calamity, and an event to be highly deprecated by all good southern men; yet we do not believe that the bare election of Mr. Lincoln, or any one else, to the office of President of the United States, according to the forms of law, under the American constitution, is sufficient legal cause for a state to secede from the American *Union,* and thereby throw off her obligations to the federal constitution, and assert her absolute independence.

2. That the secession of South Carolina, or any other state, from this Union for the above cause, would be no justification for Arkansas to follow her example.

3. That in view of the impending crisis precipitated upon us, unwillingly on our part, by the reckless spirit of northern fanaticism, it is the duty of every lover of American liberty to maintain the constitution, and to boldly assert, maintain, and battle for all of our constitutional rights in the Union, believing that we can the better secure and maintain all our rights in the Union, than out of it.

4. That if the irrepressible conflict cannot be resisted, and amnesty of feeling, and reciprocity of constitutional rights preserved and maintained by the individuals of the several states, then we should maintain our rights even at the point of the bayonet; but in so doing we should consult all our sister southern states, as well the border states as the more southern states, and present to the world a united and unbroken front upon a common cause.

DOCUMENT 13

Resolution Passed in the House of Representatives, December 3, 1860

Source: *Journal of the House of Representatives for the Thirteenth Session of the General Assembly of the State of Arkansas* (Little Rock: Johnson & Yerkes, Public Printers, 1861), 220–22.

As the secession crisis continued, many believed that federal troops garrisoned in federal installations in the South could be used to prevent states from seceding. The arsenal in Little Rock became a heated source of debate among the state's secessionists. Foreshadowing the eventual occupation of the arsenal and removal of federal troops there in February 1861, this resolution discussed the presence of those troops in the state.

RESOLUTION:

WHEREAS, The people of all the parties in the State of Arkansas, are now in a state of lively apprehensions, that their future peace may be disturbed by unusual and unknown invasions upon their rights under the administration of Lincoln, and being so, are, as an outraged people should be, jealous of all orders given by those in authority to the standing army, whereby in any event, their means of defence may be rendered less.

AND WHEREAS, it is known and ascertained by this House, that a company of infantry have, or are about to take possession of the United States Arsenal, here—a thing unusual, the same having been in the custody of but a few for many years, and in view of the likely consequent further disturbance of the peace of the public mind, by a direct line of march through the State of Arkansas, having been made by said company, to the capital for the purpose aforesaid, the reason whereof is unknown to this House and the people; in order then to prevent the already excited public from becoming more inflamed.

Be it resolved, That it is the sense of this House, that a communication from the governor to the people, informing them of the fact, if he should be so advised, that the purpose of sending the troops here, was not to fortify and strengthen the federal government against the state government, would tend much to that end—and, that if he should not be informed upon the subject to his own satisfaction, the expediency, if he should adopt such a course, of opening up a communication with the chief executive of the federal government, immediately, by which information might be obtained, would also meet with the approval of the sense of this house, as one of the means of arriving at the end desired.

Passed 44–19

DOCUMENT 14

Letter from Senator Robert Ward Johnson, December 3, 1860

Source: *Arkansas State Gazette*, December 22, 1860.

In a letter published in the *Arkansas State Gazette*, Arkansas senator Robert Ward Johnson argued that a divided Union was all but certain and that any southern state remaining in the Union would almost certainly lose any sort of political power within a generation because of the increasing power that free states would have in controlling the national government. In the end, Johnson warned Arkansans that the North would "abolish our property, elevate to the slaves in the political scale, give over the Southern white people to negro equality, and the Southern land to desolation."

. . . Blame who we may, and divide as much as we please upon the errors of the past and the authors of those errors, we must all agree that we are upon the eve of revolution, if not in it; and that with the body of the Southern States, under all circumstances must be ultimately found the true interest, the sympathy and the destiny of Arkansas.

I make no question whatever that by the 5th of March from three to six States will have withdrawn from the Union unless some action of Congress *shall induce a short respite.* I regard the secession of several States as a fixed fact. That the Southern States then left in the Union, a small minority, will be able to protect themselves for twenty-five years longer against the power and legislation of 17 Northern States, actuated by their present spirit, and the new free States annually to be admitted, no intelligent and unprejudiced mind will credit.

If this be admitted, it follows obviously as a necessity to our position, that the seceding States must be satisfied and induced to return, or the remaining Southern States will be found, sooner or later to withdraw and join them.

What then at this juncture is the most advisable course for Arkansas? Some would advise us to adhere to this Union, at all hazards. This they advocate in the face of the fact, undeniable, that our rights have been violated, the Constitution openly nullified by almost every Northern State; our social system denounced as an "evil and a crime," a national disgrace and that this "union cannot live half free and half slave," and that this war to give freedom and equality to the negroes shall never cease until that object is accomplished.

Some would say submit to everything, adhere to the Union, trust to the manifest interest and the returning sense of justice of the North, and much more of like folly, which I have not space or patience to repeat. These are *submissionists*. Their cousins would betray and destroy themselves and give up their country to a cruel ruin. They do not desire such a result, neither are they deficient in personal courage or patriotism for a different cause; they are only ignorant of the facts of the last ten years: or they are incompetent from some other cause, interest, timidity, or party prejudice, to comprehend them.

Others take fire at once, proclaim immediate disunion as the proper step for Arkansas and demand that the Executive and the Legislature now in session should proceed without delay to effect secession. These latter are too precipitate, if I do not greatly misjudge the public sentiment of this State. By the violence of their haste they would drive our State into the arms of the submissionists, which may God forbid.

The question of secession, with its justification, its expediency and rightful character as a remedy; has never been yet brought as an issue fully and fairly before the people of Arkansas.

The prevailing sentiment in this State is, that every fair and reasonable effort to obtain justice, and to reestablish effort to obtain justice, and to reestablish our rights, already violated, if not subverted, should be first exhausted by the South. That effort made, and resulting in failure, there can be no cause for doubt as to the duty, or apprehension as to the action of the state of Arkansas.

In this line of policy there is wisdom and safety for her; and a thorough unity of sentiment and action may be relied on among the people, if we pursue it. But those who counsel instant and violent action for this State, fail to recollect that our politicians have for years been engrossed with factions, rivalries, personal contentions and local interests, and that great national questions and national interests have not been the attractive subjects of debate before our people. Arkansas has not had the time or opportunity of South Carolina, with her thirty years of special devotion to the rights, interest and honor of the South, and a steady, incessant debate of all the great questions now upon us. Neither as in Georgia, Alabama, Mississippi, or Florida, have her people been called upon constantly for the last ten years, to consider of this great and grave question of secession. Neither is it recollected that Arkansas has none of the advantages of geographical position, neither the numbers, the wealth nor the credit, which render those States powerful and comparatively independent; but that on the contrary, she is wholly isolated, bounded by Louisiana at the south, by Tennessee on the east, and by Missouri on the north; three old and strong States, distinguished for their great commerce, wealth and population, and neither of whom have yet assumed a position. Would it be wise for the weakest to take the first step?

Arkansas, as represented by her delegation in the memorable contest of 1850, sustained the rights of the South, and opposed unanimously that wretched compromise which destroyed the equality of the South, and her just claims to the line of 36 deg and 30 min to the Pacific, and which by unsettling old questions and opening new ones, has entailed upon the South all her present insecurity, and upon the Union its present imminent peril. Arkansas, in the following year, after a thorough canvass, sustained the action of her entire delegation in opposing that compromise, and was the only State, except South Carolina, that did do so.

Her people are not the less jealous now of their rights, not the less true to the whole South. Arkansas demands, in a word, that this Union shall be restored to what it was in fact, when it was first ushered into existence, a union of peace of love, of equality to all the States, and protection alike to the person and property of every citizen. Our people have hoped that this may be done. They demand that the effort shall be made, before the final step is taken. But Arkansas now, as in 1850 and '51, will forever scout all talk of any further compromise on the subject of her rights. Her rights will have to be secured beyond question, and this Northern war upon them will have to cease. And if not so settled, all will then concur, that it were better that the South should dissolve with her persecutors, and that she should form a separate government, whose plain letter shall recognize our rights and property, and whose plain duty it shall be to give them protection.

At present we are bound to a Confederacy, whose various Northern members, by solemn action, executive, legislative, and judicial, destroy our property, whose people seek daily to degrade us before the world, proscribing and denouncing us in all relations of life, social, religious, and political.

I am free to say, that as one citizen of Arkansas, I would not be willing to remain in the Union with a fragment of Southern States, subject to the overwhelming power of a united North, and to the exalted fanaticism so universally manifested, and so religiously entertained by the masses as we know it to be. In the Union, after the secession of a material portion of the South, the remaining Southern States would become a small majority, and would be forever offending and provoking the one or the other of the great Northern parties. Too weak in numbers to form and constitute a great national party, every successive census would lessen Southern representation in Congress, whilst each period of ten years would augment the masses of the Northern people, and add to the number of free States, until we had become as contemptible in power, as they now regard and denounce us in the moral and religious scale. Ten years more would see us a petty slaveholding province; seeking safety under the wing of one or the other Northern party, denounced by the masses of both, and respected by neither—devoid of national principles, and from the force of circumstances reduced to become a mere band of mercenaries in every great national struggle. Defeated at last, and regarded with contempt and distrust, some great popular commotion would, in the name of God and human rights, turn us, abolish our property, elevate to the slaves in the political scale, give over the Southern white people to negro equality, and the Southern land to desolation.

Whilst yet the slaves are all in the Union we may protect ourselves; whilst yet there is hope to induce the seceding States to return, we may contend in the Union for justice and our constitutional rights at the hands of the Northern people.

But we should not condemn South Carolina and those States that may act with her. We should rather rejoice that they make the issue of our rights, before the Northern Giant shall have grown too great.

Too long the North have listened at Southern threats. The threats of the South have become masters of decision and laughter. No step less serious than that of South Carolina could have commanded a moment's notice in the political world. That State alone, if unsupported, will not command it long. It is for us to hope that a crisis has been reached, which will constrain reaction and redress. Long delay is fatal for us. Every effort to assert our rights, which fails, will serve only to strengthen the power of the government that is already in the hands of a party whose principles are the destruction of property, and of a man who reiterates in a thousand ways what he here openly declares: "We are now far into the fifth year since a policy was instituted with the avowed object and confident promise of putting an end to the slavery agitation. Under the operation of that policy, that agitation has not only not ceased, but has constantly augmented. In my opinion, it will not cease until a crisis shall have been reached and passed. 'A house divided against itself cannot stand.' I believe this government cannot endure permanently half slave and half free. . . . Either the opponents of slavery will arrest the further spread of it, and place it where the public mind shall rest in the belief that it is in the course of ultimate extinction, or its advocates will push it forward until it shall become alike lawful in all the States. . . ."

We should rejoice in the course taken by South Carolina. It is the only step to arrest a fatal end. We should hope that a few other States will accompany her, and thus manifest a power sufficient to sustain a movement throughout, if justice be not done and assurance given to us of our future safety, by all proper guards.

I now believe that this question can no longer be put aside. If the North will not give back to us the constitution amended, to declare beyond question what the supreme court declares its true and original meaning to be, when it was framed, when almost every Northern State was a slave State, and when Massachusetts even was the inflexible advocate of the slave trade, then we will know without doubt that she will never do so upon any future demand, but will continue this war relentlessly upon us; and we will also know that our time has arrived, that our only safety is in promptly dissolving this Union and forming a government of our own, whose people shall be our own people, and whose power shall be devoted to our protection.

We have grown up from our childhood in reverence for this government. We love this Union, and wish not to break it, but it is more than human to expect of us that we shall consent to see the powers which were conferred for our protection perverted to our destruction. We love this Union while it fosters and protects us as it was designated to do. We do not love it when it falls into the hands of those who refuse to us peace, respect and safety, and who proclaim our subversion and negro equality to be the "sheet anchor of American republicanism."

But there is hope for this Union, if not the South shall be true to herself. The North can never subdue us if she would. She must see, and the South should by her every act give her cause to see, that justice, equality, and future security must be the price of reconciliation. She will recognize this fact, at least and I feel some hope, though no great confidence, that our differences may now be satisfactorily and forever closed by means of a National Convention. The struggle will be fierce; but if the South be firm, and discharge from her service all paltry compromisers, men who become terrified at consequences and falter and bargain for people for a few years, as in 1850, at the cost of your rights forever, then, indeed a finality may be had, a Constitution that admits no equivocation, a public sentiment so sound as to ratify it by the requisite number of States, and a Union that may last forever. . . .

It is no time now to discuss the question of Mr. Lincoln's policy and his "overt acts," that the Northern States have committed enough of them against the Constitution and our rights, no one can deny. Enmity to our institutions and our laws, which are the same they have been, is taught at the North in all the school houses, preached in all the churches, and proclaimed in every political canvass, making of our affairs their special business, of our people their special abhorrence, and of our speedy disaster their special joy. It is no time to speak of "overt acts." The seceding States have settled that for us. They leave us. They will not return if justice be not had. We can not remain without them, and if we could

52   FROM ELECTION TO CALL FOR CONVENTION

many of our best people, impelled by their love for their children and their duty to remove them from ultimate disaster, would be forced to sell out to the new Northern immigrants and to remove to the seceding and friendly government.

Await his "overt acts!" It is a paltry device of the submissionist, invented at the expense of substantial truth, and a ten years' bitter war so palpable as to have wrought an alienation between the two sections (if not already a malignant enmity) wider than exists against England or France or any other foreign people.

I have confidence in the sound Southern sentiment and manly honor of the true citizen of Arkansas, though the State be derided abroad by ignorance and traduced at home by those who have no honest pride to shame them. . . . I have confidence in Arkansas and I invoke the love of home that resents insult to our State as a personal injury and stands faithful by the South and her Constitutional rights. I have confidence that her present Legislature . . . will not fail to speak of our wrongs with spirit—to declare and uphold the justices of the common cause which impels the seceding States to present position and which should not permit us to fold our arms and quietly suffer this government to invade their country or otherwise attempt coercion.

What position does the State of Arkansas take? Her Legislature is in session, what does she say? As represented in Congress heretofore her people have stood as soundly Southern rights as the straightest sect, and her people have never found fault with her representatives, but have indorsed their course. What will she now do? Such are the questions all over the country. Will she maintain her position, or will she break ranks and fly the field at the first onset, in the first great political battle?

. . . The people of Arkansas are Southerners, her interest and security all lie South, and her honor does not permit her to falter in this great struggle.

We should demand the prompt repeal of all legislation which is hostile to our rights and interest in every Northern State. We should refuse fellowship to every State, and deny the protection of our laws, to every people who refuse and deny them to our own State and to our own people. To this end, we should prepare and enact a retaliatory code and declare it to be "in full force and effect" after first allowing a reasonable period within which for the Northern States to retrace their steps and do us justice. We should demand protection in our rights in the territories by the general government, whilst it is our government. It owes that protection to us.

We should declare our sympathy with the seceding States, which thus sternly resent our common wrongs, and that this State will not fold its arms and quietly submit to see the great powers and forces of this general government directed towards their subversion and subjugation.

We should support the movement for a Constitutional Convention of all the States, petitioning Congress to that effect, through our legislature, that we might adjust and forever settle all such questions as threaten the peace and permanency of the Union, by means of amendments to the Constitution, or otherwise, to be submitted to the several States for their ratification.

The Northern States deny, in effect, that this Confederacy of slave-holding States . . . intended to protect and foster their own people. They deny and set at naught the decisions of the Supreme Court, our only common arbiter. . . . Should they now, in addition to all other outrages, refuse to go into council with us or refuse when in council to acknowledge our rights and give to us guarantees ample for our future security and protection from this war which is waged against us so relentlessly, it will become palpable to all that our time has arrived, that the government over us is our worst enemy, and that it behooves us as speedily as possible to dissolve it and form one of our own.

I do not believe that the Northern States will refuse to concede to us our just demands if we are true to ourselves. I do not believe that this Union will perish unless we consent to compromise and yield our rights away, or SUBMIT. . . .

But this letter is already too lengthy. There are so many points to which I would gladly have called special attention, and particularly to our Indian frontiers, and their disasters, and our troubles in prospect, when an abolition President shall have filled the agencies with abolition emissaries, and the Indian nation with abolition missionaries. The sorrow of the Indian will then come; and our peaceful frontiers will before our years elapse, find who are and what the tactics of such men as John Brown and Montgomery, with their lawless bands and Sharp's rifles.

DOCUMENT 15

Chicot Senate Resolution, December 7, 1860

Source: *Journal of the Senate for the Thirteenth Session of the General Assembly of the State of Arkansas* (Little Rock: Johnson & Yerkes, Public Printers, 1861), 215–17.

Mirroring the resolution filed with the House of Representatives the previous month, this resolution from the county with the highest percentage of enslaved residents discussed the dangers of Abraham Lincoln's election and the fears of many in the state over the perceived abolitionist intentions of the Republican Party. This resolution was also filed with the Committee on Federal Relations.

WHEREAS, The thirteen original independent states, "in order to form a more perfect Union, establish justice, insure domestic tranquility, provide for the common defense, promote the general welfare, and secure the blessings of liberty to themselves, and their posterity"— among the most important of which rights is the right of property in negro slaves—did enter into a bond of Union by adopting and establishing the constitution of the United States; and

Whereas, The Union thus formed has failed to accomplish the objects for which it was made, and is being converted into an instrument of oppression and degradation, by eighteen states against fifteen equal independent states, by the agency and machinations of a political party in the white-labor states, calling itself republican—which party, for more than fifty years, under different names, has been wresting with impunity from the slave-labor states, one constitutional right after another, one state and territory after another, in violation of solemn treaty stipulations—has never conceded a constitutional right where slave property is involved, without the surrender of some other constitution right by the slave states; has nullified, by state legislation, the laws of Congress made to secure the constitutional rendition of fugitive slaves to their owners; has trampled the constitution thus made, in the dust whenever it stood in the way of their mad fanaticism, has proclaimed a higher law than the constitution, the Bible and then blasphemed its author, and spat upon its divine precepts; has shamelessly engaged in arson, theft, robbery and murder against an unoffending people, singing paeans to its vile agents as martyrs to negro liberty; and

Whereas, This black republican party, with the aid of foreign immigration, has now attained to such huge proportions, as to be able, against all opposition, to elect *their* man to fill the office of President over an unwilling people, whose aim it will be to use all the means in his power, *covertly,* to secure the abolition of slave-labor wherever it may exist under the present government, and place the negro upon an equality with the white race. Therefore, we, the citizens of Chicot county, hereby ignore all past party names and issues, and cordially unite in the following resolutions.

Resolved, That the election of Lincoln and [Hannibal] Hamlin to the presidency and vice-presidency of the United States, by the sectional black republican party of the north, ought not to be, and will not be submitted to.

Resolved, That we believe in the doctrine and right of secession by the several states of this Union, upon sufficient cause, of which they are the sole judges, and that our only redress for past grievances, and only security in the future, is the speedy secession of the slave states.

Resolved, That in the view of constant slanders, insults and aggressions of the northern upon the southern states, to longer remain in the Union would bring upon us the merited contempt of the civilized world.

Resolved, That our legislature be requested by our representative, to announce our opinions, by resolution, as soon as practicable, and communicate the same to our senators and representatives in Congress, and co-operate with the governor in calling, at the earliest practicable period, a convention of the people of the state, to determine on the mode and measures of redress.

Resolved, That we respectfully suggest to the legislature to take immediate steps to organize and arm the forces of the state; and recommend that the surplus revenue now in the state treasury, and more if necessary, be appropriated to the immediate purchase of fire-arms, munitions of war, and the establishment of a powder-mill within the state, the more effectually to protect the state against any emergency which may arise.

Resolved, That we feel deeply grateful to our *brethren* of the north, who battled manfully, without hope, against a tyrannical majority, in the late contest for our constitutional rights; and trust, that should their rights of property be assailed, they may meet with better success. . . .

Document 16

Report of the House of Representatives Committee on Federal Relations, December 11, 1860

Source: *Journal of the House of Representatives for the Thirteenth Session of the General Assembly of the State of Arkansas* (Little Rock: Johnson & Yerkes, Public Printers, 1861), 290–96.

The members of the House's Committee on Federal Relations, after multiple petitions and surveying the political landscape in the South, submitted this report, which discussed the perceived abuses that the South had endured. Abandonment of the fugitive slave clause, abolitionist leanings, and attempts to promote black equality were included. The representatives argued that Arkansas's future was tied with the other southern states and suggested a convention of all southern states meet in Memphis in February 1861 to plan a coordinated response before Abraham Lincoln's inauguration. Of course, this meeting never happened as by early February all of the Deep South had already decided to leave the Union.

THE NORTH AND THE BLACK REPUBLICANS.

It will be admitted that the southern states have patiently endured repeated injuries and violations of their constitutional rights, by the northern states of this confederacy, in which the anti-slavery sentiment has been predominant. These aggressions have been continued until they have resulted in the present alarming condition of political affairs—until it is manifest to every man, who observes passing event, that "now is the crisis of our destiny." The existence, in great power and strength of the black republican party in the northern states, with all its sectional, odious and aggressive doctrines, is well calculated to inspire every southern man and patriot with dread and alarm. A brief statement will suffice, to satisfy all impartial men, that the aims and principles of that party are subversive of the constitution, and fraught with the greatest danger to the institutions of the South.

1. They advocate—the prohibition, as well as abolition, of slavery, by Congress in the territories, the common property, and purchased by the common blood and treasure of the citizens of all the states.

2. The abolition of slavery in the District of Columbia.

3. The prohibition of the slave trade between the states.

4 The repeal of the fugitive slave law.

5. The remodeling of the courts of the United States, that a majority of black republicans may be placed on the bench, and the constitution interpreted to suit themselves.

6. The equality of the negro with the white man.

7. The irrepressible conflict doctrine, that there will always be a struggle between the North and the South—free states and slave states, and that this Union must become all free or all slave.

8. They oppose the admission of any more slave states into the Union.

9. They have in the States of Maine, New Hampshire, Vermont, Massachusetts, Rhode Island, Connecticut, New York, New Jersey, Pennsylvania, Michigan, Wisconsin, and Iowa, by legislative enactments, nullified the fugitive slave law passed by Congress in pursuance of a provision of the federal constitution.

10. They have extended to the free negroes the right of suffrage in the States of New York, Maine, New Hampshire, Vermont, Massachusetts, Rhode Island, and Ohio.

11. They have assisted the fugitive slave to escape from his master.

12. They introduced into the House of Representatives, in Congress, at the last session, a resolution to abolish slavery throughout the Union, and it received sixty black republican votes.

13. They passed at the same session, through the same House, a bill to repeal the laws of the territory of New Mexico which protect slavery.

14. They passed an act in the territorial legislature of Nebraska, prohibiting slavery in that territory, and it was only prevented from becoming a law by the veto of the governor.

15. They passed an act in the territorial legislature of Kansas, prohibiting slavery in that territory and the same was vetoed by the governor, and they re-passed it over his veto.

16. Sixty-two members of Congress and other prominent members of that party, have indorsed the infamous Helper book, which counsels the commission of the most infamous crimes, such as murder and insurrection by our slaves.

17. They added insult to injury by attempting to elect Sherman, an indorser of that book, to the office of Speaker of the House of Representatives in Congress.

18. They have furnished us with a practical illustration of their theory in the raid of John Brown, and the butchery of a portion of the citizens of Virginia; and when the well merited punishment of death was inflicted upon him for the high crime of treason, murder, and inciting slaves to insurrection, they tolled bells, held meetings and pronounced him a martyr.

19. They have refused, on account of their hostility to slavery, to surrender fugitives from justice upon the requisitions of governors of southern states.

20. They have sent emissaries in our midst to destroy our property and incite our slaves to insurrection.

21. They have denounced the constitution and the Union, and promulgated a "higher law."

22. And to crown all, they have elected Abraham Lincoln and Hannibal Hamlin, to the Presidency and Vice Presidency of the United States.

In view of the fact, that the party entertaining the principles, and whose past history has been characterized by the acts above stated, will soon, to a great extent, obtain control of the federal government, it is not a matter of surprise that indignation, and apprehension as to the future safety and protection of their institutions, are now manifested by the southern people. . . .

THE COURSE TO BE PURSUED.

But the committee are well satisfied, from a review of the acts and principles of the black republican party, and the many concessions made by the South, which experience has taught us, have only served to increase, instead of diminish, northern aggressions; that it is time to take such a course of action as will secure an effectual demand for such guarantees as will stop and prevent present and prospective encroachments upon our constitutional rights—preserve the Union and make it answer the purposes for which it was created. It is now manifest, that there is a very strong feeling in the South against longer continuance in the Union, with those who have thus trampled on the constitution. Some of the southern states have provided for the assembling of state conventions, to consider the best course to be pursued in the present crisis, and others are taking steps to do so. In a few weeks, almost every southern state, if not all, will have followed their example. There is good reason for believing that several of these states, so soon as their respective conventions assemble, will withdraw from the Union. The incoming administration may attempt coercion, and a war will ensue for which history furnishes no parallel. The southern states are united by a common interest, and should consult together upon matters which vitally affect their common welfare. The committee believes that this should be done in a southern convention, to be held at an early day, at some point in the South. By this means rash and inconsiderate action on the part of some of the states may be prevented—an effectual demand made for such guarantees as will secure us against encroachments upon our institutions and constitutional rights—perhaps a disastrous civil war averted—the whole South united on a plan of action devised by her wisest and most patriotic sons, and the Union preserved on a firm, just and equal basis.

In conclusion, your committee would recommend as the only practicable solution of the existing and threatened disturbances of the peace of the country, the union of the southern states, for the purpose of consultation, and to demand their constitutional rights inside the Union. In order to accomplish this, the whole question must be referred to the people, and their judgment invoked in some authoritative form. This can only be effected by calling a convention, to be assembled at as early a day as practicable, for the purpose of electing delegates to a southern convention. Early action in reference to a state convention is imperiously demanded, in view of the fact that South Carolina will secede immediately, unless she can be induced to take counsel with her southern sisters. It is idle for us to say that we are not bound by her action, and that her course ought not to govern ours. Georgia, Florida, Texas, Mississippi, and perhaps Louisiana and Alabama, will resume their reserved rights, and declare themselves out of the Union. But if South Carolina should, acting singly and alone, unfurl the Palmetto standard, and resuming her sovereignty, declare her independence, how can Arkansas remain an idle spectator of such an event, and be indifferent to the consequences which will in a few months assuredly ensue?

. . . Yet, in less than ninety days, Abraham Lincoln will be inaugurated as president, and he will doubtless find *such* authority, and, if true to his antecedents, will attempt to coerce South Carolina, or any other seceding state, back into the Union. In such a contest, would not the patriotic and chivalrous spirit of the South rush to the defense and assistance of those states who are struggling for liberty.

Would Arkansas unite with those who have counseled servile insurrection, stolen our slaves, and advised the murder and ravishment of our wives and children, and assist them to destroy their brethren. Such a sentiment, we believe, finds no abiding place in the bosom of any of our fellow-citizens. In view of the fact that we may at any time be hurried into the conflict unprepared, it is proper that we should put ourselves in a condition for such an emergency.

The course of events is so rapidly hastening forward, the emergency may arrive when our people will be called upon to act promptly; and, in the opinion of your committee, the path of duty and of honor requires that the people should be called together to make a last effort to preserve the Union of the states, under guarantees of the constitution. This can be effected by assembling southern states together, and in the exercise of a clear constitutional right, demand security for the future; upon which the conservative sentiment of the nation may hereafter repose. This proceeding, instead of leading, as some affect to believe, to a disruption of the Union, will more surely perpetuate it, than abject submission to repeated and continual aggressions. . . .

To shut our eyes to the fact that there is danger of a dissolution, would be as silly as pusilanimous; to hope to avert the danger by silent submission, would be futile. The tide of events have brought us to a crisis which must be met manfully, and with a determined spirit. The people are the fountain of power, and to them we would appeal, and urging them by their love of the constitution, to act promptly in demanding their rights to preserve the Union formed by our forefathers, cemented by their blood, and transmitted to us, in the hope that it would be fraught with blessings.

We cannot appreciate the argument that it would cost too much to call a convention—to weigh money against principle, to estimate our rights by dollars and cents, may become the sordid miser, but it ill becomes the free and enlightened people of this country. The people have a right to be heard, and it is our duty to afford them the opportunity of speaking out for themselves.

Your committee earnestly recommends that a convention of delegates from all of the southern states assemble at Memphis, in the State of Tennessee, on the second Monday in February, A. D. 1861.

DOCUMENT 17

Henry Rector, Speech to the House of Representatives, December 11, 1860

Sources: *Journal of the House of Representatives for the Thirteenth Session of the General Assembly of the State of Arkansas* (Little Rock: Johnson & Yerkes, Public Printers, 1861), 300–305 and *Arkansas State Gazette,* December 22, 1860.

Referring to his inaugural address of November 15, 1860, Henry Rector advocated for preparing Arkansas for war, especially since he was convinced that the other southern states were preparing to leave the Union. Rector, like others, vividly shows how Arkansas's prosperity was tied to slavery and how integral the institution was for the state's survival. He also argued that Arkansas's future was tied to the Deep South and that it could not stand to separate from that destiny because of the institution of slavery, though he indicated that Arkansas was far more conservative in its response to Lincoln's election than South Carolina or Mississippi. Finally, Rector highlighted concerns over the state's western border, as the removal of federal troops from Indian Territory might necessitate stronger state action to quell fears that radical abolitionists would incite abolition among the Indians.

The election of Abraham Lincoln to the presidency of the United States, having been ascertained but a few hours preceding the delivery of my inaugural address to the General Assembly, and the attitude which some of the southern states would, in consequence, assume, being then in doubt and uncertainty.

I designed only to lay down in that address, as briefly as possible, my convictions touching the abstract legal right of a state to secede from the federal union, coupling with that assertion of right the opinion, that notwithstanding there was clear legal right, and cumulative moral wrong on the part of the North to justify the exercise of this right. Still, so long as there was even a remote hope that by compromise and concessions made by the northern states, the Union could be preserved and held together; that it was the duty of every patriot in the land, every functionary of the government, every citizen, rich or poor, slaveholder or non-slaveholder, the son and daughter with the parent, the parent with the child, to labor for and conserve their course and conduct to this end.

The Providence of nations, and the destinies of the world seem to will it otherwise.

The wisest and best government that has ever been allotted to man has fallen prey to the madness and fanaticism of its own children, for I am convinced that the Union of these states in this moment is practicably severed and gone forever. It seems to be impossible, upon casual reflection, that it can be so, and we realize it only by the stern inflexibility of facts, patent and palpable as when the mantle of death spreads itself upon the fair form and features of some beloved one of earth, preparatory to an eternal farewell, never, never, again to return!

I utter these sentiments in terms of solemn reverence, for I feel that I am chronicling events portentous of a gloomy future for my countrymen, for the rising generation, many of whom cluster around my own fireside.

But duty prompts me to announce to you what I conceive to be "the state of the government." Which is, I repeat, that the union of the states may no longer be regarded as an existing fact, making it imperatively necessary that Arkansas should girdle her loins for the conflict, and put her house in order.

I will not stop to discuss the remote causes in retrospect that have brought about this state of things, but proceed to look at matters as they now present themselves before the country.

In the States of South Carolina and Mississippi, the people have declared, through primary assemblages, a unanimous determination to secede from the Union.

The legislature of South Carolina has assembled and called a convention of the people, to meet on the 18th inst., to prepare the frame work for a separate and independent government.

The legislature of Mississippi, convened in session extraordinary, by the executive, has announced unanimously an unqualified determination to separate from the federal Union.

The sentiments expressed by the States of Texas, Louisiana, Florida, Georgia, and Alabama, reiterate the same determination.

Is it not madness to suppose that great governments and people like those referred to, will degrade themselves in the eyes of the world by retrograde submissive action.

But among the southern states, Maryland, Virginia, Missouri, Kentucky, and Tennessee, are disposed to be conservative.

So of Arkansas, if I am advised of public sentiment. But they and she must make a choice. Shall Arkansas remain in the Union when her sisters of the South have declared for a separate nationality? Suppose Missouri remains in the confederacy and Louisiana does not? Of which is Arkansas the natural ally, with which is her common interest, to whom must she look in the future for common sympathy and support? Can she exist in the future without a brotherhood and fraternal feeling with the cotton growing states?

Missouri may divest herself of slave labor; Arkansas never can. Without it, her fertile fields are deserts, and her people penniless and impoverished. Then the status, the destiny, the fortunes, right or wrong, of the cotton states is her legacy.

She can have no northern sympathies, nor northern affiliation, even in the Union, nor for the sake of it, after those having like climate and productions, seeking a common market, through a common channel, have gone out of it.

With the mart and channel of southern commerce in the possession and control of the states of Louisiana and Mississippi what would be the condition of Arkansas, should she determine to adhere to the Union, as will Missouri, Kentucky and Maryland? They may dispense with slave labor, and induce thereby a community of interest with the manufacturing and grain growing states of the North; we cannot. Providence has dispensed other blessings to this latitude, and it is our salvation and duty to guard them.

Thus presenting to you, in a few hastily prepared passages, the condition of the government, to my mind. The enquiry is, what shall Arkansas do; what will you, my fellow-citizens, recently returned by the sovereign people, as chosen guardians of their dearest rights, do to preserve and protect inviolate, the liberty, independence and honor of your countrymen; each hour evolved being fraught with important events, the time drawing near when the inauguration of a hostile and fanatical administration, will prove less auspicious to the free and independent action of the southern states, than is now the case, under a President whose southern sympathies have made him a martyr in our cause?

Shall we prove laggards, and listlessly sleep upon the watchtower of people's liberties! Shall we stare fate in the face, trifle with sad realities, and commit our country to a fatuitous inanity!

That we must, in ninety days, seek an alliance, as a necessity, with a confederacy of southern states, is as plain to my mind as the sun at noonday.

To do this, it is necessary, as every one must see, to put the country in a thorough state of military preparation. That the separation will be peaceful, should it occur before the inauguration of Abraham Lincoln, is guaranteed by the message of President Buchanan, recently delivered to the Congress now in session. . . .

Contemplating these events, as I do, to my mind it is highly important that an appropriation be made, at once, adequate in its amount for arming the militia with approved modern arms, and ammunition, to be stored at convenient points along the north-west border of the state, and at the seat of government. There are a few hundred stands of arms subject to the order of the governor, now deposited at the United States arsenal at this place, and other additional ones, to which the state is entitled, at the City of Washington, amounting in all to 1,400 of antique structure and *doubtful* capacity.

I am not for war, but I am in favor of preparing for war, in times of peace, and recommend to you, who have authority to provide the means necessary for the defense of our citizens.

The money in the treasury belongs to the people, and they ought to be permitted to use it for the protection of their property, and the security of their wives and children.

Our western border is in imminent peril now, from the incursions of [James] Montgomery,[2] a freebooter, sent down by the people of the northern states, with common designs against Missouri, Arkansas and Texas. The protection afforded by the federal government, even in the Union, is contemptibly spurned by any bandit who sees proper to invade us.

Imagine the condition of our border people, then, when we strike for our liberties, and declare for separate nationality. Immediate legislative action, calling a convention, is earnestly recommended, that the state, by the authority of the people, may define her position at as early a period as possible—other states of the South, with whom we must share a common fortune, being far in advance of Arkansas in this important movement. Party prejudices and recrimination ought to be buried and forgotten, in so momentous a crisis.

Let the people speak through their delegates, fix the destiny of the state, and all will unite in the verdict. If there are any among us who are deaf to the admonition of plain facts and reason, false to the honor, glory and independence of their state, which is their rightful sovereign, let them speak, also, that we may know ourselves.

To prevent the migration from other states, having anti-slavery tendencies, I advise the passage of a law prohibiting the importation of negroes into Arkansas, from any source whatever, unless accompanied by their owners, who shall settle and become permanent citizens of the

---

2. James Montgomery led a Jayhawk free-state group in Bleeding Kansas and frequently raided pro-slavery settlers, using violence to advance free-soil and abolitionist ideology.

country. The object of which is to compel the border states to take care of and protect their own slave property, and ultimately to look to the cotton growing states as confederates and allies, having like institutions and common interests. Such a law need have only temporary application, to be repealed or modified in future, as circumstances require. When Missouri abolishes slavery, Arkansas becomes a border state. She is likely to do this before a great while, unless inhibited by such a statute as this, united in by all the cotton growing states.

The Indian nations on our western border will do the same thing, unless their free soil proclivities are forestalled by such statutory enactments. . . .

DOCUMENT 18

Resolutions from Desha and Jefferson Counties, December 15, 1860

Source: *Journal of the Senate for the Thirteenth Session of the General Assembly of the State of Arkansas* (Little Rock: Johnson & Yerkes, Public Printers, 1861), 290–93.

Submitting identical resolutions to the Arkansas Senate, citizens of the heavily slaveholding counties of Desha and Jefferson called for a convention so that Arkansas could openly discuss secession. These resolutions not only referred to the fugitive slave clause and cited the lack of support the North had given to the South, but made the case that Arkansas had to act in concert with the other slaveholding states. They proposed that representatives from the slaveholding states meet in Atlanta, while they also cautioned South Carolina, preparing to hold a secession convention, not to push toward open conflict without first consulting the other slaveholding states.

Resolved, That, while from patriotic considerations, we are inclined to treat, with respectful consideration, the expressed will of the constitutional majority of the people of the United States, in the choice of a chief executive officer, still a proper regard for sincerity and truth forbids that we should disguise the fact, that the election of Mr. Lincoln, under the existing circumstances, by a purely sectional vote, looking to sectional aggrandizement, sectional domination, blind to the spirit, if not to the letter of the constitution, has produced a profound sensation in all the slaveholding states; because the principles upon which Mr. Lincoln was elected, are at war with the constitutional rights of the South.

2. *Resolved*, That the fifteen slaveholding states are united, not only by common language, common origin, common history, but by common institutions, productions and interests; therefore it is not only their safety and protection, but their duty and their interest, that they should act in concert and harmony, in the present emergency; wherefore, we regard any individual, inconsiderate, impulsive action on the part of any or either of said states, tending, whether so designed or not, to coerce their sister states into their support, without previous consultation or advice, as injudicious.

3. *Resolved*, That in view of the fact that several of our sister slaveholding states, have felt it to be their duty, under existing circumstances, to take counsel of their people, by holding state conventions, in order the better to protect our rights in the Union, shield and protect the constitution under which we live from assault or aggression from the North or from the South, we therefore respectfully submit to the governor and legislature to call a convention of the people of the state of Arkansas, at as early a day as practicable, to take into consideration the threatening political condition of the country, and to prepare the state to act in concert with our sister states, in devising and carrying out such remedial measures as may be deemed necessary and appropriate to maintain the integrity of the Union; but more especially the rights, all and singular, of our own state in or out of the Union.

4. *Resolved*, That this convention, when assembled, in addition to the business and duties before alluded to, shall advise and request all the slaveholding states to meet in convention, at the city of Atlanta, in the State of Georgia, by such a number of delegates as each states, respectively, may deem proper, to devise the most appropriate and efficient means to arrest the spirit of nullification, insubordination, and disloyalty to the constitution of the United States, evidenced by several of the northern and western states, in their efforts to embarrass the execution of the fugitive slave law, by a system of legislation, not only anti-patriotic,

anti-social and unjust towards the southern states, but unconstitutional and insulting to the majesty and sovereignty of the federal government.

5. *Resolved*, That in this emergency, we intend to forget all past differences of opinion, growing out of our former party political organization, and unite as one man, in the support and vindication of our interests and institutions, as God and our fathers gave them to us, through evil and through good report, come weal or come woe.

6. *Resolved*, That while sympathizing with South Carolina in feeling, we respectfully request that she will not precipitate us into revolution or secession, without a calm consultation with her sister southern states.

7. *Resolved*, That we respectfully submit to the legislature, the propriety of appropriating a portion of the surplus revenue now in the treasury, to the purchase of arms, and to the putting of the state into a proper attitude of defense, believing that the best way of avoiding trouble or danger, is to be prepared for them. . . .

DOCUMENTS 19–21

Contrasting Ideas: Resolutions of a Union Meeting in Benton County and a Secession Meeting in Jefferson County, December 18, 1860

Source: *Journal of the Senate for the Thirteenth Session of the General Assembly of the State of Arkansas* (Little Rock: Johnson & Yerkes, Public Printers, 1861), 324–30.

While pro-secessionists in eastern Arkansas expressed extreme concern over the future of Arkansas after Abraham Lincoln's election, this first resolution from Benton County in Northwest Arkansas pushes a conservative approach to the crisis. Citizens there found no real threat that indicated a need to leave the Union and instead favored working with the other states in the Union to ensure the proper operation of the fugitive slave clause. The resolution from Benton County, where just over 4 percent of the population was enslaved, contrasted with that of Jefferson County, where almost 48 percent of the population was enslaved. The latter took a much more pessimistic view of Lincoln's election. Between these two citizen petitions is a resolution introduced in the Arkansas Senate on the same day that sarcastically encouraged the state capital be moved to Bentonville. In reality a political ploy, the resolution painted the more conservative Benton County residents as far wiser than those who advocated for secession.

Resolution of the Citizens of Benton County

WHEREAS, The conviction is forced upon us by every issue of our weekly periodicals, but more especially by the reckless and incendiary documents which are being sown broadcast over our lovely and patriotic land—documents overwrought and in many instances concocted without a due regard to the facts; fostering an already morbid sentiment, and arraying in a spirit of defiance one section of our country against the other. That there is being nurtured in the South a spirit of anarchy, which, unless chastened and modified by *southern conservatism*, will set at defiance all law, all rights, and involve our country, our whole country in civil war and irremediable ruin. Therefore,

Be it resolved by the citizens of Benton county assembled, That we, as a people venerate and hold as sacred, our constitution and Federal Union, purchased by the common blood, baptized by the tears, and consecrated by the "lives, the fortunes and sacred honors" of the purest and most devoted band of patriots that ever honored the face of the earth.

Resolved, That in our judgment, *the constitution* by the purity of its principle, the justice of its requirements, and the liberal spirit of its articles of confederation, has rendered us the most prosperous and glorious nation under the broad canopy of heaven.

Resolved, That we are firm and enthusiastic adherents to a democratic form of government, in which we believe it to be the duty of the minority to submit cheerfully to the will of the majority, *constitutionally expressed*, and in which redress for grievances may more readily and certainly be obtained by discussion and legislation, than by dictation or resort to arms—the common arguments of tyrants and despots.

Resolved, That, whereas a number of northern states have by legislative action nullified the fugitive slave law—a safeguard granted and guaranteed to us by Congress and by our *constitution*, that of which no state has the right or *constitutional power* to deprive us. We, as citizens of Arkansas, *with a common South*, appeal to those states, who, we cannot believe are yet lost to every sense of justice, and calmly, but *firmly insist* and *demand* that they forthwith repeal those enactments which are so palpably in violation of the constitution, and work to us so great injustice.

Resolved, That we cordially indorse and adopt the principles laid down by President [Andrew] Jackson, touching the South Carolina nullification acts of 1832, as a true construction of the constitution, viz: "No state has the right to nullify the acts of Congress, or to secede from the Union."

Resolved, That we repudiate the system of appealing to arms for the redress of our casual grievances, whether by Sharp's rifles in the hands of the hirelings of Kansas aid societies in the North, or Minnie rifles in the hands of minute men in the South, recommended and detailed by the Beechers, the Sewards, the Sumners and the Hales, North; or the Yanceys, the Rhetts, the Toombs, and Wigfalls of the South.

Resolved, That we esteem the ultra spirit of the extremes both North and South, alike subversive of the harmony and compromises of our government, and the perpetuity of our liberal institutions, and by a blind persistence in such course, we demonstrate to the world that we have constituted *passion umpire* in our deliberations, and are no longer capable of self-government.

Resolved, That we see in the present issues, no justifiable grounds for secession or revolution, or even the morbid apprehension and agitation of the South. That we regard it as an anomalous and unwarrantable step in diplomacy to declare war on the *mere anticipation* of an issue.

Resolved, That in secession we see no alternative but civil war, naught but the inevitable and immediate extinction of that very institution of which we are so jealous. . . .

Resolved, That we venerate and love the South which is our home, and southern institutions. But we shall never feel justifiable in setting at naught the Federal Union, with all its fountains of immunities and emoluments, teeming with rich blessings to our common country and the whole world, merely from the fact that a majority of the enfranchised citizens of our *democratic republic* have elected to the Presidency of these United States, a man whose principles are inimical to our institutions,

and whose election we deplore, but who is rendered harmless by constitutional safeguards, nor yet by legislative enactments of sister states
which are "a dead letter," a nullity from their unconstitutionality, *so long
as they make no effort to execute those enactments*.

Resolved, That we consider ourselves loyal and devoted subjects of
this confederation, common and *equal* in the *rights*, the honors and
the blessings of this heaven prospered country. Until the spirit that has
manifested itself in the North shall have been more fully developed in
organised and official violation of our rights and property; then when
we have exhausted every legal and honorable recourse to procure redress
and indemnity, and not till then will we give up this glorious Union. . . .

Resolved, That we most earnestly conjure our fellow-citizens to exercise a spirit of moderation and forbearance in these troublous times,
feeling that we have *justice on our side and must prevail*.

Resolved, That we watch with jealous eye the myriads of reckless and
irresponsible demagogues, who, with fiendish energy and industry are
sowing the seeds of estrangement and bitterness; and whom we esteem
as equally dangerous enemies to our country with those who procure
"republican" enactments.

Resolved, That we rely on the intelligence and virtue of a conservative
people, and a free and independent exercise of their franchises, untram-
meled by *reckless politicians* and their unholy combinations, as our sheet
anchor in the storm that is upon us.

Resolved, That we hereby pray our legislature to memorialize our
national Congress now in session, to take the constitutional steps to
national convention, for the purpose of adjusting the vexed question of
slavery upon *equitable terms* to the *south*, and to the satisfaction of all
sections, if *possible*, and place *forever* beyond the power of politicians to
drag it into the political arena, or into our national councils.

Resolved, That from the spirit manifested by the patriotic and better
portion of the north, we are led to hope that by honorable negotiation,
conducted in a liberal spirit in such a convention, the South may procure the repeal of obnoxious laws—entire satisfaction for past grievances
and ample security against their recurrence—thus our beloved county
would be snatched from the abyss that is yawning to receive us; whilst
an intolerant course of crimination and wholesale denunciation would

foster a similar spirit on the part of the North, and hasten the consummation of all that we most dread. . . .

Resolution on Location of Capital City

WHEREAS, In this day of great peril to our beloved Union, the stoutest hearts and wisest minds of our country should be placed as the head of public affairs; *and whereas*, we have in one of our counties, a few distinguished statesmen who have sprung like Minerva from the brain of Jupiter; *and whereas*, to secure their services, and as a measure of economy, be it therefore

Resolved, That the state capital be removed to Bentonville, Benton county, and all public offices and officers shall be and reside at that place.

Resolutions of Citizens of Jefferson and Arkansas Counties

WHEREAS, The election by a large majority of the northern voters of Abraham Lincoln, a determined abolitionist, to the presidency of the United States, in utter disregard of those fraternal feelings which should actuate the people of all sections of the country in their choice of federal officers, in the culminating wrong of a long series of injuries, to which the South has been *called* to submit to a black republican triumph of mere numbers, against right, constitutional guarantees, and the vital interest of the largest producing portion of the Federal Union; and is a triumph of a party which has never scrupled to declare that its mission is to *exterminate slavery*, and desolate the fairest and most fertile regions of the country, and to substitute their higher laws, for the supreme law of the land, the constitution upon which this government was constructed;

And whereas, The time has come when the states of the South are called upon to provide measures for the effectual protection of their rights and safety and of their persons against the invasion of their territory by their hordes of anti-slavery propagandists, who are now more emboldened than ever, to carry on their cherished schemes of inciting insurrections and servile war: the first practical fruits of their principles was the John Brown raid in Virginia, and now followed by the Montgomery raid into our sister state Missouri—murdering the peaceable citizens for no other cause than they are owners of slaves, and threatening our own State of Arkansas, we are called upon, unmistakably by the signs of the times, to provide for our own safety, even if in so doing, we should present a hostile front to the aggressive states of the North. There are interests dearer to our hearts than any nationality, however glorious it may be, and believing that in the future we have no better remedy for our wrongs than a stout, bold and united resistance, we do resolve,

1st. That the southern states ought to resist this election, since a quiet submission to it would be sacrificing their equality in the Union, and the respect due a free and independent people.

2d. That we do believe this sectional triumph will but give courage to embolden the fanatics of the North to continue and increase their treasonable attempts to rob the citizens of the South of their property.

3d. That our senators and representatives are requested to introduce a bill in our legislature and urge its adoption, to appropriate the sum of five hundred thousand dollars for the purpose of procuring arms and munitions of war to place the state in a position of defense.

4th. That all the counties in the states are requested to hold primary meetings, with a view of obtaining the sentiments of the people on the all important subject now agitating the country.

5th. That in the event of the southern people, or any portion of them, being driven to the necessity of vindicating their rights and honor by an appeal to arms, we will rally to their aid, to battle with them against a common foe, and share with them a glorious victory, or a no less glorious death.

On motion, the preamble and resolutions were voted for one at a time, when each one was adopted by the whole meeting, without one dissenting voice. . . .

DOCUMENT 22

Telegraph from US Senator Robert Ward Johnson and Congressman Thomas C. Hindman, December 22, 1860

Source: *Journal of the House of Representatives for the Thirteenth Session of the General Assembly of the State of Arkansas* (Little Rock: Johnson & Yerkes, Public Printers, 1861), 424–25.

Two of Arkansas's congressional delegation reported back to the Arkansas legislature in Little Rock in late December their view that most of the South would secede. Indeed, South Carolina had seceded from the Union on December 20. Additionally, they enclosed the credentials of Commissioner David Hubbard of Alabama. Commissioners like Hubbard began coming to Arkansas in December 1860 and brought with them news from their home states and served as advocates for secession once their states had left the Union, frequently highlighting the perceived antagonism of the federal government to slavery.

It is now manifest that the other cotton states will secede. North Carolina moves towards the same end. The people of the border states are taking steps to call conventions. The spirit of the present Congress forbids a reasonable hope of any adequate remedy. We believe it to be our public duty to state our present conviction, which is, that it is the imperative interest of the state to pass an act calling together a convention, to enable the people of Arkansas to join in the common councils of the South, for her protection and future safety.

R. W. JOHNSON and
T. C. HINDMAN

I am also instructed to transmit to your honorable body the following certificate from the governor of Alabama, accrediting Hon. David Hubbard, as a commissioner, to consult with the governor and General Assembly of this State, touching political affairs:

EXECUTIVE DEPARTMENT, *Montgomery,* Dec. 10th, 1860.

WHEREAS, The election of Abraham Lincoln, a black republican, to the presidency of the United States, by a purely sectional vote, and by a party whose leading and publicly avowed object is the destruction of the institution of slavery as it exists in the slaveholding states; *And whereas,* the success of said party, and the power which it has, and soon will acquire, greatly endanger the peace, interest, security and honor of the slaveholding states, and make it necessary that prompt and effective measures should be adopted to avoid the evils which must result from a republican administration of the federal government; and as the interests and destiny of the slaveholding states are the same, they must naturally sympathize with each other; they, therefore, so far as may be practicable, should consult and advise together as to what is best to be done to protect their mutual interests and honor.

Now, therefore, in consideration of the premises, I, ANDREW B. MOORE, Governor of the State of Alabama, by virtue of the general powers in me vested, do hereby constitute and appoint Hon. David Hubbard, a citizen of said state, as commissioner to the sovereign State of Arkansas, to consult and advise with his excellency Governor Henry M. Rector, and the members of the legislature, to be assembled in said state, as to what is best to be done to protect the rights, interest and honor of the slaveholding states, and to report the result of such consultation in time to enable me to communicate the same to the convention of the State of Alabama, to be held in Montgomery the 7th day of January next.

DOCUMENT 23

Resolution from Hempstead County, December 24, 1860

Source: *Journal of the Senate for the Thirteenth Session of the General Assembly of the State of Arkansas* (Little Rock: Johnson & Yerkes, Public Printers, 1861), 377–78.

At the end of the year, pro-secession meetings in the largest slaveholding counties in Arkansas, including Hempstead in southwestern Arkansas (38.6 percent enslaved), continued to press the legislature for action before Abraham Lincoln's inauguration. This resolution specifically linked slaveholding and states' rights together and pushed for Arkansas to work in concert with other slaveholding states to press Congress for constitutional protections, specifically concerning fugitive slaves.

Resolved by the people of the county of Hempstead, in the State of Arkansas, in a primary meeting convened, That the stability and perpetuity of the union of the states composing the United States of America, is dependent upon the equality of said states, and the rights thereof as secured and recognized by the Constitution of the United States.

Resolved, That the institution of slavery, as it exists in the present slaveholding States of this Union, is a constitutional right, secured and recognized by the Constitution of the United States, and that the right of property in such slaves is coeval with the existence of the government of the United States, and ought of right to be so recognized by the states that now exist or which may hereafter exist, and that it is the duty of the Congress of the United States to protect this right of property in such slaves in all the common territory belonging to the United States throughout their territorial existence, and until they shall be admitted into the Union with or without slavery, as their constitution may prescribe.

Resolved, That the rights of the owner of any such slave escaping from any one state or territory to that of another, shall not be impaired in the right of property in such slave, so escaping, but such slave should be delivered to the owner, and that the law passed by the Congress of the United States, known as the fugitive slave law, is a valid and constitutional law, made to secure and protect constitutional rights, and that all state laws, impairing or defeating this constitutional right, are consequently null and void.

Resolved, That it is the immediate and imperative duty of the Congress of the United States to propose amendments to the Constitution of the United States, fully embodying the principles and sentiments set forth in the foregoing resolutions, and that such amendments should be adopted, and thereby become part and parcel of the Constitution of the United States of America, in accordance with the mode pointed out by the Constitution of the United States, and that such amendments be declared unalterable and irrevocable, without the consent of all the states of this Union.

Resolved, That the election of a man to the presidency of the United States, upon sectional principles, warring against declared and well defined constitutional rights, is antagonistic to the principles upon which the government of the United States was created, and is a just cause of alarm for the safety and perpetuity of the rights of the slaveholding states of the Union, and imperatively demands immediate remedial action by all just and law-abiding citizens. . . .

Resolved, That in the event that the proposed amendments to the Constitution of the United States, or such others embracing the same rights and principles, and securing the equality of the states, as hereinbefore designated and specified, shall not be immediately and favorably received and acted upon by the Congress of the United States, that the State of Arkansas will, in justice to herself, take such immediate action, in conjunction with the slaveholding states of this Union, as may be deemed just and equitable by a convention of said states, under such form and system of government as may be agreed upon between them for their future security in the enjoyment of life, liberty, happiness, and property, and which has been denied to them by the aggressive and lawless policy of a large majority of the free states of this Union. . . .

DOCUMENTS 24–25

Contrasting Resolutions from Meetings in Sebastian and Johnson Counties, December 29, 1860

Sources: *Journal of the Senate for the Thirteenth Session of the General Assembly of the State of Arkansas* (Little Rock: Johnson & Yerkes, Public Printers, 1861), 419–22 and *Arkansas State Gazette,* January 5, 1861.

Residents of Sebastian County, along the state's western border with Indian Territory, had far fewer slaves than Arkansans in the Delta. Residents of Johnson County had only a small percentage more but came to radically different conclusions in these two resolutions presented to the Arkansas Senate on the same day in late December. The Sebastian resolution, like the Benton County Unionist petition earlier the same month, indicated that no perceived violations discussed by the pro-secessionists warranted armed revolt. The Johnson County petition agreed wholeheartedly with the Committee on Federal Relations' report and Governor Henry M. Rector's comments on the need for secession.

Resolution of the Residents of Sebastian County

WHEREAS, The election of Abraham Lincoln to the presidency of these United States, by an entirely sectional party, has given just cause of offence to the southern states of this Union; *And whereas,* The consequent agitation thereupon, is but too likely to result in a disruption of our glorious government, and a destruction of the brightest hopes of mankind; therefore,

Resolved, That deeply as we regret it, yet we regard the election of Mr. Lincoln as entirely constitutional, and therefore no just ground of revolution or secession on the part of any of the southern states of this government.

2d. That we do not recognize in the constitution of these United States, any such right as that of secession, except in a sense synonymous with the inherent right of revolution.

3d. That revolution, or a resort to arms to redress our wrongs, would be the greatest curse that could possibly befall our peaceful and prosperous country, and should only be resorted to when every other honorable expedient has failed.

4th. That we do not regard the present as, in any sense, a proper occasion for such an expedient, but on the contrary, there is now no evil of which the South complains, which, before a christian and civilized world, would justify revolution, or for which revolution would furnish a remedy.

5th. That, granting the existence of such a right as that of peaceable secession, we yet have rights *in the Union,* which it would be cowardly in the extreme to abandon.

6th. That we regard the scheme of a "southern confederacy" as a chimera wholly impracticable, if desirable, and wholly undesirable if practicable, existing only in the imagination of disappointed aspirants to political office.

7th. That it may be, and doubtless is true, that the interests of those politicians (whose success depend upon the ruin of social order,) are with a "southern confederacy," but the interests, and the hopes, and the happiness, and the honor of the *people* of this government are identified with the *Union as it is!*

8th. That we will yet watch with jealousy, the administration of

Lincoln, and resist even to death, any attempt at an unconstitutional aggression upon either our rights or equality in the Union.

9th. That we instruct our representatives in the legislature, to request our representatives in Congress, and to instruct our senators, to use all honorable means of avoiding a dissolution of the Union, and to effect a compromise between the contending sections, upon such terms as shall be just and honorable to all parties.

10th. That Arkansas is quite competent to take care of herself, and her destiny is not "hitched on" to that of South Carolina, or any other state; nor will she allow herself to be "dragged" into any cause contrary to the wishes of her own people, but that she will pursue her own counsels, and shape her own conduct, irrespective of either the wishes, or the precipitate action of any other state. . . .

Resolution of Residents of Johnson County

WHEREAS, the people of the southern states, for the last thirty years, have borne and submitted to the outrage and contumely of the northern states, beyond what could be expected of any people. To recapitulate the many aggressions, studiously committed by the people of the northern states, and also by the states themselves, would only be a rehearsal of the chapter of wrongs a thousand times told, which shows how the rights of southern men have been outraged, and the political rights of the southern states disregarded and trampled on; this not being the time or place to set forth and make an array of the many outrages and untold grievances that the southern people have been made to submit to, time and again—we content ourselves with promulgating the following resolutions as the sentiments of the citizens of Johnson county:

Resolved, That we fully, cordially, approve and indorse the report of the committee on federal relations, in the House of Representatives, now in session at Little Rock, recommending the assembling of a state convention under sanction of law; that said report is an able expose of many of the wrongs committed by the northern people, and the northern states, upon the most sacred rights of the South and her people, showing, as a conclusion, that these aggressions have been studiously planned, and have been rigorously executed for a continuous number of years, until the overt acts already committed and leveled at the peace, quiet and tranquility of the southern people, cannot be any longer endured or tolerated by a free people, whose Anglo-saxon origin entitle them to an honorable position in all political connexions.

Resolved, That we hereby instruct our members in the state legislature to vote for the law to call a state convention, and to urge its immediate passage, so that people may have a legal and a legitimate chance to resume their organic rights, so they may speak forth and enumerate their many wrongs, and show up the numerous grievances to which thus far patriotically submitted to for the vain hope of preserving, *in tact*, the Federal Union, bequeathed to us by the fathers of the republic; nothing less, at this time, than the passage of said law will satisfy our reasonable desires.

Resolved, That the late special message sent to the legislature by Gov. Henry M. Rector, shows conclusively that he is ever watchful of the dearest rights of the southern people, and to see that they shall be properly vindicated against the aggressive and overbearing spirit evinced by the northern people; while our rights are in such hands, we may quietly rest assured that our every right will be patriotically vindicated.

Resolved, That we heartily indorse and approve of the three measures of national policy submitted to Congress by our chief magistrate, in his recent annual message, and believe that the principals involved in them, can only be made the just and equitable basis of settlement between the North and the South, and that we accept *none other*.

Resolved, That immediate efforts should be made to discipline and arm the militia of the state, so that we may be prepared for any emergency that may arise.

Resolved, That the federal government of the United States is nothing more than the creative or political machine of the sovereign states as a federative agent, to perform such national functions as is specifically delegated in the constitution of the United States, made by the thirteen original states, and which have affirmatively granted, and no other power can the general government exercise whatever—there being no grant or affirmative organic law in the constitution of the United States which, in any manner, impliedly or otherwise, gives any authority whatever to the general government to coerce or force a sovereign state to any position or condition, less than supreme and equal power to be exercised by such a state.

As a corollary to this—no state having surrendered the reserved right to withdraw from the federal compact, to which they were a voluntary party; they still retain that supreme power to judge of any infraction of the federal constitution which may be injurious to the vitality of their rights. The social condition and rights of the citizens, and the protection of life, liberty and property. When this fails to the injury or destruction of the rights of the people of any state, by the people and sanction of law and authority of any other state, it then becomes the duty of any such state whose rights are thus wantonly outraged, to put themselves in position to demand immediate and satisfactory guarantees for all such violated rights; and, upon failure, that the same shall be satisfactorily adjusted alike honorable to the parties interested. Such state, exercising and retaining all her sovereign power and rights, ought to withdraw from the federal compact; and form such alliances with other states as will best conduce to the success of human liberty, and in protecting life, liberty and property.

Resolved, That sovereign states, in forming a new federal compact, should specifically reserve the right to withdraw upon the violation of constitutional rights by a majority of states forming the same.

DOCUMENTS 26–27

Majority and Minority Resolutions from Clark County, December 31, 1860

Source: *Journal of the Senate for the Thirteenth Session of the General Assembly of the State of Arkansas* (Little Rock: Johnson & Yerkes, Public Printers, 1861), 426–28.

Residents of Clark County, including Arkadelphia, where 23 percent of the population was enslaved, submitted two resolutions to the Arkansas Senate, which were read on December 31, 1860. The first, from the majority, asked the legislature to call a state convention and work with other slaveholding states on a southern convention in order to protect Arkansas from Abraham Lincoln's opposition to slavery. The second, from the minority of Clark County residents, advised caution and a preservation of the Union. However, it advocated a southern convention be assembled that would present an ultimatum to the northern states to create "final settlement of the agitation of the slavery question."

Majority Resolution

WHEREAS, The people of the northern or free states of this confederacy have elected Abraham Lincoln president of the United States solely upon the ground of his hostility and opposition to the institution of slavery, thereby confirming the determination heretofore evinced on their part, to no longer regard our rights or their constitutional obligation; and whereas, some of our sister southern states have recommended separate conventions preparatory to a southern convention for the purpose of taking common council in order to protect our rights— therefore, the people of Clark county in primary meeting assembled, hereby ignore all past party names and issues, and cordially unite in the following resolutions:

1. *Resolved*, That we recommend to the legislature of this state the passage of such laws as may be necessary for assembling a state convention for the purpose of considering the momentous questions which now agitate the public mind.

2. That we recommend the assembling of a southern convention, to be composed of delegates from each slaveholding state, as shall choose to be represented, and that said convention shall have all necessary powers to do such acts and things as shall be by them thought necessary to protect the rights of the South.

3. That we earnestly recommend such measures as shall unite the South, and to this end, in case a southern republic be determined upon, recommend such a constitutional provision as shall protect the rights of the border states.

Minority Resolution

WHEREAS, In this momentous crisis in the affairs of the nation it becomes the duty of every patriot and patriotic community to speak forth their sentiments, and declare what they should think best to be done in this serious emergency; therefore, we the people of Clark county, in mass meeting assembled, do adopt as the sentiments of this county, the following resolutions:

1. *Resolved*, That we are in favor of preserving our present great and glorious Union, provided it can be done with honor and safety to the South and southern institutions.

2. We are in favor of exhausting all honorable means to save this Union, and in order to do this more effectually and promptly, would recommend a convention to be called by our state legislature for the purpose of agreeing upon some general plan of *action*.

3. We would further give it as our opinion that the only hope now of saving the Union, is through a general convention of the southern states, made up of the wisest, ablest and most prudent statesmen, selected by the conventions of the different states; whose duty it should be, when convened, to agree upon the least demands that the South should make to the North consistent with her safety, and submit the same as a firm and *united South* to our northern brethren as our *ultimatum*.

4. *Resolved further*, That unless the North should be willing to accept such *ultimatum*, or grant us such measures of redress, and such guarantees as will insure our safety in the Union, and final settlement of the agitation of the slavery question, we are in favor of forming a separate republic, composed of all slave states.

5. That we are of opinion that the time has come when a decided position should be taken; but we consider calm deliberation much more expressive than hasty action, however tempestuous may be the enthusiasm manifested. Such a people as those of the South, united in a firm, decided, unwavering determination to maintain their rights, carry a moral force that is irresistible; and possesses a physical strength that is invincible. . . .

Documents 28–29

Resolutions of Citizens of Monroe and Union Counties, January 1, 1861

Source: *Journal of the Senate for the Thirteenth Session of the General Assembly of the State of Arkansas* (Little Rock: Johnson & Yerkes, Public Printers, 1861), 431–35.

On the first day of the new year, the Arkansas Senate considered the petitions of residents of Monroe and Union Counties. The Monroe petition, where slaves represented about 40 percent of the population, advocated that all southern states secede effective March 4 (Abraham Lincoln's inauguration day) unless the federal government ensured through constitutional guarantees that fugitive slaves would be returned, that slave property would be protected in the territories, and that slaves could be brought onto federal property and into Washington, D.C., without harassment. The petition from Union County, where slaves represented roughly 50 percent of the population, asked for an immediate convention and used vivid language to do so, citing the slave insurrection in Haiti and John Brown's raid on Harper's Ferry as reasons why Arkansas should move to protect the economically important institution of slavery.

Resolution of the Residents of Monroe County

WHEREAS, In the present important crisis in public affairs, in order that the sentiments of all the people may be obtained, it is necessary and proper that every community throughout the southern states should make known their views on matters in which each individual is so vitally interested; we, the citizens of Monroe county in mass meeting assembled, hereby declare the following to be our views and sentiments, and to this end be it

Resolved, 1st. That we regard the election of Abraham Lincoln to the presidency by an exclusively sectional vote, predicated upon a deep rooted and long cultivated hostility to southern institutions by the people of the North, as but the realization of the fears and predictions of the father of his country in his farewell address to the American people, to-wit: that such a consummation would end in the severance of these states.

Resolved, 2d. That any people of a sovereign government who would consent to commit their destinies to the rule and direction of a power deriving its source in a section foreign to it by locality and antagonistic to it in interest, and hostile to it in feeling, are unworthy of the name of freemen, and in reality slaves.

Resolved, 3*d*. That we regard the recent action of the convention of the people of the sovereign state of South Carolina, as the exercise of a reserved and inalienable right of the states composing the confederacy, to-wit: the right to judge of infractions of the constitution as well as the mode of redress, each state for itself being only responsible to the federal government for their acts as any other sovereign independent government, and that it is not the official duty of the federal government to exercise coercion against a seceding state without regard to the justice of her action in taking such a separate existence, and that the converse of this doctrine would have justified the action of the British government in their attempt to coerce the colonies in the American revolution.

Resolved, 4*th*. That South Carolina had good and sufficient cause to justify her in the severance of the ties that had previously bound her to the Federal Union, and that every southern state is indissolubly bound with her destiny, and that her success will be but the success of the South, and her failure but our failure, and that her conquest or coercion would be but the enslavement and subjugation of the whole South to the abolition fanatical power of the North, and in such a contingency, we would feel that every interest of the South would be at the discretion of the North, and that representatives of southern states who counsel such coercion should be regarded as base traitors to their country, and that their names should be infamous.

Resolved, 5*th*. That under the present state of affairs, the only safe or practical course for the South to pursue, is the separate secession of each state for itself, to take effect on the 4th day of March next, with the ordinance of secession conditioned that if the North will consent by that time to give us good and sufficient constitutional guaranties of our rights and our honor, to-wit: The faithful execution of the law requiring the return of fugitives from justice, and of fugitive slaves, an efficient protection of our persons and property in the territories, and an equal participation in the same; our rights of property and person to be protected in the District of Columbia, in the forts, in the dock yards, or upon the high seas, or wherever else the federal authority may exclusively extend; non-interference with the slave trade between the different states or in the same; no tariff except on strictly a revenue standard; no internal improvements by the general government, except for general defence or the improvement of the harbors and rivers traversing the different states with specified limitations, and a constitutional guarantee for the future; that in election of a president and vice-president of these Untied States, before they should be declared elected, that they should receive a plurality of the electoral vote of both slave and non-slaveholding states, or failing in this, a plurality of the representatives in the House or of the senators of both sections in addition to the present regulations of the constitution or the equivalent of these specifications, or such guarantee as may be agreed upon by a convention of the southern states, provided one should be assembled, then, and in that event, the ordinance of secession or the government established by it to cease its force and effect, otherwise provision to be made for the union of the seceding states and means of defense provided for. . . .

Resolution of Residents of Union County

WHEREAS, It being evident that the North not being content with violating the compact of the constitution, as well as the comity of nations between themselves and the South as independent sovereignties, and time and again refusing their assent to that *law* of Congress commanding the rendition of fugitive slaves, and absolutely nullifying it in various ways, nine or more of them having denied by positive statutes the authority of such a law, the remainder obstructing its execution in some form or other, thereby robbing the South annually of five hundred thousand dollars worth of slave property, without the possibility of redress in the Union; they have incited the negroes to insurrection, burned our towns, poisoned our wells, distributed poison among the negroes of the southern states with which to poison their masters; trampled upon the decisions of the supreme court that were in favor of slavery in the South, murdered or imprisoned, and imposed fines upon our citizens when attempting to regain fugitive slaves from the northern states; they have called upon the non-slaveholders of the South to aid them in their infamous designs; they have formed societies, and sworn their members that they will never cease to war upon the South until slavery is extinct, and to surround the South, if in their power, with free states, so that slavery, like an adder in flames, will sting itself to death; they have murdered our citizens in the territories; they once took possession of an arsenal in

Virginia, have caused San Domingo's scenes of blood shed and horror to be again enacted in the same state; they have heaped ungenerous and hellish epithets upon the slave holders of the South, denounced them from the sacred desk, both upon the sea and land, at home and abroad, from the political stand, from the press, from every place of discussion and private station; they have divided all the orthodox churches of the Union, thereby unchristianizing and denouncing the southern christians as heretics, mansteakers, and hell-deserving people, declaring that there must be an anti-slavery God, Bible, and constitution; and now to complete their ungodlike purposes, they have elected over all conservative men, a man to occupy the highest position in the gift of the American people—Abe Lincoln as president of these United States, who has pledged himself to carry out the principles of the republican party, which will fast hasten the ultimate doom which awaits the South in the Union, unless averted by the southern people, therefore be it

Resolved, 1. That we, the citizens of Union county, do recommend to the legislature of this state to authorize the governor to call a convention immediately, to obtain the will of the people of the state in regard to the present political issues which are now shaking the government to its very center, and to determine upon what course should be pursued by this as one of the slave holding states in regard to the great issues that now await us.

2. That our representatives in Congress from this state, be instructed to do all in their power to bring about a reconciliation or speedy adjustment of affairs between the two sections of the government, in such a manner that the South may maintain all her rights guaranteed to her under the constitution, and be never again proscribed by the North, and that the wrongs done the South as set forth in the above preamble, be redressed before the fourth of March next.

3. That believing that South Carolina has even now dissolved her connection with the federal government, and believing that Alabama, Mississippi, Georgia, Florida and Texas will do likewise, we, a portion of the citizens of the State of Arkansas, pledge our lives, our fortunes, and our sacred honors, to sustain them against coercion by the federal government or any other power.

4. That we acknowledge and hold the right of a state to secede at will, and that we cordially sympathize with South Carolina, Mississippi,

Georgia, and other southern states, which expressed a determination not to submit to the domination of the republican party, and that the *State of Arkansas should not submit*. . . .

Document 30

David Hubbard to Governor Andrew Moore of Alabama, January 3, 1861

Source: US War Department, *The War of the Rebellion: A Compilation of the Official Records of the Union and Confederate Armies* (Washington, DC: GPO, 1900), series 4, 1:3.

David Hubbard, Alabama's commissioner to Arkansas, reported back to that state's governor in early January that he had engaged in debate with Arkansas legislators regarding secession. He indicated that at this point Arkansas was on a conservative course, not yet ready to abandon the Union, especially because the state's western counties (Benton, Washington, Sebastian, and Crawford) were concerned with the influence of the federal government on the Indian tribes. Of course, these counties also had some of the lowest percentages of slaves, though the fear that Indians under federal encouragement could be employed to put down any secession movement resonated with Arkansans.

MY DEAR SIR: On receipt of your letter and appointment as commissioner from Alabama to Arkansas, I repaired at once to Little Rock and presented my credentials to the two houses, and also your letter to Governor [Henry] Rector, by all of whom I was politely received. The Governor of Arkansas was every way disposed to further our views, and so were many leading and influential members of each house of the Legislature, but neither are yet ready for action, because they fear the people have not yet made up their minds to go out. The counties bordering on the Indian nations—Creeks, Cherokees, Choctaws, and Chickasaws—would hesitate greatly to vote for secession, and leave those tribes still under the influence of the Government at Washington, from which they receive such large stipends and annuities. These Indians are at a spot very important, in my opinion, in this great sectional controversy, and must be assured that the South will do as well as the North before they could be induced to change their alliances and dependence. I have much on this subject to say when I get to Montgomery, which cannot well be written. The two houses passed resolutions inviting me to meet them in the representative hall and consult together as to what had best be done in this matter. When I appeared men were anxious to know what the seceding States intended to do in certain contingencies. My appointment gave me no authority to speak as to what any State would do, but I spoke freely of what, in my opinion, we ought to do. I took the ground that no State which had seceded would ever go back without full power being given to protect themselves by vote against anti-slavery projects and schemes of every kind. I took the position that the Northern people were honest and did fear the Divine displeasure, both in this world and the world to come, by reason of what they considered the national sin of slavery, and that all who agreed with me in a belief of their sincerity must see that we could not remain quietly in the same Government with them. Secondly, if they were dishonest hypocrites, and only lied to impose on others and make them hate us, and used anti-slavery arguments as mere pretexts for the purpose of uniting Northern sentiment against us, with a view to obtain political power and sectional dominion, in that event we ought not to live with them. I desired any Unionist present to controvert either of these positions, which seemed to cover the whole ground. No one attempted either, and I said but little more. I am satisfied, from free conversations with members of all parties and with Governor Rector, that Arkansas, when compelled to choose, will side with the Southern States, but at present a majority would vote the Union ticket. Public sentiment is but being formed, but must take that direction.

Contrasting Resolutions to the Senate from Saline, Marion, Carroll, Newton, and Searcy Counties, January 9, 1861

Source: *Journal of the Senate for the Thirteenth Session of the General Assembly of the State of Arkansas* (Little Rock: Johnson & Yerkes, Public Printers, 1861), 495–97.

In another contrasting set of resolutions to the Arkansas Senate, pro-secession advocates in Saline County, in central Arkansas where slaves represented 11 percent of the population, argued that slavery, as protected by law, needed to be defended after Abraham Lincoln's election by all southern slaveholding states. In contrast, the second resolution from four Ozark counties, where slaves represented less than 5 percent of the population, rejected secessionism and disapproved of the legislature's move to arm the state for war.

Resolutions of Residents of Saline County

WHEREAS, Abe Lincoln has been elected President of the United States by a sectional party, whose avowed principles are declared to the world to be to legislate against the rights and institutions of all those of the United States wherein African slavery exists by law; *And whereas*, the southern states have a common cause to resist the continued aggressions upon their inherent rights as freemen; *And whereas*, we deem it highly essential that the people of the different portions of this state should give free expression to their views and sentiments on the present disturbed condition of our federal relations to the general government; therefore,

Be it, by the people of the county of Saline, in primary convention assembled, resolved, That the people of the different southern states have the same right to extend and expand their institutions into the territories as the northern states have to extend their institutions into the same, and this right should be secured to them, and enforced by the general government, as long as the said territories remain in a territorial condition, and that when the people of a territory have the requisite population, and apply for admission as a state into the Union, as to slavery, they should be admitted with or without slavery, as their constitution may, in that respect, provide.

Resolved, That the general government is one of delegated and limited powers, and can exercise none except those delegated to it in the constitution of the United States, and the claim of the black republican party of the North to legislate and enforce the policy asserted in their platform of principles, is despotic and tyrannical in its character and tendency, totally at variance with the spirit of constitutional and free government; that governments are instituted among men to protect, and not destroy the property of its citizens, and that said platform declares a principle of government which, as such would in our judgment, be beyond that of even a sovereign state, viz: to legislate against the rights of the citizens of a division of its domain to their property, much less can the United States, which has more limited delegated powers to do so.

Resolved, That the condition of our federal relations absolutely require that the General Assembly of this state make immediate provisions for the assembling of a state convention, to take into consideration all matters relating to her connection with the general government at as early day as practicable, allowing sufficient time for the delegates to the convention to canvass their respective counties, in order to become acquainted with the views and sentiments of their respective constituents . . . and that, in the meantime, until the assembling of said convention, our senators and representatives in the Congress of the United States should remain in Congress, and do all in their power to bring about a reconciliation and adjustment of sectional animosity, and the recognition and settlement upon a firm basis, of the constitutional rights of the southern states; which have been so grossly and wantonly violated by the northern states.

Resolved, That we cherish a firm and sincere attachment to the Union of all the states, north and south, of this great nation, that we are profoundly sensible that the union of all the states, under the present constitution of the United States, when its provisions are carried out in its true spirit, is the firmest and surest basis for prosperity and security at home, as a people, and respect and protection abroad, and is even one of the main bulwarks for the preservation of our liberties, and that our northern states should ever be reminded that we are ready and willing to adjust the existing difficulties between us, and live in peace and amity on an equality, as states, but not otherwise.

Resolved, That the southern states, having a common cause, in resisting the encroachments of the northern states upon their rights, we are in favor of consultation with the respective southern states, in order to effect a concert and union of action of all of them.

Resolved, That provisions should be made by the present General Assembly, to organize, arm and equip the militia of this state, with as little delay as possible, without resort to further taxation at present for that purpose.

Resolution of Residents of Marion, Carroll, Newton, and Searcy Counties

WHEREAS, By the constitution of the United States . . . the people of the United States did enter into a bond of union, which has so far succeeded in the accomplishment of its objects in that we have grown to be a great and prosperous people; *And whereas,* by the recent election of President and Vice President of the United States, the country has been violently agitated, the perpetuity of the general government endangered—the peace and prosperity of our country imminently imperiled, and the social relations of our people involved in almost inextricable difficulties; therefore, be it

Resolved, That we regard the continuous agitation of the slavery question, by partizan demagogues, both North and South, as a means of self-aggrandizement, unworthy the patriot and statesman.

2d. That the perpetuity of the general government should, and of rights ought to be preserved; that we regard the prospective disruption of the United States as one of the most dire calamities that could befall the American people.

3d. That a suspension of commercial intercourse with the North would but tend to alienate and estrange those who, by a less rigid course might preserve and maintain a feeling of reciprocity, by which peace and prosperity would again prevail.

4th. That we will abide by the constitution, and will support the President in the discharge of all constitutional duties.

5th. That we do not regard the election of Mr. Lincoln to the presidency as a just cause for a dissolution of the Union.

6th. That the doctrine of secession, as taught in the resolutions of 1798–'9 is dangerous, and calculated to subvert the ends and aims of the articles of confederation.

7th. That we are opposed to the present and unconstitutional secession, and regret the position taken by our representative in Congress, the Hon. T. C. Hindman, in favor of immediate secession.

8th. That we disapprove of the appropriation, by our legislature, of $250,000 for the purchase of arms and munitions of war, as recommended by Hon. T. C. Hindman. . . .

DOCUMENT 33

Resolution of December Meeting at Fort Smith, Presented in the Arkansas House, January 10, 1861

Source: *Journal of the House of Representatives for the Thirteenth Session of the General Assembly of the State of Arkansas* (Little Rock: Johnson & Yerkes, Public Printers, 1861), 550–51.

Residents of Fort Smith in Sebastian County, where slaves made up 7 percent of the population, met in December of 1860 and endorsed this resolution that was read before the Arkansas Senate in January. The residents stressed their desire to support a strong Union and "speak in moderation," but in the end they supported a convention to cooperate with other southern states and ensure that Arkansas's rights were protected.

WHEREAS, Several of our sister southern states have either called conventions, or are about calling conventions of delegates fresh from the people, to consider what is best to be done under the existing and alarming state of public affairs; therefore,

1st. *Resolved*, That the State of Arkansas feels no less interest in the prosperity of the South than her sister southern states, and sympathizes with them in their efforts to place themselves in a situation to guard and ward off the blow, which may well be anticipated from the antecedents of the executive elected, as soon as he comes into power; but such proposition should always come from the people, and the only legitimate mode of arriving at the will of the people is by state conventions.

2d. *Resolved,* That we are in favor of the immediate call of a state convention, to consider and settle what the people of this state desire to be done under the existing state of our federal relations, before Mr. Lincoln's inauguration.

3d. *Resolved,* That it is the duty of all good citizens in the impending crisis, to examine candidly the great issue now before us; to speak of it with moderation, and to act in reference to it in full view of all the momentous consequences; and we will use all honorable means likely to result in success to obtain a peaceable adjustment of our present difficulties, but failing in this, our interest and feeling alike dictate to us our duty to unite and co-operate with our southern brethren, to secure our rights out of the Union, the rights denied us in it, and to present to friend and foe, at home and abroad, a united and invincible South.

4th. *Resolved,* That while we admire the ability of our brethren of South Carolina, and are disposed to extenuate the motives which induced them to secede from the Union, we think they should defer to the judgment of their southern brethren, and act with the deliberation necessary to secure the hearty and undivided co-operation of those equally interested with themselves in maintaining the honor and rights due them, as integral parts of this great confederacy.

5th. *Resolved,* That we condemn any attempt on the part of the federal government to coerce a seceding state.

6th. *Resolved,* That we are fully aware that there are thousands of Union loving and conservative men in the North and East, who are ready to assist us in maintaining our constitutional rights. . . .

DOCUMENT 34

An Act to Provide for a State Convention, January 15, 1861

Source: *Journal of Both Sessions of the Convention of the State of Arkansas* (Little Rock: Johnson and Verkes, State Printers, 1861), 3–4.

After much discussion and debate, the state legislature asked Arkansas voters to determine the necessity of a convention at a special election on February 18, 1861. By this time, South Carolina, Mississippi, Florida, and Alabama had already left the Union, and Georgia, Louisiana, and Texas would leave before the February vote.

Section 1. Be it enacted by the General Assembly of the State of Arkansas, That the governor shall issue his proclamation, ordering an election in all the counties in this state, submitting to the people the question of "convention" or "no convention" to be held on the eighteenth day of February, 1861, which election shall be conducted as state elections are now conducted; Provided, That the sheriffs of the several counties shall be required to give but ten days' notice of said election.

Sec 2. Be it further enacted, That, at said election, the people shall also vote for a delegate or delegates to said convention, and each delegate elected shall be made a special returning officer, and shall bring up the certified vote of his county on the question of convention or no convention . . . on the second day of March, 1861; and if, on counting the vote of all the counties of this state, it shall appear that a majority of all the votes cast are for a convention, then the governor shall immediately issue his proclamation, requiring the delegates elected as aforesaid to convene in the capital on the following Monday, and organize themselves into a state convention, by the election of a president, and such other officers as may be required. . . .

Sec 5. Be it further enacted, That each county in the state shall be entitled to elect as many delegates to said convention as it is now entitled to members in the lower branch of the General Assembly, and the qualifications for a delegate shall be the same as now required for a member of the House of Representatives. . . .

Sec 8. Be it further enacted, That upon the organization of said convention, it shall take into consideration the condition of political affairs, and determine what course the State of Arkansas shall take in the present political crisis. . . .

[Chapter 3]

Campaigning for a Convention

January and February 1861

After the legislature agreed to hold a vote on a secession convention on January 15, 1861, candidates campaigned until the election for the convention on February 18. Candidates published broadsides and spoke openly about their stance on the crisis. This chapter reproduces many of these appeals to voters that detail a wide range of opinions. The Unionists, however, did not reject secession but instead argued that at the present moment it was the wrong choice for Arkansas and, thus, are more aptly termed cooperationists. They, like their secessionist opponents, indicated that the federal government had abused the rights of slaveholders and pledged to solve the property crisis and eliminate challenges to the South's racial hierarchy. Secessionists, emboldened by the continued secession of the rest of the Deep South during the campaign, continued to argue that secession was the only viable option for the state if it wanted to defend its property rights and racial order. The election on February 18 allowed for a secession convention but elected a majority of Unionists/cooperationists.

DOCUMENT 35

Fort Smith Broadside for Delegate Samuel Griffith, January 21, 1861

Source: Broadside Collection, Arkansas History
Commission, Little Rock, Arkansas.

Samuel Griffith, a farmer with twenty-nine slaves, published this broadside to announce his ultimately successful candidacy to represent Sebastian County at the
convention. Borrowing some language from a December
1860 Benton County resolution, Griffith supported the
need to preserve the Union at all costs and for more consultation with other southern states. However, he advocated that as a conservative Unionist he would work for
the repeal of northern personal liberty laws as well as to
prevent "the loathsome disease called negrophobia" from
destroying the Union.

I have before me yours of yesterday inviting me to become a candidate to represent you in the Convention to be held in Little Rock on the
fourth of March next, the object of which Convention (if the people by
their votes should decide to call one) is to take into consideration and
determine what stand Arkansas shall take in the present political crisis.
Were I so selfish as to consult my *personal* feelings or so mercenary as to
allow pecuniary considerations to influence me, it is an honor which I
should decline without hesitation.

I have never taken an active part in political affairs, nor is it my
intention to do so in the future; but "clouds o'er lapping clouds, are
weaving o'er our house an evil woof—a fearful canopy." Our country is shaken by a political earthquake which threatens ruin to all that
Americans hold sacred. But yesterday we were the most happy and prosperous Nation under the broad canopy of Heaven. A Nation offering
and affording a home, a refuge, for the down-trodden and oppressed
of very part of the globe—a Nation whose Flag commanded respect
on every sea and in every land; with a Government standing on the
broad basis of Justice and Equality—a Government which allows and

encourages the poorest boy to aspire to the highest place in the gilt of a free and independent people. Now, as if by the touch of a magician's wand, all, all is changed; and we are threatened with the most terrible of all scourges of which the human mind can conceive—Civil War, with all its attendant horrors.

Fellow citizens, under this state of things I hold it to be the duty of every man, however humble or private his previous position may have been, to come forward and make every sacrifice in his power to assist in bringing peace to our unhappy country, and save our glorious Union, if possible to be done, by means honorable, just, and equitable alike, to all sections of the country. We should, in my humble opinion, stand firm in the support of our Constitutional rights—rights guaranteed to every American citizen (whether by adoption or native born) by a Constitution made sacred and consecrated by the blood, fortunes, and honor of the noblest patriots of any age of any land—not by such agreements as tyrants and despots use, nor by inconsiderate, extreme, or hasty action, but by prudent, wise, and conservative counsels.

That the South has been wronged, no candid man can deny; but in our efforts to redress those wrongs, let us not forget that there are thousands upon thousands of Union loving, conservative men in the non-slaveholding States, who are ready to stand shoulder to shoulder with us in the battle for our just rights. We should act in concert with such friends, promptly and with firmness; but in the name of all that is sacred, let us not suffer demagoguing politicians (who would sacrifice their country to elevate themselves) nor fanatical abolitionists who have cast aside the Holy Bible and placed on their pulpits the infamous Helper book—who constitute passion umpire, by their unholy means tear down in a day the noblest fabric ever erected by the wisdom of man.

Arkansas should not allow herself to be dragged headlong into trouble by the Beechers, Sewards, Sumners, or Hales of the North; nor by the Yanceys, Rhetts, Toombs, or Wigfalls of the South.[1] We have men enough in Arkansas capable of appreciating our rights and of understanding our wrongs; and who, knowing the right, dare pursue it.

---

1. The northerners mentioned were prominent abolitionists, and the southerners were prominent fire-eaters.

I regret that our Legislature did not pass the Act calling a Convention, earlier, so as that in the event that that body pass an Ordinance of secession, it could have then been referred back to the people for their ratification or rejection. In this way, the voice and deliberate decision of every man in the State, could be had upon the all important question now before the country, in which all free men have an equal interest. And I do firmly believe that had this plan been adopted in those States that have already seceded; they would all have been yet in the Union. In other words, that they have gone out contrary to the will and wish of a majority of their citizens. Fellow citizens, we have time for sober second thought. Let us not be precipitated. I am opposed to this wholesale muzzling the mouths of those whom unprincipled demagogues call the *dear people* (until they get their votes) and it should be submitted to no longer.

I have hoped and I still hope a Southern Convention will be agreed upon, wherein the best and true men of the South (not now occupying political position) can agree upon and present to the North a plan of adjustment, as our ultimatum, which would be:

First—A demand of the repeal of the mischievous Personal Liberty Bills which now disgrace the statute books of many of the Northern States.

Second—By the amendment of the Constitution, so as that the loathsome disease called *negrophobia,* can never again darken and disgrace the Halls of Congress. . . .

But five of the States have already gone out. The question now to be considered is, what stand shall the remaining States take. Arkansas has a mind of her own. Let her act as her duty to her sister Southern States, to herself, and to the Union; and as honor and justice dictate to be right, in view of the momentous consequences—asking nothing more than her just rights, accepting nothing less. Then we shall be justified in the eyes of the civilized world, by God and man.

But gentleman, I have already prolonged my reply to your complementary note, I fear, to a tedious length. Allow me then, in conclusion, to say to you, and through this medium, also to my friends in different parts of Sebastian County, who have expressed a wish that I should become a candidate for the Convention, that I had hoped that some one better versed in the political affairs of the country than myself, would have been called on. Nevertheless, I have only to say, that I am a Southern man by birth, education and feeling. Western Arkansas has been my home for the past twenty two years. Her interest is my interest—come weal or woe, her fate shall be mine.

... It being distinctly understood, that I prefer to fight *in the Union*, under the *Constitution* and that *spotless Flag*—the broad Stripes and bright Stars bequeathed to us by our forefathers. At all events, until all hope (the last thing that leaves the human mind) is gone, for an honorable settlement of the grave question now agitating the public mind.

DOCUMENT 36

Letter from David Walker to David C. Williams, January 29, 1861

Source: D. C. Williams Papers, Arkansas History Commission, Little Rock, Arkansas.

David Walker, from Fayetteville, the future president of the secession convention, wrote to David Williams, a merchant and Unionist from Van Buren, and remarked on the way the convention was organized, specifically, that it did not allow for the convention's decision to be referred back to the people. Moreover, Walker advocated that Arkansas should stand with the slaveholding states that had not yet left the Union, creating common cause with them. Walker was no stranger to Arkansas politics or slavery. He had previously been active as a Whig senator, as a member of the original constitutional convention in 1836, and as an associate justice on the state supreme court for eight years. He owned twenty-three slaves in 1860.

... The convention bill has come to us since you wrote and makes no provision for referring the action of the Convention back to the people for their approval. This was a great and grave error. If this government is ever broken up as it is threatened to be, the sovereign power will not revert to the kin apparent to the Crown, as it would in a monarchy, but the power reverts to the people and such individuals taking back to himself an equal part with any other. And when a new government is formed, they delegate certain powers to the several departments of government to exercise for the common good. It therefore naturally and properly follows that they should know what powers the new government is to possess and ratify and affirm them or they may well claim that they have parted with the powers and will not sanction the act. North Carolina, Tennessee, and Missouri entertaining a decent respect for the rights of the people, provide in their bill calling a convention that should the convention decide that a change in the relations between the State and the federal government was proper, that they should refer the question of Union or disunion back to the people for a direct vote. And let them say whether they would sanction such changes. Kentucky and Virginia will doubt less do the same. This was all right and will not only afford time for an adjustment of our difficulties but will enable the people to decide directly for themselves. This bill of ours, however, makes no such provision but gives a quorum of 50 men called to gather under an apportionment made ten years ago absolute power to dissolve all connection with the federal government and to inaugurate a new government such as they may see fit and which is to be binding upon us whether we approve it or not, this is a gross outrage and one to which I never will subscribe.

My opinion is that we should have taken our stand with Missouri, Tennessee, Kentucky, and the other border states. And if a convention must be called, that we should have followed their example if they determine to remain in the Union by all means we should join them. We should encourage them to take the stand and have united with them. I am confident in six months the folly of the outcomes would be manifested to themselves so forcibly as to bring about settlement of all difficulties. But how is it now they have all resolved that if their diligents in Convention think it necessary to secede that the question be referred back to them. Arkansas holds her convention at the same time, no such obligation is imposed upon her. If she goes on and acts, she thereby places it out of her powers to act with the other border states. She in effect throws them off and discourages them from all further efforts. Whilst she encourages the disunionists to preserve in this disloyal cause towards the nation.

Thus situated it seems to me that we should make the issue hardly at the polls, in the approaching election and to enact of every candidate who runs a *positive irrevocable pledge* that in no event will he take any step to disrupt our present federal relations or to inaugurate any new government . . . before it is referred back to them to be voted upon and approved. This is reasonable and just and it seems to me that the great mass of the people will approve it. I am confident they will. . . . If this is done, then the members of the Convention will do what the legislature should have required them to do, and as will still stand side by side with the border states to act with them. . . .

I have no doubt but that if the Northern people could have a chance now to elect members to Congress they would send men who would vote for Crittenden Compromise measures.[2] Then Southerners don't want the Compromise to be effected and if the Northern members were to come over now and vote for the Compromise, I doubt not but that a goodly number of the Southern members would find some excuse to vote against it. Indeed in anticipation that such might be the result, several have said that they would not abide any compromise that did not receive a majority of Northern votes.

These men want to open the African Slave Trade. They want free trade and as a necessary consequence direct taxes. This has been their favorite policy for years.

It is probable that I will run for the Convention. If I do, or whether I do or not, I will do all in my power to restore peace, and prevent extreme measures in this state. I owe this to posterity and my children more than to myself. My own race is too near run to hope to see our country prosperous as it was 12 months ago. . . .

---

2. An attempt to stave off secessionism by Kentucky's US senator John Crittenden. In December of 1860, Crittenden proposed constitutional amendments that guaranteed slavery in the West by extending the Missouri Compromise line, protections to ensure orderly return or compensation for fugitive slaves, and guarantees that slavery could not be abolished in Washington, D.C., or on federal property in slave states. The proposal failed in Congress.

DOCUMENT 37

Governor Henry Rector to John Ross, Principal Chief of the Cherokee Nation, January 29, 1861

Source: US War Department, *The War of the Rebellion: A Compilation of the Official Records of the Union and Confederate Armies* (Washington, DC: GPO, 1880), series 1, 1:683–84.

Henry Rector, countering perceived attempts by northerners to agitate abolition in Indian Territory, wrote to Cherokee chief John Ross to encourage him to side with the South in order to protect Cherokee slave property from northern abolitionism. Many Cherokees, along with the Choctaw, Chickasaw, Creek, and Seminole, allied with the Confederacy and fought alongside it.

SIR: It may now be regarded as almost certain that the States having slave property within their borders will, in consequence of repeated Northern aggressions, separate themselves and withdraw from the Federal Government.

South Carolina, Alabama, Florida, Mississippi, Georgia, and Louisiana have already, by action of the people, assumed this attitude. Arkansas, Missouri, Tennessee, Kentucky, Virginia, North Carolina, and Maryland will probably pursue the same course by the 4th of March next. Your people, in their institutions, productions, latitude, and natural sympathies, are allied to the common brotherhood of the slaveholding States. Our people and yours are natural allies in war and friends in peace. Your country is salubrious and fertile, and possesses the highest capacity for future progress and development by the application of slave labor. Besides this, the contiguity of our territory with yours induces relations of so intimate a character as to preclude the idea of discordant or separate action.

It is well established that the Indian country west of Arkansas is looked to by the incoming administration of Mr. Lincoln as fruitful fields, ripe for the harvest of abolitionism, freesoilers, and Northern mountebanks.

We hope to find in your people friends willing to co-operate with the South in defense of her institutions, her honor, and her firesides, and with whom the slaveholding States are willing to share a common future, and to afford protection commensurate with your exposed condition and your subsisting monetary interests with the General Government. . . .

Document 38

S. J. Howell to Jesse Turner, January 29, 1861

Source: Jesse Turner Papers, University of Arkansas Special Collections, Fayetteville, Arkansas.

Jesse Turner was elected to represent Crawford County, where 11 percent of the population was enslaved, in the secession convention. A supporter of the Union, Turner had been involved in Arkansas politics since the 1840s, serving as a Whig in the state legislature and as the US attorney for the Western District of Arkansas. In this letter, S. J. Howell, a resident of Pittsburg in Johnson County, discussed with Turner the problems with immediate secessionism and again linked Arkansas to the non-seceded slaveholding states that he believed held "the balance of power."

Yours of the 13th Instant is before me and the contents noted my absence is my apology for not answering sooner. You seem to be anxious to know whether we have all turned disunionist. I can answer for one I have not as long as there is hopes of getting our rights in the Union. I think the Border States hold the balance of power in their hands and if they will hold a convention claim up to 36 30 [36 deg. and 30 min. north latitude]. Alter the Constitution so as to make all the states slave up to that line South and free north and the subject to be taken out of Congress forever in the future, then if the north will not or does not give us this we will secede and go with the South as our interests are identified with them. Immediate secession on our part could be attended with no good. It could only saddle us with a large state debt that perhaps we would not get clear of for the next fifty years and would not affect any good by it. Besides this if the Border States were to secede the government would have nothing to protect west of us, consequently they would withdraw the Troop and we would be exposed to savages as well as an internal element aged on by Abolition emmisarys. I have been to NC. In the midst of secession the ultras do not want a compromise but to form a southern confederacy open their ports free and raise revenue by direct taxes, property qualification to vote. This I think is mity near monarchy. I subscribe to nearly all your doctrine except the calling a convention of all the states, that I think would do no good as there are ultras North and South, and if the Border States saw Texas, Arkansas, Missouri, Kentucky, Tennessee, Virginia, and North Carolina, Maryland, and Delaware would meet, declare their rights in the Union and say this same we will go and no further the thing would be brought to a compromise. Or we would then be compelled to dissolve I think from what I can see and here that the People or a majority of them in this county are for this policy. I have not seen the candidates nor do not know how ultra they are, hope they are more conservative than you think, though I have not much room will write you when I hear them speak which will be next Saturday. In looking over your late papers yesterday I was proud to see you requested to be a candidate for Convention as you clearly show in your letter that you are conservative but not submissionist. I can not become a candidate unless there can not be another man who will on the side of the Union. . . .

DOCUMENT 39

Letter from Mark Bean to David Williams, January 30, 1861

Source: D. C. Williams Papers, Arkansas History Commission, Little Rock, Arkansas.

Discussing the impending election in Washington County, Mark Bean, one of Washington County's largest slaveholders, presented a personal opinion on the election of David Walker and the fate of secessionists in Washington County. Washington, with four delegates, was the third most populated county in Arkansas in

1860, but only 10 percent of the population was enslaved. Bean's support of Walker and the Unionist/cooperationist ticket illustrates that the individual decision to support secession was multifaceted, not just related to one's own slaveholding.

Dear Friend,

I have received your letter also one from our good friend Judge Walker and also your letter to him embracing the same subjects, and which I as fully endorse as any man in Ark. Walker spent the night with me last week, he was extremely anxious for me to run for the Convention. I told him that nothing would give me more pleasure than to stand by him as I did in the State Convention and battle side by side with him when the South with Billy Cummins at the head, contended that the basis of representation should not be upon the free white male inhabitants only, but two thirds of their negroes should be represented. I told him that it was impossible for me to run owing to my feeble state of health. Last Saturday we nominated Mr. JB Reussell for the convention and recommended Walker unanimously and Doctor Dean. Also JH Stirman. All eyes are turned to Judge Walker here. There is a mass meeting in Fayetteville next Saturday to nominate conventioneers. We passed a resolution or platform for our candidates, that our candidates must be strong union men. Walker will have nothing to do with the convention in Fayetteville. The wire workers I think or secessionists will be defeated. I hope so at least. I have and still will urge the importance as you suggest the decision back to the people and have every candidate pledged to this affect. I hope that Gen. Thomason will run for one man in Crawford. What have we to gain in a division of our glorious union. I see no compromising spirit by any of our members in Congress are they reflecting the will of Arkansas, or are they sympathizing with poor South Carolina, which I can not do. I would be glad to hear from you at anytime.

DOCUMENT 40

Jesse Turner of Crawford County and the Secession Crisis, February 4, 1861

Source: Heiskell Broadsides Collection, Center for
Arkansas History and Culture, Little Rock, Arkansas.

The Unionist Jesse Turner, as part of his electoral strategy, published this broadside in Crawford County to discuss his views on secessionism before the February election. Turner responded to two important questions: Does the convention have the right to take the state out of the Union? And if it is approved, should secession be referred back to the state's voters for popular approval? He, like many Unionists, did not agree that a state had the right to leave the Union; and, even if the convention approved such a course, he believed the decision should be returned to a vote of the people. Turner hoped that the South would give the North time to "repent" and provide safeguards to slaveholders to avert war.

. . . I have to say, that I do not recognize the Constitutional right of a State to secede from the Union, while I do recognize the right of revolution as an extreme remedy, which would be an appeal from the cancelled obligations of the Constitution to original rights and the law of self preservation. If however, I recognized the constitutional right of a State to secede from the Union, or believed that an occasion had arisen justifying a resort to the extreme remedy of revolution, I should still in the event of the Convention passing an Ordinance of Secession, insist on its submission to the votes of the people, for their ratification or rejection. But, denying as I do the Constitutional right of a State to secede from the Union, and utterly denying that any adequate cause exists, justifying a resort to the extreme and original right of revolution, I should the more earnestly insist on submitting such Ordinances to a direct vote of the people, before the same shall become final.

It is a defect in the Convention bill that it does not provide expressly for referring the action of the Convention to the people. But the programme of its authors no doubt was, to precipitate Arkansas out of the Union, at a time of unprecedented excitement, without giving the people time for sober and deliberate reflection, and thus commit the State to the mad and revolutionary schemes of other seceding States. But the Convention will have complete control of the whole subject matter, and I hope will act in the premises as though the Legislature had made express provision for a reference of its action to the people.

. . . [P]ermit me to express my ardent desire for the preservation of our Federal Union, if it can be preserved consistently with the honor and rights of the slave-holding States. We ought not to be in haste to pull down and destroy the noblest Government the world has ever known. We ought to give the people of the Northern States, reasonable time to repent of their follies, to retrace their steps, to expel from power their reckless and fanatical leaders, and to yield to the South such guarantees of their rights as their safety may require. We ought to confer with, and abide by the fortunes of the border Slave States, and as a last resort we ought to hold a National Convention in order that a great and final effort may be made to preserve the unity of our great American Republic.

And now Gentlemen, in conclusion, I beg of you not to despair of the Republic, for although dark and angry clouds are above us, and all around us, let us hope that a bright light will ere long stream through the thick darkness, bringing joy and gladness to the hearts of patriots every where, and that our Federal Union, the palladium of our liberties, to which we are indebted for our greatness, glory, and happiness as a people, may endure for ages and ages yet to come, blessing and blessed of all our race.

DOCUMENT 41

Broadside: To the People of Washington County, J. H. Stirman, February 5, 1861

Source: Broadside Collection, Arkansas History Commission, Little Rock, Arkansas.

J. H. Stirman, a Fayetteville merchant, was elected to represent Washington County in the convention. Stirman asserted that Arkansas's rights within the Union must be defended, but he believed that at this time immediate secession was not the answer: secession should only be used as a last resort. In this way, Stirman reflected the views of many Unionists who were not opposed to the idea of secession but did not see it as a viable course of action in February 1861. These cooperationists, like their pro-secession counterparts, understood that the South needed to come to an accommodation with the North. Stirman also referenced concerns of Indian attacks along the state's western border, which, since he represented a border county, his constituents would have appreciated. He also linked Arkansas to its regional economic partners since he believed that the system of slavery that linked Arkansas with Louisiana, Tennessee, and other bordering states needed to be taken into consideration when thinking about secession.

Fellow Citizens: Having been requested to submit my name as a candidate for the approaching Convention, I have not, in my view of the numerous solicitations from all parts of the county, felt at liberty to decline the call.

I am no politician, and would prefer the retirement of private life; but I hold it to be the duty of every good citizen to occupy the post which the people may choose to assign him, especially in times like these. It is hardly necessary to mention that the darkest period in the history of our Republic is upon us, and that it is the duty of all patriots and lovers of their country, to be up and doing, to avert, if possible, the dangers and calamities which threaten. Already six States of the Confederacy have unconditionally seceded therefrom, and others may very soon follow in their train.

Our Legislature has wisely proposed that a Convention of Delegates from the several counties of the State assemble at Little Rock on the 4th March to "take into consideration the condition of affairs, and determine what course the State of Arkansas shall take in the present political crisis."

I hold it to be the duty of every candidate for the Convention to state his views clearly and explicitly, in reference to the troubled condition of our country. I shall attempt to do so.

I hold that the Union, as bequeathed to us by the Fathers of the Revolution, is of inestimable value—politically, socially, and in every respect which can affect the peace, prosperity, and happiness of the American people; yet no true and loyal citizen of this State, would desire that Arkansas should remain in the Union, unless her Constitutional rights in that Union were fully recognized, guaranteed, and secured. The people of this State and of the whole South agree in this; so there is no issue upon that point. I think it possible that our rights may yet be secured in the Union; and holding this opinion am opposed to the secession of this State until every effort shall have been exhausted to secure them *in* the Union. Let secession be the last remedy.

I am not one of those who would *hurry* Arkansas out of the Union, fearing perhaps lest some terms of adjustment might be agreed upon that would be just and satisfactory to the whole country; nor do I believe that the best way to save the Union, is to *destroy* it, and then reconstruct it.

At the present moment, by the suggestion of the State of Virginia, a Convention is in session in Washington City, composed of some of the wisest statesmen and purest men in the land, both from the North and the South, who are engaged in a noble effort to restore harmony and concord to our distracted country. From this effort we have much to hope; should this fail however, then in this emergency—having regard to all the interests of our State, I should be in favor of co-operating with Missouri, Tennessee, Kentucky, Virginia, Maryland, North Carolina, and Delaware in their action, whatever it may be. It would seem to me, that their destiny must be ours, whether for good or evil. The western portion of our State is but sparsely settled, bordered by Indian Territory, and from this circumstance, will be more exposed to hostile incursions and military forays than any one of the Southern States. The States above named are our natural allies, and by their geographical position, can come to our aid in time of extremity and danger. While statesmen are so busy with the plans of Free Trade and Direct Taxation, with the perfecting of systems by which they hope to build up on the Atlantic sea-board, Cities of enormous wealth and splendor, let not the *inland* State of Arkansas, abandoning her natural and local allies before alluded to, be dragooned into the support of these systems and plans, to the neglect of her own citizens, their homes and firesides. Arkansas must act for herself and consult her own interests.

While holding these views, I would have our State take a firm and unalterable position along with the other border States against coercion by the General Government, or any one of the seceding States.

The Legislature wisely submitted to the people of the State, the propriety of holding a Convention. This was right. How much more important is it then, that the *action* of the Convention, affecting our relations with the General Government should be submitted to the people for their ratification, before it becomes valid. I hold that "all power is inherent in the people," and that all questions of such magnitude, should be sent back to them for their approval or rejection. I therefore pledge myself, should I be elected a Delegate to the Convention, to vote for no *Act, Ordinance, or Resolution* of said Convention, having for its object, to change or dissolve the political relations of this State to the General Government, or of any other State, until a majority of the qualified voters of this State, voting upon the question, shall ratify the same. . . .

DOCUMENT 42

Address of Senator Robert Ward Johnson, February 7, 1861

Sources: Robert Ward Johnson, *Address to the People of Arkansas* (Washington, DC: H. Polkinhorn, 1861), 1–8 and the *Fayetteville Arkansian,* March 1, 1861.

Robert Ward Johnson, a member of Arkansas's political dynasty the "Family," represented Arkansas in the US Senate from 1853 to 1861. Johnson was first elected to Congress from Helena and served in the House of Representatives from 1847 to 1853. He was a fiery secessionist, and his speech countered the opinion of the Unionists/cooperationists who believed that there could be a compromise to protect southern rights within the Union. Johnson argued that Arkansas should join the new Confederacy, which on the next day would be formed in Montgomery, Alabama. This government would be "relieved of the doctrines of negro equality, intolerant religious hatred, and a partial sectional legislation"; and Arkansas would therefore not be "sunk powerless beneath Abolitionism, Emancipation, Negro equality."

The people of Arkansas are to decide on the 18t instant whether they will assemble in convention by their delegates, on the 4th of March, to adopt such measures as the public welfare may demand; and they are at the same time to elect those delegates. All eyes are turned towards her, as the eighth and last Cotton States, to see what, in the present great emergency, she will consider demanded by her interest and due to her honor.

I am, I may say without impropriety, a native of our State, with all my interests inseparably connected and interwoven with hers. If this, and the best years of my life faithfully spent in her service, can entitle my counsels to any share of respect, I feel, without vanity or presumption I am sure, that it is my duty to offer them, whether they may win me thanks or odium.

Within the limits of a letter, it is not possible either to discuss all the questions involved in the present controversy or to recite the hundredth part of the fact and circumstances that have brought about the present crisis. I can only select and allude to a few of each; and say plainly what, in view of them ought to be the determination of the people of Arkansas, if they desire to care properly for their future welfare, and to control their future destinies.

A revolution is in progress. This all admit. In less than ten days the Southern Republic will have been fully organized and in action, beneath its own national flag. It will be the same Government that this was designed to be by our forefathers—the same Constitution, laws, and forms—relieved of the doctrines of negro equality, intolerant religious hatred, and a partial sectional legislation, which has made us the mere tributaries and commercial vassals of the North.

This has been produced and justified by a long-continued and systematic disregard, denial, and violation of the just rights, interests, and equality of the people of the Southern States. It has been hastened by the fact that on the 4th of March next, the powers of the General Government are to pass into the hands of those whose rancorous hostility to our interests and social institutions we are not permitted to doubt. Thus, those who are resolved to confine domestic slavery within the present limits, and to expel it from the Border States, to make it odious everywhere, and to deny it protection everywhere, will then have complete possession of those great powers by which such results are to be effected, after a thirty years' bitter struggle to obtain them.

None but those who are experienced in the operation and effect of systematic legislation, and who are close observers of the vast influences of executive power, can comprehend the hopeless condition of any people that are, for a series of years, to be subjected to their joint exercise in hostile hands. That we are soon to be placed in that position, if we do not act promptly and effectually, is well known to every well-informed citizen.

Our Statesmen disagree, not as to the justice of our complaints, or of those apprehensions that oppress the minds of the Southern people; but as to the remedy by which they may most effectually defend and protect themselves.

The people of seven States, connected with us by the strong ties of race and lineage, of common pursuits, and the same habits and manners and modes of thought, have elected Secession as the only adequate remedy. It is a rightful remedy, and resort to it is amply justified by the systematic violation of the Constitution by the Northern States. It is a constitutional remedy; since, that each party to a contract shall keep it honestly is no more a part of the contract than that if part of them do not, the other may at their option consider it rescinded.

The doctrine of the Kentucky and Virginia Resolutions, 1798–99 and separate "States Rights," always asserted and maintained by ourselves, and by the Jeffersonian Democracy of the Northern States, now furnish to us an adequate and peaceful remedy, and we have no other remedy except forcible Revolution.

The Northern people and parties assert that this General Government is a Government of *majorities* and that the majority, must and shall rule. We deny this proposition, and while we admit that majorities inside of each State must rule . . . we claim that the Federal Government is a Government of States, each people being distinct, and represented in the Federal Government as a separate mass by its own State Authorities, and not to be merged in the masses, or subverted by the will of other communities more numerous than itself. It is a "reserved right," that each State shall judge for itself of all infractions of the Constitution, and give all proper protection of life, liberty, and property, against the unscrupulous tyranny of the *majorities* in other States.

This is the contest; and it is a contest which involves the successful assertion of our equality in the Union, our social system, our property, our liberties, everything: if we fail, that failure must result in our absolute submission to a Northern fanatical majority, a popular Despotism that is hostile to us, and the gradual if not rapid loss of all these blessings.

The "*State Rights*" doctrines have been openly and ably sustained by the greatest American statesmen for the last sixty-three years. They were suited to the protection alike *of any and every oppressed State*; whether it lay to the North or South. The time when, or the occasion upon which, or the party by whom, a resort to them might first become necessary was foreseen by no one. It is the misfortune of the South that she has been marked as the victim to oppression. It is the good fortune of the South that in prosperity she was just to all *and maintained these principles*, and that in her adversity she can consistently appeal to them, and protect her rights.

Seven States, as I have said, have put an end to the discussion as to the right of secession, by exercising the right. Whether it be a Constitutional or a Revolutionary right, is a question that has disappeared. They have decided, and we know that it was, at least, the only adequate and effectual remedy.

Admit that "Co-operation," or joint action of the Southern States, instead of separate State action would have been better, and the fact remains that if Co-operation had been waited for, we would have sunk powerless beneath Abolitionism, Emancipation, Negro equality, &c. And, with us, the question of "Co-operation," can scarcely be said to remain, since it is now only left to be determined, whether we will cooperate with *seven* States who are out of this Union, and with whom we will be free and equal, or with *seven* States yet remaining in the Union, who have lost all semblance of equality, and who are undoubtedly subject to a future of Abolition rule, and a dangerous if not degrading inferiority. I have no idea that *seven*, or even one, will consent, after the present commotions, to settle down and remain in the Union; but if it should be so, I would never be willing to share with them the destiny which, sooner or later, must inevitably be theirs.

Let us decline to discuss with the Northern States the question of the right to secede. Let us only inquire if it be the only effectual remedy; and settling that for ourselves, if we hold it to be so, maintain our right to resort to it, even by arms, if that necessity be forced upon us.

Some of our public men (not many of any mark in the South) still hold that we could obtain ample and perfect security, without secession, if we would but give the North time to provide it for us. Neither the States of the North, nor their public men of the dominant party, make such pledges. Congress has been in session more than two months, and during all that time certain southern men have continually besought and implored obdurate Black Republicanism to yield something to the South, if it were only plausible, admitting of two interpretations; if it were only to reiterate more specifically what the Constitution, properly understood, already contains. But they have yielded nothing, proposed nothing, promised nothing.

They will allow the vote on the Crittenden, resolutions to be taken, they say, about the 3d of March, perhaps if it is taken at all, and they stand pledged to defeat them by a solid party vote. The Crittenden proposition is another *compromise*; it will not protect us five years; and the south ought not to accept it. I cannot vote for it in your name. But they will yield nothing that we can or ought to accept. We, the weaker party to this irrepressible conflict, are made by the mouths of southern infatuated men to present all the propositions for compromise, with our humble prayers to the deaf ears and stony hearts of Black Republicanism, and finally, to the mortifying sense of humiliation is to be added the ignominy of failure, and the bitter consciousness of contempt.

Nothing less than secession could have compelled the North to give us the guarantees and security that we are compelled to demand. Whilst Congress does nothing, and the Border States, deluded by the Peace Congress and the idle hope that the Crittenden propositions may be adopted, are allowing the golden opportunity for efficient action to pass away, LINCOLN announces that he is opposed to any compromise and will execute the laws; and as an earnest of his resolution he selects WILLIAM H. SEWARD for his Secretary of State. His followers in Congress and our, pronounce for coercion: the laws of the States, in violation of the Constitution, and which annul the act of Congress passed to prevent the stealing of our property, remain unrepealed; and Pennsylvania, New York, Ohio, Massachusetts, and others, tender to the incoming President men and money to enable him to subjugate the South.

And if any promises were made to us, why should we put trust in them? If they have violated the once sacred Constitution and their oaths, what obligation, more sacred and superior to them, can man devise? All pledges are met with a punic faith if in conflict with the northern policy and religious hostility. Their policy is the extinction of four thousand million dollars of southern property, and the *freedom, and the equality with us* of the four millions of negroes now in the South. All obligations have, and all future promises will give away before that policy.

For thirty years the politicians have had this controversy in their exclusive charge; and all the time while it has been going from bad to worse, and the Constitution has been helpless to protect, and the Union has been to us a mere hollow truce, a treacherous armistice, the praises of that Union and the glories of our flag have been vociferously chanted by those who were vigorously violating the one, and shattering the other into fragments.

We have had compromises enough, equivocating platforms enough, while in every contest the South have lost more and more of their just rights, and more shorn of their strength. . . .

At last, thank God, the People of the southern States have taken the matter into their own hands; and I have faith in them. They will settle it. They will have their just rights, peaceably if they can, forcibly if they must. Heart and hand, with my whole soul, through every trial, I am with them, as I am of them, until the end. Urged by their ablest and purest public men, these people are taking charge of their own interests through their State governments; and as a result we see that, for the first time, since 1789, the South is resolutely and successfully maintaining her rights and equality against the great "irrepressible conflict." Whatever differences of opinion among our public men there were originally, in regard to separate secession, they are rapidly disappearing. . . .

The Northern States are alarmed. They feel the truth of the significant remarks of the London Times, that if the Border States unite with those that have seceded, and form a new federation, it would be the real United States, so far as the territory present and prospective is concerned, and reduce the North to what our ancestors would have termed "a rump," with a future hardly greater than that of Canada, a narrow slip of country as straggling as that of Prussia, and ready soon to fall to pieces; *in which future separation of the territory North,* we are to find, and in nothing else perhaps, perfect peace for ourselves and perfect security for the future.

Even the present reluctant admissions of a few of the people of some of the northern cities, would never have been obtained, if the Southern people had not put Congress (in which they were powerless) to one side, and themselves assumed the conduct of the controversy; and if they were now to halt, and again commit it to Congress, to calculating friends and timid compromisers, the patched up truce would soon be broken, agitation for the repeal of all concessions would shake the North, the Statesmen who had conceded anything would be every trace of our equality obliterated, and we should have again to resort to secession, under increased disadvantages, and far greater hazard, while all the world smiled and anticipated for us a new defeat.

It sounds well of no Arkansian to reproach the States that have adopted separate action, aside from the fact that the complaint will be found to come invariably from the very men that will show themselves, if not already well known, to be opposed to action of any kind. Arkansas made no effort to co-operate with her sister Southern States though invited to do so; and therefore has no right to complain that each has acted for herself. Each is sovereign as she is. But they and she are embarked in one common bottom, and must sink or swim together. Honor and decency would not allow us, if our interest would, to separate ourselves from the Cotton States. We could not without being lost to all sense of shame, forgetful of the desperate destiny to which we would consign our children, and devoid of self-respect adhere to the Northern States.

Therefore it is my well-considered opinion that Arkansas ought to secede, and that at the earliest practicable day, and to unite her fortunes with, and become a member of the new Confederacy and Republic of Southern States, to which we rightfully belong, and whose National Flag beyond question is already flying.

If it be dangerous for us to secede in case the Border States do not, it will be equally dangerous for us to remain in the Union with them; and we shall not avoid danger by accepting dishonor, and abandoning those who are only fighting in a cause that is as much ours as theirs. Besides, if war is to be made on us, if we are to be coerced, every Border State stands pledged to resist it, and of course to secede even if they should not do so *immediately*. We must consent, if we continue under an abolitionized

Government, soon to see our Indian country abolitionized, and possibly even Missouri. . . .

But I do not anticipate serious hostilities between the North and the South. If the Border States secede, the Southern Republic will be so powerful that coercion will be hopeless, and a peaceful separation and the benefits of a friendly commerce too desirable, to admit of war. And if the Border States do not secede, war and coercion are not to be thought of by the North, since its immediate result would be to drive every Border Southern State into secession.

But if, nevertheless, war shall come, we will not be the first people who have had to fight for liberties. We shall have to accept the necessity, and do our duty manfully. For that necessity will in no wise lessen our rights, nor make it wrong in us to vindicate them. Worse calamities may befall a people than war; of these are submission and Negro equality, and the subversion of our social system which makes of the humblest and poorest white man, a proud man, and the peer and the equal of the wealthiest and greatest in the land. Arkansas has all the material requisite to make her a great, prosperous, and powerful State. Her future is full of promise, if she but act wisely and manfully in the present exigency. She may find wiser counsellors than I; but she can find none more loyal, none more devoted to her interest and her honor. I believe I urge her to that straightforward and manly course that alone will redound to her good fortune and her glory. It is for her to decide. I at least avoid no responsibility when I say to her "ARM THYSELF! SECEDE FROM THIS UNNATURAL UNION! UNITE WITH THY SISTER STATES AND SHARE THEIR FORTUNES."

DOCUMENT 43

Broadside: An Appeal to the Voters of Benton County, February 12, 1861

Source: Oversized Small Manuscript Collection 41,
Arkansas History Commission, Little Rock, Arkansas.

The author of this broadside spelled out some clear differences between the Unionist and Secessionist platforms, indicating that the difference was not whether or not to secure rights for Arkansas within the federal government, but that Unionists believed that there was a way within the current federal system to do so, as opposed to secessionists who believed that immediate secession was the only option available. Addressed to the largely non-slaveholding population of Benton County, this message also appealed to class and regional divisions in the state as it indicated that a new nation formed by the southern states could result in only slaveholders having the right to vote.

. . . [Y]ou are called on to vote for or against the most important measures that have ever been brought before the People of Arkansas; nothing less than deciding not only your own destiny, but that of your children after you. Then, as the matter is so momentous, let us see what we are deciding. Let us look the question full in the face, get all the information we possibly can, in so short a time and then each of us, for himself, cast his vote as he may think best for the interest of the whole country. The question, then, simply and fairly stated, is this: Are you in favor of remaining in the Union, or seceding from the Union? This I conceive is a fair statement of the matter at issue, on which you are called to vote. For the sake of brevity, I shall call those in favor of remaining in the Union, UNIONISTS, and those in favor of secession, SECESSIONISTS. Both the Unionists and Secessionists agree to this proposition, that the South should not remain in the Union with the North, unless her constitutional rights in the Union are RECOGNIZED, GUARANTEED, AND SECURED. We all agree upon that proposition, and on that question there is no issue. But the mode of securing those rights, is where the two parties differ. The Union party think it is possible to secure the rights of the South in the Union, and to that end they are willing to make one more effort before they give up the OLD SHIP. The Secessionists believe that the argument is exhausted, that it is impossible to obtain the rights of the South in the Union, and they propose secession as the remedy.

Let us examine these questions calmly and deliberately, for your verdict must determine your destiny. The Unionists believe it possible, the Secessionists believe it impossible to secure the rights of the South in the Union, and the latter propose secession as the remedy. And what are the rights we are contending for so strenuously?

1st. An equal right with our property in the common territories. Now I ask any candid man, if we abandon that right, and secede from the General Government, can Arkansas claim any right in the common territories of the United States? Does South Carolina claim any right to the public domain? Do any of the seceding States claim any part of the common territories?

2nd. We claim the right, and it was secured to us by the adoption of the Constitution of the United States, that when our slaves escape from us and get into a free State, they should be delivered up on being claimed; not only delivered up, but the US Government stand pledged to use all its power, if necessary, in assisting us in securing our rights. Then, as we secured that right by adopting the Constitution of the U.S. if we overthrow, abandon, or secede from that Constitution, have we any right to go to another State and demand our escaped slaves? None whatever. The States then are foreign governments. These are questions that concern you and they must be met. There is no escaping them. And now let us examine this doctrine of secession: The Secessionists claim that any State in the Confederacy has the right to withdraw from the Union peaceably, at her own will. That is the doctrine, fairly stated. If one State can at any day break up a confederacy of States, I ask any candid man, is it not almost impossible to form a federal Republic?

Again: We all admit that the United States have the right to acquire territory, either by conquest or purchase. We also admit the right that that territory so purchased has the right, on certain conditions, to be admitted into the Union on an equal footing with the other States. These are propositions we all admit. Then Arkansas was purchased by the United States from France, and admitted into the Union. And now has she a legal or moral right to withdraw, or secede? Florida was purchased by the Federal Government, and millions upon millions spent by that Government in protecting her people, removing the Indians from her territory, erecting forts, arsenals, navy yards, light horses, &c, and admitted on an equal footing with the other States. I ask, has she a right to withdraw? Again: The Government paid Texas some $10,000,000, admitted her into the Confederacy, became engaged in a war with Mexico in consequence of her admission, lost some ten thousand as brave men as ever went forth to battle, spent about $100,000,000, and now has Texas a right to secede?

Again: The President recommended Congress to make an appropriation of the small sum of three hundred millions for the purchase of Cuba; tomorrow we admit her, and if we admit the right of secession, the next day she has the right to secede, and sell herself to another power, provided she can find a purchaser. And this is the doctrine you are called upon to sanction and establish by your vote. One word in relation to the origin of this doctrine of secession: I believe South Carolina claims the honor of originating the doctrine—Now I would ask how many men in South Carolina ever had the privilege of voting for a President of the Republic? Answer: the members of the Legislature only. How much property does a man have to own in South Carolina, before he can vote for a Senator? Ans: Landed estate, and, under the new regime, a negro qualification. Again, let me ask, What do we gain by secession? We often hear it answered by the Disunionists, that if we secede, the North will come to us; we will reconstruct the Government, secure our rights, and all will be well. In reply to this, it is sufficient to refer to the answer South Carolina made Virginia, and the resolutions passed by the Convention now in session in Alabama, that THEY WANTED NO CONNECTION WITH THE UNITED STATES. Then, is it not time that each of you ask himself, Where are we going, and whither are we drifting?

It may be asked what the Union party propose to do? To act in concert with the Border Slave States. We think we can safely follow where Virginia leads. To stand by each other in every trial, and NOT ABANDON OUR RIGHTS. In regard to the seceding States, we shall oppose coercion, and think, as to Louisiana, the repeal of the tax on sugar, in connection with her geographical position, must in a short time bring her voluntarily back. As to Texas, her extended frontier withdrawn from the protection of the Government, and the discontinuance of the mail service, must of necessity act as a powerful motive to induce her to again come under the stars and stripes. As to the other seceding States, it will be so utterly impossible, with the doctrine of secession established, to inaugurate a permanent federal union, on Republican principles, to command strength at home and respect abroad, that we dismiss even the consideration of the subject. The General Government now pays for transportation of the mails in the seceding States, over and above what she receives from the Post Office Department in those States, some $3,000,000 annually. She spends immense sums in garrisoning the forts on your frontier. I ask, then, what do we gain by secession? We abandon our rights in the Union; we create ten offices where we now have one; we assume the privilege to be taxed twenty-fold; we give up our privileges, immunities and franchise, which we now enjoy, and are secured to us.

And for what? That we form a Southern Confederacy!! Do you KNOW that in that confederacy your rights will be respected? That you will be ALLOWED A VOTE unless you are the OWNER OF A NEGRO? These things you do not know. Where then, is your compensation for all the rights you are asked to abandon? Should you not rather with the Union party co-operate with the Border Slave States? Never abandon the old ship so long as there is hope, but after every effort has been made, every honorable means exhausted, and we cannot obtain our rights, then call a convention of all the States, make a fair division of the common territory, forts, and all other public property, and go in PEACE. Monday you are called on to settle this great question. We feel confident, if the Union Party succeeds, all will be well. If they fail, we much fear our boasted Republican system fails with the day. Our leading Union men at Washington saw that there is more hope now for an adjustment than there has been since Congress met. Then let us all make one more effort to save the UNION! One word in relation to men: It is almost useless for us to make an effort, unless we act in concert. You being for Union, I for Union, you voting for one set of men, I for another, we accomplish nothing; we neutralize each other's influence. Then let us all unite on one set of Delegates, and not be influenced by personal considerations, or wilful and malicious falsehoods circulated over the country to influence your VOTE.

The report in circulation that the Government is already dissolved between the Free and Slave States, and that the Union party want to submit to and go with the Black Republican party, is simply ridiculous, untrue, and false in every particular, and could only have been put in circulation to influence your vote. . . .

DOCUMENT 44

Albert Pike's Address to Arkansans, February 17, 1861

Source: Albert Pike, *State or Province? Bond or Free?* . . .
Addressed particularly to the people of Arkansas (Little Rock,
1861).

Albert Pike, a lawyer, railroad supporter, and newspaper
writer, had been active in Arkansas politics since the
1830s, writing newspaper editorials and serving as a lawyer in Little Rock, usually very critical of the Family, the
organization that dominated the state's political system.
By the 1850s, he had written staunch defenses of southern
rights, challenging the idea of popular sovereignty and
arguing that secession was legal if property rights were not
being respected, though he himself remained supportive
of the Union. By early 1861, Pike altered his stance; and
in this pamphlet, he discussed the right of secession in
detail, pulling from the founding era as well as from the
Virginia and Kentucky resolutions of the 1790s. Also vividly displayed are the perceived injustices that the North
had placed on the South. The "virtually annulled" fugitive
slave law was prominent as well as the dangers caused by
slavery's lack of movement into the western territories.
Pike very vividly indicated that if the increasing slave
population were to remain within the current borders of
the South, a "swarming negro population" would "light
the torches of servile insurrection and Earth and Heaven
shudder at the hideous atrocities and horrors that follow."
This appeal, published right before the election, hoped to
encourage Arkansans to support immediate secession as
the only viable strategy to ensure the state's safety.

We are in the midst of a revolution; and, as is usual, those who are
hurried along in its vortex are, for the most part, ignorant of the real
causes that have produced the revolution, and of the depth to which the
questions involved in the controversy have struck their roots downward
among the very foundation-stones of the Republic.

. . . It is well when a great crisis occurs, that compels the discussion of the first principles of the Government; and when great Constitutional propositions are debated, without appeal to lower or meaner considerations. Then the debate is lifted above the low flat level of ignominious and angry disputation, and we breathe the thin clear atmosphere that wraps the mountain tops where Truth and Reason sit enthroned. . . .

This, which is now in progress in our country, is clearly a Revolution. It has marched with swift steps. The Southern States are rapidly retiring from the Union, and preparing to seek peace and safety in a new confederacy. We can now look back and see that the current of events has been incessantly drifting us towards this consummation for forty years, little as most of our statesmen believed or even expected it. The Northern States look on, amazed, incredulous, almost distrusting their own senses, busily conjecturing what can be the cause of this movement. They assign for it this or the other reason—that power is passing away from the South, and therefore it is for revolution; that the slave oligarchy are indignant because they cannot have protection for their chattels in the common territory. It is a mere temporary ebullition, many think, that wills soon pass away, and then the waters be calm and still again. The Union is too strong in the affections of the people to be permanently dissolved: a little wholesome chastisement of the refractory States will soon bring them back into the national fold: a few ambitious politicians have led the South astray, taken it by surprise, and obtained only unreal majorities for secession, while the mass of the people were in favor of the Union; it is a rebellion of the slavery propagandists; but still the mob has taken everything into its own hands; and there is a genuine Reign of Terror.

All this is the merest babble. . . . The present movement is a general, and for the most part spontaneous, uprising of the People; and he is a very shallow pretender to statesmanship who supposes it to be the ebullition of a mere temporary fit of passion. We all act very much from instinct; and peoples do so no less than individuals. . . . The Border States do not appreciate the questions involved in this controversy; but reproach those further south that they have lost no fugitives, and yet secede because the North refuses to comply with its obligations to return them. The question of southern rights in the Territories, too, they say, is an abstraction, because we have now no longer any Territory into which

Slavery can go. This is, in the truest sense, to mistake the mere symptoms for the disease.

So men tell us that these troubles are altogether owing to the rash and violent course of politicians north and south, and chiefly to the passage of the Nebraska and Kansas bill. They say that it could all have been avoided, if our public men, and especially the Democratic leaders, had only been wise and patriotic. That may be true. If the ship has not sunk, the man would not have drowned. All men, as well as all circumstances, are instruments used by Providence to effect its great purposes. Why and to what use blame the instrument? But for too much or too little rain, the grain-fields would have laughed with their golden waves. If George III and Lord North and the British Parliament had been wise, the Colonies would not have revolted—*then*. Was it not as well for them to revolt *then*? Could they *always* have remained Colonies? Was it not well that king and minister and Parliament would not listen to Chatham and Barré?

Mr. [William] Seward,[3] who is ambitious to wear the honors of philosophic statesmanship, and thinks to attain them by antithesis and paradoxes, pronounced, a year since, that there was an "irrepressible conflict" begun between the North and the South. It was true; but it was not true in the sense in which he applied it. The real controversy between them is as old as the Constitution itself. For it is a radical difference as to the very nature of the Government; and it arrayed against each other the first parties formed in the Republic. The Southern States hold, as Jefferson and Madison and all the Anti-Federal party held, that the General Government is the result of a compact between the States . . . amendable by the states only, and dissolvable by the States whenever it fails to answer the purposes for which they created it. The earliest symbol of the Union—a chain, composed of thirteen circular links, each perfect in symmetry and complete it its separate identity—well expressed the true nature of that union, and the Southern States'-rights doctrine. The Northern States, on the contrary, hold that there is no such compact; that the *whole* people of *all* the States, as an aggregate and unit, made the Constitution; and that there is no right of secession retained

---

3. US senator from New York, soon to be the secretary of state to Abraham Lincoln.

by a State; from which, by our American common law, it results as an inevitable corollary, that whenever the majority of voters of the whole Union choose to exercise the power, notwithstanding the mode provided by the Constitution for its amendment, they may call a Convention, not of the States, nor in each State, but of the whole People of all; and, the majority being there represented, may set aside the present Constitution of the United States, and make a new one, making, if they please, of the whole Union not a single State, and the States mere Counties.

For it is fresh in our recollection that the People of New York, not many years since, held a Convention, in utter contempt of their Constitution, and of the mode which it provided for its amendment, and made a new Constitution, which the highest Court of that State held valid; and it governs that State now.

And it will also be recollected that it was earnestly argued, by Southern men, only two years ago, that the People of Kansas would have a right to change their Constitution, in defiance of the provision contained in it, prohibiting any change for a certain length of time.

. . . There is a difference as wide and substantial between this Government, as its nature is understood by the fifteen Slaveholding States, and the same Government, as its nature is understood by the nineteen Non-Slaveholding States, as there is between Constitutional Monarchy in England and Imperial Absolutism in France.

We should not consent to remain a day in such a Government adds Mr. [Daniel] WEBSTER[4] confirmed the North in holding this to be. We do not believe that a centralized and consolidated government, built on the theory that the people of all these States were massed into one in order to make it, can have perpetuity or even continuance. To us the value and only recommendation of the Government are that it is the result of a compact between the States, that no individual action, but only State action, is constitutional, felt in the General Government, and that the States remain as they were when they achieved their independence, "FREE SOVEREIGN, EQUAL, AND INDEPENDENT STATES."

This radical difference of opinion, as the very *nature*, and of course as to the *powers*, of the General Government, could not help

---

4. Senator Daniel Webster (Whig-Massachusetts).

but continually develop itself in legislation as well as in the creeds of parties. Upon it, as I have said, the first parties in the Republic were formed; and parties degenerated into factions when other and pettier questions pushed it to one side. *It is a difference of opinion that cannot be reconciled;—and the Northern people are nearly two to our one.*

While they hold that this is simply a government of popular majorities, and degrade the States to the rank of Parishes or Counties, they have become too strong for us, outnumber us in people and States, receive a hundred thousand emigrants per annum, have more open space wherein to make six or seven new States, and announce it as their ultimatum that *we* shall not expand southwardly or southwestwardly, but slavery shall be prohibited in all territory hereafter acquired.

He who reflects on all this, cannot well fail to see that separation was but a question of time. Sooner or later the North and South could not help but divide, unless the powers of Government were placed and kept in the hands of the wisest Statesmen of each. If they were habitually intrusted to second-rate men, disintegration was inevitable. How much more so, if possible, when the pulpit in the North assumed the powers of legislation, and stirred a practical question that jeopardized the safety of every home in the South, aroused its pride, and touched its honor? It became as easy to destroy the Union as the crazed incendiary found it to burn the Temple of Diana at Ephesus.

The party which calls itself Republican has at length succeeded to power. In the controversies that have finally resulted in that election of its obscure candidate to the Presidency, the questions chiefly discussed have been those provoked by the feeling in the North against Slavery; and particularly that of the rights of the Southern States and their citizens in the common territory.

If it was then important, it is now still more important to understand the real issue between the North and the South, and the reach and extent of the principals involved. For now we are about to sever the bonds that have for seventy-three years held us together, and to create and set on foot a new government for ourselves; and it is especially essential that the ground of separation should not be misunderstood by any considerable portion of our own people, that a mere corollary should not be mistaken for the essential principle involved, and that a part of our people and some of our States should not imagine that there is no more vital principle or broader question at issue, then the interests of slave-owners and the right of emigration into uninviting and inhospitable territories. . . .

I, for one, have not deplored the agitation of the question of slavery. For in its discussion have been all the time involved the very essential nature and terms of the compact under which our national system exists. The questions to which Slavery has given rise could not have remained unsettled, nor been ignored, and the real issues are far graver than that of the right of a Southern citizen to emigrate to a Territory with his slaves.

The theory of the North, that the People of *all* the States, as *one* People, made the Government, has become a living reality in practice. The doctrine of the North as to the Territories is but an application of it; and if the Southern States, from Delaware to Texas, do not mean to abandon their Constitutional faith, admit that there is not union of *the States*, and submit to the worst of absolutisms, that of a foreign majority, they must stand shoulder to shoulder, one firm unbroken phalanx, in this great emergency, and prove to the world that they are strong, wise, and patriotic enough to form and maintain a Constitution and Government for themselves.

This issue concerns little Delaware as much as it does Louisiana, if not more; and Kentucky and Virginia as much as it does Alabama and Georgia. And it concerns the man who owns no slaves quite as much as the man who owns them, as I think can be demonstrated; and this is what I wish to show. . . .

There is the great *theoretical* question now at issue. It is the most fundamental of all questions; since the construction and consequences of every compact must chiefly depend upon the question, *who* made and are the parties to it. Its decision must decide what is the proper *name* for the system we are under; what is citizenship of the United States; what our paramount allegiance; what, treason; where is the proprietorship of our territories and the rights and relations of those who go thither; what, the rights of the States and their citizens therein. . . .

The Constitution, it is true, created one Nation for certain purposes, and "a Government proper, founded on its adoption by the People" [of each State separately as one political unit], "and creating direct relations between itself and individuals;" but it does not, *therefore*, follow that it is not *itself* a compact between the several States, in their sovereign Capacities.

. . . The first question to be determined, evidently is, "*Who* made the Constitution?"

When the Delegates from twelve of the thirteen States met together in that Convention which sat in 1787, and framed our present Constitution, each of the thirteen States was an independent Republic, formally so acknowledged by each other, by England, and by all the world, all being simply linked and leagued together by "*a firm league of friendship with each other, for their common defence, the security of their liberties, and their mutual and general welfare.*" It was expressly stipulated by the articles of confederation of the year 1777, that "*Each State retains its Sovereignty, freedom, and independence;*" and their joint or general interests were managed by "*The United States in Congress assembled,*" that is, by a meeting or coming together of Delegates, not less than two, nor more than seven in number from each State; in which Congress or meeting each State had one vote, and paid its own Delegates. Each State raised its necessary quota of all moneys needed for general purposes, in proportion to the value of land within it held by private title. No judiciary was provided for, except Prize Courts, and Special Tribunals or Boards to try controversies between the States. If moneys were borrowed, the debt was due by the States as joint debtors. To exercise the most important of the powers delegated, the assent of nine States was necessary. Each State retained the title to its land, and it was finally provided in these words: "and the articles of this Confederation shall be inviolably observed by every State, *and the Union shall be perpetual; nor shall any alteration at any time hereafter be made in any of them, unless such alteration be agreed to in a Congress of the United States, and be afterwards confirmed by the Legislature of every State.*"

Under these Articles of Confederation, all acts of a national character were done by all the States jointly. It was declared to be a simple league or partnership of the States; and *in contemplation of law*, the States concurred in and *themselves* did every act done, and exercised every power of Government. . . .

But the powers so to be exercised were not sufficiently extensive, nor intrusted to efficient hands. The States discovered that larger powers must be conceded, that there must be something more than a mere partnership of the States, and that another Body Politic must be created, for the management of the national affairs, with the necessary officers and machinery to render it efficient. But we may safely challenge any one to show that they meant that this new system should be created, not by themselves, not by the States, but by the *People* of *all* the States, amalgamated for the purpose and occasion, and for all future time into one mass. They still intended *a union of the States*, but a *more perfect* union—a term which imports that the self-same persons or members before united, were to be drawn more closely together; and not that a *new* union was to be made, of *other* persons.

The phrase, "THE UNITED STATES OF AMERICA, *in General Congress Assembled*," was adopted in the Declaration of Independence: and the Articles of Confederation provided that "the style of the Confederacy" should be, "THE UNITED STATES OF AMERICA." This term, no one will doubt, under *that* system at least, did not mean one political *Unity* or *Entity*, but a mere union and concurrent action of the States *as* States, each acting as an Individual. No body corporate or politic, distinct in law from the members, was created; and the style of the Confederacy was in substance the same as if it had been, "*The Thirteen American States, united in a firm league of Friendship, and for certain purposes acting in concert.*"

The Delegates from twelve of the these States (Rhode Island not being represented), who assembled in Convention in 1787, had no power to *adopt* a Constitution, to carry into effect any change in the existing system, or to put in operation a new Union or Government. . . .

The Convention did settle and frame a draft of a Constitution, which provided that its *ratification,* i.e., the acceptance and adoption of it as the act of their States, by the Conventions of any nine States, should be sufficient for its establishment "*between the STATES so ratifying the same.*"

. . . Each of the twelve States in question was a political and moral Being, Person, and Entity, in law, separate and distinct in its individuality and action from each and all of its citizens or people. . . . The Delegates of 1787 were agents, *each of his own State*, AND OF IT ALONE; and they declared, at the end of the Constitution, that what they had done, was "done by the unanimous consent of the STATES present."

. . . It was not the Constitution of 1787, but of the 21st of June, 1788; on which day the ninth State, NEW HAMPSHIRE, accepted and ratified it; and on which day it was delivered as their deed, and became a binding and operative compact between Delaware, Pennsylvania, New Jersey, Georgia, Connecticut, Massachusetts, Maryland, South Carolina, and New Hampshire; those States *then* solemnly and in unison making this declaration (in which Virginia untied *five* days, and New York *thirty-five* days after). . . .

This, it is continually reiterated, shows that the *States* did not create the Government, but the *one* People of all the States, not the People of *each* State, giving the *State's* consent; but all the *individuals*, in all the States, each individual giving *his own* consent. The argument is pardonable, in the mouth of a man innocent of all knowledge of the law; but *only* there. It is simply a question whether the word "*People*" is to be taken collectively or distributively; and every lawyer who knows anything, knows that the expression, taken by itself and unexplained, admits as naturally and legitimately of one construction as of the other. The use attempted to be made of it has simply been a fraud on unlearned men, which a lawyer would never have tried to practice on a *court*.

The Constitution itself declares who made it, in the most positive and unmistakable terms. "The ratification of the *Conventions* of nine *States*," it declares, "*shall be sufficient for the establishment of this Constitution*, BETWEEN THE STATES SO RATIFYING THE SAME." He that ratifies, makes: and if the *States* did not ratify and so make the Constitution, *it never has been in force at all.*

In ratifying the Constitution, each State has one voice; and it would have been defeated, if eight States only had ratified it, though by the unanimous vote of every man in their limits; and though these were a large majority of all the voters of all the States. . . .

The *States* exercise, or at least *should* exercise, all the powers of the General Government, under the Constitution. The *Legislative* power is vested in "a Congress of the United States." The same phrase was in the Articles of Confederation,—"The United States in Congress assembled;" and there pains was taken, as it were, to impress it on the mind that the *States*, THEMSELVES present as Peers, in this Amphictyonic Council, met face to face and transacted the common affairs. It was a fine idea, not thrown aside by the Constitution. Our acts of Congress are still enacted by "The Senate and House of Representatives of the United States of America in Congress assembled." It is not the *Senate* and *House* that are assembled in Congress, but *the several United States of America;* often as we now lose sight of that fact, that *great* fact, which is the distinctive characteristic of our government, and in which alone was hope of safety and assurance of continuance. . . .

And, in short, there is no political act done by the United States, in which the voices of all the people of all the States are taken as one mass, and concur, the majority governing. The People only act through their organizations as States.

These have always been the Southern Democratic or States-rights doctrines.

The celebrated Virginia resolutions of 1798, to which the Democratic party has ever since adhered, were drafted by MADISON, but submitted and defended in the State Legislature by JOHN TAYLOR, of Caroline, the great apostle of strict construction. These resolutions thus announced the opinion of Virginia as to the nature of the Constitution itself, and the limit and extent of the powers of the National Government; and the South now claims no more than the Mother of States then claimed. . . .

. . . The resolution still asserted that the Constitution was a *compact*, and a compact between the *States*. So did the Kentucky Resolutions of 1798, reaffirmed in 1799, and said to have been drafted by Mr. Jefferson; for, as drafted, they declared:—

"1. *Resolved*, That the several *States* composing the United States of America, are not *united* on the principle of unlimited submission to the general government; but that by *compact* under the style and title of a constitution for the United States, and of amendments thereto, *they* constituted a government for special purposes, delegated to that government certain definite powers, *reserving each Sate to itself,* the residuary mass of right to their own self-government; and that whensoever the general government assumes undelegated powers, its acts are unauthoritative, void, and of no force; *that to this compact each State is an integral party;* that this government, *created by this compact*, was not made the exclusive or final judge of the extent of the powers delegated to itself; since that would have made its discretion, and not the constitution, the measure of its powers; but that as in all other cases of compact, among parties having no common judge, each party has an equal right to judge for itself, as well of infractions as of the mode and measure of redress."

. . . Now, as the power or powers, the party or parties, that so ordained and established the Constitution, were those that had an actual and legal existence *prior* thereto, inasmuch as the creator must exist before the creature, and the ordainer before the thing ordained, the phrase "*We, the people of the United States,*" necessarily meant the people of those United States *previously* existing, under their *previous* Confederation, acting as such, in the only mode of action then competent for them, and through their *then* existing lawful organs. Consequently, it *was* the people of each State, acting by themselves as a unit, or one party, separate and distinct from the people of every other State—that did ordain and establish the Constitution.

That is, the States, such as they were while confederated, created the new Government; and the preamble is essentially and exactly the same as if it read: "We, the States of Virginia, Massachusetts, &c., now united in a Confederation, do, acting in concert, but each for itself ordain and establish this Constitution." And thus, it was that the states reserved, each to itself and to its people, all powers not granted by it and its people to the General Government."

But it does not follow, because the *States* made the Constitution, and assemble in Congress, that therefore this is *simply* an alliance or a league of those States. There is only one language in which their action in making it, and the results of that action, can be intelligibly described; and that is *legal* language. Let us look at the matter by the light of legal principles; not by that of mere precedent, or of narrow technicalities, but of those accurate modes of consideration and definition of the nature of political and social aggregations, which the law has adopted, in order to attain justice, and, as a means to that end, to give clear, distinct, just, and adequate ideas of the relations of associations to the individuals who compose and create them.

. . . When the Constitution was made, each State was a corporation, with such powers and franchises as the people of each had chosen to invest it withal. When the Constitution took effect, and the United States began *its* corporate national existence, *it* took such powers and was invested with such prerogatives as the people of the several States, acting in their corporate capacity as States, chose to confer; and those of the States remained as before, except so far as they were limited and narrowed, or wholly taken away by the new charter.

Thus it was that the Fathers succeeded in effecting what had never before been attempted, or suggested as possible—the forming, at one and the same time, of a *Union* of independent confederated States, co-equals, and retaining their individuality as States; and a national Unity or single nation, for all necessary national purposes. They did not create some non-descript creature, *in part* a League or Confederation, and *in part* one nation and one people; but they created that which was *at one and the same time,* BOTH a League and Union of many States, and ONE State. The motto, "*e pluribus unum,*" did not mean that the many were fused together or chemically combined into one unity; but that, continuing *many,* they were *at the same time one.* . . .

If this was *not* what the Fathers effected—if the States did *not* create the Government, and continue to be the only members of the Union—if the Constitution made the People of a State to be distinct and different from the State, so that *they* could act, and the State not act—then the government could not help sooner or later becoming the unbridled rule of a mere majority, a pure Democracy, with only imaginary checks and balances; and the Constitution could only be a frail and feeble barrier of shifting sand, against the hungry waves of Passion, Ambition, and Fanaticism.

If the States did not compose this Union, and were not the members of it, then, called by whatever name, they were mere municipalities, and their crown and robes of sovereignty the mere tinselled trappings of the theatre. It was then folly to prate of State rights and State pride. The old Commonwealths, in whose bosom it was deemed an honor and good fortune to be born, had laid aside their greatness and their glory, and could no longer demand allegiance of their sons, nor extend to them protection. If they were so emasculated and reduced in circumstances, so far below their original high estate, as to be mere images and counterfeits of States, then there was little hope for the perpetuity of our institutions, and little in them for other nations to admire or for us to boast of. And it is because the South finds it impossible longer to resist this wretched and degrading doctrine *in* the Union, that it is now seeking safety *out* of it, and on the point of creating a new government, that shall repose on the solid foundation of the equality, independence, and sovereignty of the States. On which side shall Arkansas stand in this great controversy?

If the Union could have continued, as it ought to have done, and would have done, if men had been wise, we should insensibly have become more and more one nation. Our common flag would have made us so. Time and habit would inevitably have consolidated us, and the antagonisms of race would have died out, or combined in harmonious action. Every war we engaged in would have made the feeling of *oneness* more and more irresistible. None, I think, ever served under that flag, who did not for the time feel, with a conviction more potent than all the arguments and logic of statesmen could produce, that we were one nation, in name, fame, and destiny; who did not feel that our national motto, *E Pluribus Unum*—ONE, made up of many—was a true definition of the nature of our Government—the *manifold* welded into the *one*—oneness grown out of the manifold.

There was no necessity for any irrepressible conflict between the sections. There was no necessity for hatred, jealousies, and wrong-doing. We have been unnecessarily set against each other, by fanatical folly and unprincipled ambition in the North, and passion and rashness in the South. The harm is done. The silver chain of Union is broken; and the restoration of harmony is now as impossible as it is between husband and wife, when, estranged by their own tempers or evil counsellors, their domestic dissensions have been paraded in court, and divorce granted, not alone from bed and board, but from the bonds of matrimony. That they could and ought to have lived together in peace, makes the sentence none the less irrevocable, the separation none the less eternal. But if we had not been estranged, argument and logic would soon have become powerless against the *feeling* that we were one Nation and one People; and it would have become necessary for all men, whatever their theoretical opinions, to make up their minds, and reconcile themselves to it the best way they could, that, as the years glided past us, the Union continuing, we should regard ourselves more and more as one nation, whatever might be the true meaning of the Constitution; and this consequence would have been the inevitable result of circumstances, and a mere act of forced obedience to the great laws of God, which constitute what we call human nature.

. . . Thus, whenever the United States became, in any mode whatever, by purchase or conquest, the owner of land, that land was in substance the land of the several States. Its legal capacity to act as an individual, the fiction of its identity separate from the States, would be sued to give effect to, and make fully available, all the rights of the States and the people of each State, in and upon that common property. They *could not* be used to annul or render ineffectual those rights. Whenever the effectuation of those rights demanded it, the *fiction* would vanish, and the States be regarded as the *real* owners of the lands, the Lords Proprietary.

When a portion of country thus became the common property of the States, it was held in trust for them by the United States; and in the same sense, somewhat inaccurate, in which the property of a corporation is said in the law to be held in trust by it for the corporators. The meaning is, that *in law* it is *its* property, but *in reality* it is theirs; that, so far as it is necessary, in order to carry out their intentions and subserve their interests, the law will *use* the legal fiction, and *regard* it as *its* property; but when justice and convenience require the fiction to disappear, it will regard it, as it *really* is, as *theirs*.

Now, besides their real ownership of the land, the States had great political and social interests in the territories, considering them as nascent or embryotic States. Each State had the right to demand that they should be opened as wide to its own citizens, as to those of any other State or number of States; and the *Southern* States, that *they* should have a *fair* chance in the peaceful struggle for additional political weight and power in this confederacy. The duty of each to its own citizens also gave it a right to insist that they should not be directly or indirectly excluded from the common territory. It had necessarily the right to demand that they should be there protected in the enjoyment and possession of whatever they carried thither, that was their property by its laws. And, if the Constitution really warranted the Northern States in Congress, or the people of a Territory, in denying the South these equal rights in the common territory, then it was the duty of the Southern States at once to withdraw from a Union in which they never were equals.

Short-sighted men imagined it was we, who, insisting in 1860 on these rights of the South, brought upon the Country the dangers of Disunion; but a truer wisdom taught us, that only in the principle we proclaimed was safety, and that we were the truest Defenders of the Constitution and the Union. Whether present victory or defeat awaited us, was of little moment. Truth would still march onward in serene majesty, whether we stood or went down in the shock of the battle. The South would at last rally to the flag of the equality of the States and the protection of all the constitutional and legal rights, when the passions and angers of the contest should have passed away; and its States would stand with linked shields, in one compact and solid phalanx, demanding in the calm tones of conscious power the maintenance of the Constitution as the condition of the continuance of the Union.

They have demanded that, if indeed some of them have not condescended to beg for it. What is the result? The Republicans in Congress refuse Concession and threaten Coercion. They accept no propositions of Compromise. The personal-liberty laws of many Northern States, that make it an infamous crime in a master to reclaim and recover his slave, legally, under the laws of the United States, still remain unrepealed. Although the Supreme Court solemnly decided, if it decided nothing else, in the Dred Scott Case, that a negro cannot be a citizen of the United States, fifteen thousand of them voted in Ohio for Lincoln. The whole North with one voice declares that there shall be no more slave territory; and its most powerful States tender arms, men, and money to the General Government, wherewith to subjugate the South. What was it the right and duty of the Southern States to do, when it thus became evident that folly and fanaticism, rapacity and lust for power and office, taking the Northern men captive, have rendered it impossible for them longer to remain in the Union as the equals of the Northern States, or without abandoning the cardinal tenets of their political faith, unless new and ample guarantees can be obtained? And what mode of procedure offered a rational hope of obtaining of such guarantees?

It is the deliberate opinion of at least seven of the Southern States, that withdrawal from the Union is the course most proper to be adopted, the only remedy of efficacy sufficient to cure the disease and bring the North to its senses, if indeed any remedy can effect that. In those States and others, the only question has been, not as to the right or propriety of secession, but as to the expediency and policy of separate secession, as compared with the separation by the conjoint action of all or several of the Southern States. It is evident that the right of all or several to secede, must depend on the right of *each* to do so. For the right, if it exists at all, flows from this, that the States are the parties to the compact, and a gross violation of it by the majority of the States, to the injury of any one, gives that one, and each one so injured, the right, at its option, of regarding it as at an end and rescinded. The right must needs be the individual right of each State. Certainly it is qualified by the interests of the other States that have not violated the compact. . . . But still, each State having the right to secede, must determine for itself as to the propriety or expediency of the act; and that right has already been exercised by six States, and will in a few days be exercised by one more.

This right of secession is strenuously denied by the Northern States, and even by a respectable number of persons in the South; but as a right to be exercised only in an extreme case, of grave violation of the Constitution, when there is no other sufficient remedy, it seems to me that in the very nature of things it *could* not have been parted with by the States; and that its exercise is neither treason or rebellion.

The right to secede flows necessarily from the fact that the States *made* the Constitution. If one party to a compact violates it, the other may at his option treat it as rescinded; or, as WEBSTER once said: "A bargain broken on one side is a bargain broken on all sides."

. . . If it were to be procured to sustain the Constitutionality of an Act of Congress abolishing Slavery in certain States, would there still be no right to secede on the part of those States? If, acting upon the notion that one people made the Constitution, Congress should call a Convention of Delegates from all the States, and, the South refusing to sit there, the Convention, representing the popular majority, should proceed to change the Constitution, and annul important rights of the South, would there still be no right to secede? The States are equally as much bound by any amendments to the Constitution regularly made, as by the original articles. If the North were to multiply its States until it had three-fourths of all, and then change the basis of representation in the Senate, fixing it according to the population of each State, and so depriving every Southern State of that whereof the Constitution expressly declares no State shall ever be deprived, "its equal suffrage in the Senate," all other remedies failing, would there be no right to secede? The new Senate is the sole judge of the elections and qualifications of its members. It admits, for example, ten from New York, and decides that Delaware is entitled to but one. There is no remedy for this *in* the Union, no appeal to the Courts; Power is lawless, and majorities unreasoning. Is there still no right to secede?

Absolutely to deny the right of secession, is to say that the constitutional rights of the Southern States may be denied, and they continually insulted and outraged; that all remedies in Congress, in the Courts, and elsewhere may fail them; that the other States may violate the Constitution at every point, and yet that they may hold the Southern States in the bonds of obedience to it; and that the latter will yet have no right to throw off this intolerable yoke, and escape from this humiliating serfdom, by saying that "a bargain broken on one side is broken on all sides," and that they withdraw from a union that no longer deserves that name.

Admit the right in the extremist case, and you concede the whole principle. Then it only becomes a question of the sufficiency of the cause. I admit that the cause must be grave to be sufficient. I admit that the remedy is a severe and extreme one, fit to be used only in the last resort, and when all others have failed; and I am now satisfied that no *other* remedy could cure the disease under which the body politic now labors, if indeed that of Secession has that virtue. No remedy less sharp and decisive could have brought the North to its senses. Indeed, it still seems to be far from sane. I am now satisfied that even Secession, even the formation of a Southern Union, will not cure the Northern people of their fanatical delirium, unless it bring upon them such ruin as nations have rarely experienced, and experiencing lived.

That the South has, and has long had, ample cause for separation, few men, at the South, will be disposed to deny. We need not fear, on that point, to demand the judgment of an impartial world. For that our rights have long been jeopardized and denied, and the Constitution shamelessly violated by the Northern States, it is in vain for any one to endeavor to dispute.

The provision of the Constitution that guarantees the return of fugitive slaves, is virtually annulled. It costs as much to reclaim a slave as he is worth, and exposes the owner, in many of the Northern States, to be harassed by suits civil and criminal, that make his remedy worthless to him. For this deliberate, shameless violation of the compact, persisted in and become habitual, the South has the present right to dissolve the Union. A State that so nullifies a part of the Constitution, loses all right to any of its benefits; and the Southern States might well have insisted that Connecticut, Vermont, Massachusetts, Wisconsin, and other of the Northern States should be expelled with ignominy from the Union, as the condition of their own continuance in it.

A person who speaks for Massachusetts in the Senate has lately arraigned the Southern States as "the Barbary States of the Union," before the bar of the world, and impeached the courage, the honor, and the decency of all their people, in stilted Ciceronian sentences, steeped with gall and bitterness, and reeking with malignant falsehood. No one should have replied a word. And when his State formally, and with the intention of branding the insult in upon the South, endorsed his harangue and made it her own, either *her* Senators should have been expelled, or those of all the Southern States ought in strict justice to their constituents, to have withdrawn from that desecrated and dishonored chamber. If they had done so, the whole South would have leaped up with one great cry of joy and applause, and have made the act their own. . . .

At any rate, the question of the right of secession is receiving a practical solution. South Carolina, Florida, Alabama, Mississippi, Georgia, and Louisiana have already, by formal ordinance adopted in convention, withdrawn from the Union, and become each a foreign country to us, if it is possible for a State to do so by her own solemn act; and in a week or two more, Texas will have in like manner severed the bonds of union, and resumed her independence.

There may be different opinions as to the necessity, wisdom, policy and expediency of this measure. I, for one, did not believe that the necessity of resorting to this extreme remedy was as yet upon us. I thought we ought not to despair, so long as there was hope of a returning sense of justice in the Northern States. I doubted whether secession would prove a remedy for any of our evils, or given any additional security to our rights; and above all, I was enthusiastically attached to the Union, under whose flag I had fought. Disunion seemed to me equivalent to downfall, disaster and ruin, whereby we should become a mock and a by-word all over the earth.

And I thought, that, when separation should become inevitable, the Southern States ought not to secede separately, but that they should act in concert, meet in convention, decree the separation, construct and set on foot a new government, and thus, being strong to repel attack, make it insanity on the part of the Northern States to attempt to dragoon them into submission.

That was my individual opinion. Perhaps Arkansas thought so. But the other Cotton States did not think so; and they have acted for themselves. Can they ever return into the Union? Is any compromise possible, with which they and we ought to be satisfied? And how can such a compromise be effected? These are the only questions that now concern *them*. The rest are obsolete; and these equally concern *us*; for the inexorable decrees of destiny will compel us to unite with them. . . . The Republican leaders have made compromise for the present impracticable. . . .

No concessions would now satisfy, and none *ought* now to satisfy the South, but such as would amount to a surrender of the distinctive principles by which the Republican party coheres, because none other or less would give the South peace and security. That party would have to agree that in the view of the Constitution, slaves are property; that Slavery might exist and should be legalized and *protected*, in territory hereafter to be acquired to the Southwest; and that negroes and mulattoes cannot be citizens of the United States, nor vote at general election in the States. They would have to repeal their laws that make it a crime in a master to reclaim his slave, that menace him with the penitentiary, and are meant to rob him of his property; and instead they would have to agree to deliver that property up in good faith.

For that party to make these concessions would simply be to commit suicide; and therefore it is idle to expect from the North, so long as it rules there, a single concession of any value. They will not be made, if ever, until the *People*, impoverished and distressed, if not invaded by universal ruin and general bankruptcy, with starvation in the cities and destitution in the fields, shall have learned no longer to intermeddle with what in nowise concerns them. Then proper concession may be made, by the general consent of the people; and if so made, the settlement will be permanent. But if made sooner, under the influence of a temporary terror, or by the management of politicians, the immediate result could not fail to be, as indeed it would most probably be in any event, after whatever solemn settlement, that, as soon as the danger of disunion was over for the time, as soon as the seceding States had returned into the Union, an agitation would commence in the North, stirring it to its profoundest depths. The compromise would be denounced from every pulpit and rostrum and in every canvass, as a league with hell and a covenant with the Devil. Those who made it would be politically slaughtered; and after such convulsions as the country has never felt, the whole work would be undone, and the Southern States be forced again to secede, when secession would have become a farce.

It is certain that none of these concessions can be had at present; and events will not wait until they can be obtained. Perhaps a compromise might be brought about, if we had breathing time. It would require a year or two, at least. Except so far as they tend to prove to the South that it is impossible now to obtain any guarantees from the North, thus urging upon the Border States prompt and vigorous action, all the propositions, plans, and projects for a compromise are not worth the paper they have been written on.

We were often enough told in 1860 that the territorial question was a mere abstraction, since we had no territory as to which the matter was not actually settled. Strange! How much men are like bats in the daylight!

The Northern States are now nineteen to our fifteen—counting Delaware as one of ourselves. They outnumber us, in white population, nearly two to one. They increase, principally by foreign emigration, in a much larger ratio than we do. They have a great country yet to be peopled, sufficient to make six or seven States. British America will, in all probability, desire to become, at no distant day, a part of the Union, if it continues; and a simple act of Congress will admit it. The North announces it to be its fixed determination, that there shall be no more slave territory; and, therefore, we must either acquire no more from Mexico, or, if we do, we must consent to see it made into Free States. We may fight for and help to pay for more territory; but we must do so for the benefit of the Pharisees among the States, alone. How long would it be, under that system, before the union of North and South would be like that between England and Ireland; which, obtained by bribery, has been always maintained by force?

It is strange that statesmen do not see that here is the great question between the sections. To expand is the destiny and necessity of every young and growing nation. It is a law of its being. You cannot repeal it; and if you oppose it, it will crush you. By the law of growth and by natural right, the Southwest is as much *ours*, as the Northwest is the heritage of the Northern States. This law is more imperative with us, because another law is superadded, by which slavery gradually drifts off to the southward, seeking more profitable fields of labor. . . .

We have *four* millions slaves. How many years will elapse before we have ten millions? These—all—are to be henceforward confined to the present Southern States. No doubt it will be well enough so, during *our* lifetime; *but how will it be with our children?* Are we ready, in order to purchase quiet and peace for ourselves, to bequeath such a curse and calamity to *them*, as the perpetual confinement of slavery within its present limits would be? Shall we, to avoid a present danger, and that we may be permitted to fold our hands and sleep in our dishonor, devise to them that accursed legacy of a superabundant, swarming negro population, denied outlet, until their labor, like that of white men elsewhere, is not worth their food and clothing, and hunger and discontent light the torches of servile insurrection, and Earth and Heaven shudder at the hideous atrocities and horrors that follow? I, for one, will not consent to it. Better even Treason against an unrighteous Government, than Treason against our own children!

Here is the *true* and *great* issue; and it concerns *every* man and every woman in the South. We cannot sign the bond which the North insolently demands, to this effect, that because we are "the Barbary States" of the Union, and "Slavery is the sum total of all villainies," therefore we shall not seek to expand and grow. For it is both our right and a necessity to grow and plant new States. It is God's law; and the attempt to stay its operation has already shivered the Union as one shivers a vessel of fragile glass.

Devotion to the Union was for a long time an almost idolatrous sentiment with nearly the whole South; and secession seemed the sum of all horrors and disasters. But we are at last compelled to look separation in the face. Most dangers seem greater at a distance, than when we grapple with them. Secession, at hand, and in part consummated, does not seem to the South one tenth so terrible, as when it frowned upon us while yet in the future. The act once accomplished, or become inevitable, men begin to find more and more reasons whereby to justify it; to prove its necessity and its expediency; to show that a much longer continuance of the Union was impossible; and that the evils of separation were chiefly imaginary, or at any rate vastly exaggerated. . . .

They begin even to say, that as the North entertains views of the nature of the Government, radically and essentially different from those which have always been the political religion of the South, this must ultimately have divided the Republic; that the people of the South and those of the North are essentially two different races of men, with habits of thought and action very unlike; that the Southern States are essentially homogeneous, and perhaps no people in the world is so much so as that which composes almost their entire population; there being among them but a very inconsiderable percentage of foreign blood, except in Louisiana; and none of them having much in common with the character and habits of New England, and of the States chiefly populated by the swarms that have flowed forth from that teeming hive; while the immense and incessant influx of Teutonic and Celtic blood into the North, plays no unimportant part in making it and the South more and more two separate and distinct peoples.

They begin to say that this North, so unlike the South, and with its different theory of the government, is becoming too strong for us; that the present form of government has lasted its full time, and separation is a merely natural process; since the country is too large and has too many varied interests for us longer to continue one household; that the Union never was anything more than a truce, maintained by continual bribery of New England, on the part of the other States, from the very first, with protective tariffs, the carrying trade, fishing, bounties, and other gratuities that she has continually clamored for.

If we add to this fixed determination of the North to intermeddle with slavery, and the equally fixed resolution of the South not to permit such interference, which, while dangerous, doubles the wrong by coupling it with insult, it is not strange that Southern statesmen begin to think and say that it is well that separation has come now, before the North has become strong enough to prevent it, and the South too weak to resist, with her public men debauched perhaps by the manifold bribes that a great nation can offer to avarice and ambition; and before Mexico had been occupied by the North or a foreign power.

There is still a possibility of reconstruction and reunion. But it will not last long unless wise men have control on both sides; and it will disappear at once and forever, if resort is had to the arbitrament of arms. Surely no man of ordinary intellect can be so blind as not to see that if from disunion civil war results, that will amply justify disunion, because, as there is neither desire nor motive on the part of the South to aggress upon the North, hostilities must be initiated by those who were lately our allies, must be unjustifiable, malicious, revengeful—springing either from a determination to intermeddle with slavery after they have ceased to be responsible for it, and so to excite servile insurrection, with all its multiplied hideous horrors; or from a fixed purpose to whip us back in the Union, in order that we may afterwards be their serfs. In either case, hostilities thus initiated will prove that the alliance between us and them was unnatural and unfit, and its longer continuance dangerous and disgraceful to us.

If disunion is *not* followed by war, there is no reason why it should entail upon us any serious disasters. The Southern States are large enough for an empire, and wealthy and populous enough to maintain a government that all the world must respect. And surely no true man in the South will believe that there is not wisdom enough or patriotism enough among its people, to enable them to construct, set on foot and maintain a constitutional government, republican and conservative.

I can see only one mode in which peace can be maintained. The border States ought to hesitate no longer. If they do, coercion will be attempted by the Northern States, and they will be parties to it. They should at once unite with the States that have seceded and are yet to secede, meet them in convention, and aid in framing a Constitution, and setting on foot a Government. When thus united, the matter will have assumed quite a different aspect from that which it wears at present. There will no longer be half a dozen seceded States, but a new and powerful Confederacy, to attempt to coerce which would be simple fatuity. A war against it would be too expensive a luxury for the North to indulge in, and would moreover defeat its own purpose; since it would not only render a restoration of the present Union impossible, but would also make enmities eternal, which otherwise would be only evanescent. A treaty of amity and reciprocity, easily made if no blood is shed, will keep open the door, at least, for complete reconciliation, and in the mean time make an alliance more profitable to each country than an inharmonious Union; and when their people were no longer responsible, as they now think or pretend they are, for slavery within our limits; when the outrages they now perpetuate with impunity would be acts justifying war, those among them who are regarded their substantial interests would *compel* the fanatical and rascally to attend to their own affairs, and let our property alone.

I do not see how war is otherwise to be avoided, or reconstruction hoped for. The delay of the Border States encourages the Republicans.

As soon as Lincoln is inaugurated, he cannot help but attempt to coerce the seceding States, if the Border States still delay. *Laws will be passed in time, giving him men and money*, and requiring "the enforcement of the laws, and the collection of the revenue." Emboldened by the hesitation of Virginia, Kentucky, Tennessee, and Maryland, we can see that Republicans become more insolent, and speak in bolder tones of rebellion and coercion. . . . Lincoln objects to any compromise; and the very fact that any States have seceded is ignored. The names of their members are still called in both Houses.

Action, action, action, is necessary. The Southern States must make common cause. Blame South Carolina as much as you will, the attitude of the North, and all the acts of the Republican party, go very far to prove, even to those most reluctant to believe it, that the separation of the Southern States has not occurred a day too soon.

. . . More has been done in the last six weeks to satisfy the people of the South that the mass of the people of the north are their enemies, and that the continuance or restoration of fraternal relations with them is simply impossible, than had been done in ten years before.

Whatever we may have thought or wished, Fate has been too strong for us; the die is cast, and the act *done*. The Past is no longer ours. The Present and the Future alone belong to us. It is profitless to inquire who are to blame for the present condition of affairs, or to disclaim responsibility on our individual part. . . .

Reconciliation, by means of amendments to the Constitution to be made or agreed to by the North, being simply impossible for the present; first for want of time, and next because they cannot be carried by three-fourths of the States, only one possible mode remains. If the Southern States adopt the Constitution, with no other amendments than such as are necessary for their protection, and as experience has shown to be necessary, with none that can be unfair or injurious to the Northern States; if they establish and set on foot a government under the Constitution so amended, and invite the other States to unite with them under it, a restoration of the Union, and a better Union are possible. There is, in my opinion, no other hope whatever.

In the meantime, since the States that have seceded will surely frame a constitution and establish a government, the Border States, including Arkansas, are called upon to decide what course of action on their part will be most consistent with their honor, and most conduce to their safety. . . . Shall Arkansas share the fortunes of her sister States, from whom most of her people come, who have heretofore defended the same Constitution against a common enemy, and who are connected with her by all the ties of one blood, the same habits of thought, the same prepossessions and customs, the same interests, and a common destiny? Will she stand aloof, and await the issue of the struggle, before determining with which side she will cast in her fortunes? Or will she adhere to the North, and become a party to all that may be done in order to subjugate the seceding States? Will she assist to do that? Would she even look on as a neutral, and without striking even one good blow in their behalf, see them crushed under the brutal heel of Power, or lashed back into the Union?

If Arkansas and the other Border States mean to unite with the Seceding States, in case proper guarantees are not given by the North, they may as well do so at once. If any compromise is patched up, somebody will be sold. No such guarantees can be had. Accept such as you can get; and you will soon see what convenient things words are, to cheat withal. Surely you will not let the Seceding States alone make a final Constitution for the Southern United States. . . . Surely that would be beneath the dignity even of a young State like Arkansas, and much more beneath that of Virginia. For even Arkansas, let us hope, has sons whose wisdom and judgment might be of some value, and whose opinions might exercise some influence and command some attention. . . . It is of the utmost importance that *all* of the Southern States should co-operate in making the new Constitution, lest rash experiments should be tried and the old landmarks injudiciously removed.

The fourth of March is near at hand. If Arkansas is then found in the Union, she will be a party to whatever may have been or may then be done by the Government of the United States. Its acts of coercion, its denials of the rights of the States, its claims of more than Imperial powers, will be her acts, her denials, her claims. When the Senate is convened by the new President . . . Arkansas will be a party to whatever acts of oppression may be done there by the nineteen Northern States, and the jubilant Abolitionists and Republicans who will then fill that gaudy gilded chamber.

It must not be forgotten, that, if the South returns into the Union, she too will have to make, by implication as strong as express agreement, certain concessions on her part. She will never afterwards be permitted to protest against protective tariffs, nor against laws securing the coasting and carrying trade to Northern bottoms; nor against fishing bounties; nor against a homestead law, to give land to the landless, offer bounties to foreign emigration, and carry out Seward's project of peopling the Territories with foreigners in preference to native-born; nor against grants of land and money to build a Northern Pacific Railroad withal; nor against internal improvements in the Northern States by the General Government; nor against the erection of light-houses, and the construction of harbors, breakwaters, forts on the Northern Lakes and North Atlantic Seaboard; nor against the making of hot-beds, in which to force new States into a precocious maturity; nor against the acquisition of British America; in short, that we shall in all the future never escape the necessity of aiding with all our might in building up and strengthening the North, until, a hundred-armed Briareus,[5] only the feeble barrier of its good faith shall restrain it from strangling us in its embrace.

If this, or much of it, will probably be the fruit of even a compromise and settlement, we may readily imagine how powerless to resist in all these respects we shall be, how ludicrous any future attempt to resist will be, if we stand by and permit the seceding States to be subjugated by the Federal Power. After that, it would be supremely absurd for us to whisper even to ourselves in our chambers, that this government is the result of a compact between the States. The Virginia and Kentucky doctrines of 1798 would have become utterly obsolete; and the most ultra Federalism the universal orthodoxy.

We cannot separate from the cotton growing States. As well expect a limb severed from the human body, to live. "Sink or swim, survive or perish," our destiny and theirs must be one. We must manfully accept our destiny, meet the danger half-way, and if overcome by it, *deserve*, at least, to have conquered. . . .

If the worst should come, and re-construction of the Union be at the last found to be impossible, there will still be no reason for despair. Let the occasion and the State's necessity demand Wisdom and Patriotism, and it will be found that men are as wise and patriotic now as they were eighty years ago. Who is there that is willing to admit even to himself, that the Southern States are not wise enough to make and strong enough

---

5. Briareus was a hundred-armed and fifty-headed giant from Greek mythology.

to maintain a free government? When they meet in Convention to frame one, they will, fortunately, not have to *discover* the great principles of Constitutional Government. These are already embodied in our present great Charter; and the experience of seventy years has developed its few defects, and shown in what respects and how it needs amendments.

Let us concur in making these amendments, or adopting this Constitution, in establishing a Government for the Southern States. Let us arm, and perfect our military organization. Let us invite the North again to unite with us, and offer them, if they decline, a treaty of amity and reciprocity, peace and the mutual benefits that flow from friendly intercourse. And having thus done our duty, and provided for every emergency, we may tranquilly await the result, sure in any event that we shall not be dishonored.

It is the common cry that the dissolution of this Union will be the signal failure of our experiment of free government; and make us a by-word and an object of contempt all over the world. On the contrary, we are now proving that our institutions are not a failure. The world never saw such a drama as is now being enacted here. Without anarchy, without disorder, without interruption of the free and ordinary course of the laws, without martial law or suspension of the habeas corpus act, or troops to prevent or punish popular excesses, or even an increase of the police, the separation of a great Confederation of Sovereign States goes quietly on, with all the forms of law, all the solemnities of deliberation, all the decorum that could characterize the most ordinary proceedings in a period of profound peace.

Here only, in all the world, could such a spectacle be exhibited. If war results from it, it will not be by our fault; but in consequence of Northern avarice reluctant to let those who have so long been it tributaries go free, and resolute to substitute another government for that which our forefathers made. And, whatever their determination, if the present Union be not restored, and we are such men as have heretofore built up empires, we shall establish a new Republic, that shall outlast us and our children, and vying with its Northern Ally or Rival in arts and arms, surpassing the proudest glories of their common Ancestor, shall still prove to the world that the great experiment has *not* failed, and that men *are* capable of governing themselves.

[CHAPTER 4]

The First Convention

MARCH 1861

The secession convention opened on March 4, 1861, in the Old State House in Little Rock, the same day Abraham Lincoln was inaugurated president. By this point, seven states had left the Union and others were actively discussing secession. Resolutions, speeches, and remembrances from the convention all refer in some way to the need to prop up a racial barrier and defend the institution of slavery. By the convention's end, cooperationists had foiled Arkansas's secession. Instead, delegates adjourned on March 21 with an agreement to refer the secession question to voters in an August election. The convention would then meet again later that month to review the election results and act, if need be, though the president of the convention could recall it earlier if national events warranted.

DOCUMENT 45

Governor Henry Rector's Message, March 2, 1861

Source: *Journal of Both Sessions of the Convention of the State of Arkansas* (Little Rock: Johnson and Verkes, State Printers, 1861), 41–49.

Two days before the secession convention opened, Governor Henry Rector issued this message to the delegates, which put aside the legality of secession since other states had obviously already taken that course. Rector identified "the extension of slavery" as "the vital point of the whole controversy between the North and the South" and discussed Arkansas's place within this larger debate. Also important, Rector reported on the seizure of the Little Rock arsenal, which occurred the previous month.

. . . The constitution of the State of Arkansas declares "that all power is inherent in the people, and all free governments are founded on their authority and instituted for their pace, safety, and happiness," and to these ends, may be abolished or reformed at pleasure.

In deference to the uniform precedent, and with great respect to an assemblage, charged with such important duties, I have conceived it to be my duty to address you touching the momentous questions that imperil the honor, the lives, and the fortunes of our people.

No period in American history, nor any connected with the administrative policy of the civilized world, has imposed more solemn, more responsible, or more delicate duties upon an assemblage of men, than those which now devolve upon you whom I have the honor of addressing. . . . Unfortunate it may prove in future for the cause of civil liberty, that the American government, made up of confederated states—peopled from a common ancestry, and deriving the inestimable blessing of republican liberty from a common fountain, have from antagonistic, domestic and social institutions become alienated—distrustful and inimical to each other—until the ligaments of the Union, once like hooks of steel, have been severed so insensibly as almost to defy realization. On the 12th of December last, then, whilst American history had not recorded the separation of the United States—I communicated to the General Assembly what seemed to my mind an inevitable result, to-wit: that the union of the states was no longer an existing fact, and which succeeding events have too well testified; and that Arkansas, surrounded by inauspicious circumstances, should not hesitate to prepare for coming events, through a council of her people assembled in convention. Procrastination, however, and delay ensued, the legislature seeming to rely chiefly upon the hand of Providence, to stay the wind and dissipate the storm. . . .

The question at issue before the people of Arkansas is, whether their honor, their future safety and happiness now and forever, impels them to separate from the Federal Union, and unite their fortunes with the seven seceding states, or, on the other hand, whether prudential motives shall admonish them to take refuge amidst the fragments of the old Union, hoping for a reconstruction of the government upon terms of honorable equality to the slaveholding states.

Surrounding circumstances are the true indices of all human action. What might have been of dubious propriety on yesterday, often becomes of paramount importance on tomorrow.

The United States, as they originally stood, were composed of thirty-three independent sovereignties—each one the judge of its own wrongs, and of the mode and measure of its redress. Upon this principle and none other, the original compact was formed, uniting each state with the general government. It was a treaty, or alliance of separate and distinct governments, for the purposes of mutual protection against the inroads or aggressions of the more powerful European powers—each state preserving its equality with either, or all the other states combined—inferior to none—the voice of its own people being the superior and ruling authority. The right of secession so implacably assailed, is but the fruit of the American Revolution, announced to the world by our forefathers in their declaration of independence, and sealed by their blood at the battles of Monmouth, Bunker Hill, and Lexington.

In our own constitution, by the "bill of rights," the right of the people to reform or abolish their government, is distinctively announced, and is the sheet anchor of their liberties; What would American liberty be worth, if the kingly prerogative existed in the general government to oppress a state, or a section or states, if the power of redress was not held in their town hands? If the states are not the judges of their rights or wrongs, who is the arbiter? Who is the umpire? Some point to the judicial arm of the government as an authority constituted to decide upon the relative rights of the states and the general government. That tribunal, organized to determine the civil rights of individuals, was never intended by its creators as a repository of political power. But whether in legal contemplation, the states have a right to secede or not, has become entirely unimportant—they have done so, fully, emphatically, and completely—the enigma has been solved by practical demonstration. The golden chains once bracing up the lions of the Union, have been rent in twain by the very hands that forged them. Georgia and South Carolina, matrons among the original thirteen states, have thrown off the galling fetters, and struck a second time for unrestricted liberty.

Since they have exercised this abstract right, are they morally justified in what they have done? Have they in the light of heaven been sinned against, or are they sinning against others? Their offence, like our own, in the eyes of the northern people, is *slavery.* This institution, co-existent with the remotest periods of civilization, and sanctioned by divine authority, is declared by the president elect, to "be in the course of ultimate extinction." He has declared, and that truly, that the United States government "*cannot exist half slave and half free.*" An irrepressible conflict, says he, is going on between freedom and slavery. That institution is now upon its trial before you, and if we mean to defend and transmit it to our children, let us terminate this northern crusade, by forming a separate government, in which no conflict can ensue.

But if, upon the other hand, we are prepared to admit the argument, that slavery is a sin—that the melioration of the white and the black races requires us to abolish it, we shall keep in the true line of policy marked out by the incoming President, by remaining in the Union.

Great solace is indulged in by some, that it is the avowed purpose of black republican domination to permit slavery to remain unmolested in the states where it now exists; whilst it is as distinctly announced upon the other hand, that the institution shall be denied all power of expansion over territory now possessed or hereafter to be acquired.

The laws of physical science perceive no stand point, from which there is neither progression nor retrograde action. Peoples, governments, and the institutions of government, must either recede or advance. The area of slavery *must be extended correlative with its antagonism,* or it will be put speedily in the "course of ultimate extinction." It must invest the southern portion of North America, from the Atlantic to the Pacific, south of 36 deg and 30 min north latitude, to be permanent; else when hemmed in by a cordon of fire, "like a scorpion, it will sting itself to death." Put in the bounds; and it will soon have a general goal-delivery.

The extension of slavery is the *vital point* of the whole controversy between the North and the South, as is plainly manifested by the persistent opposition of the northern people to its being engrafted upon any newly acquired territory, whether south or north of the negro line. Does there exist inside the borders of Arkansas any diversity of sentiment, as to the religious or moral right of holding negro slaves? Do any imagine that the non-slaveholder will be less involved pecuniarily and socially, in the extirpation of this institution than the slaveholder himself. The productive portion of the soil of Arkansas is so geographically circumstanced as to preclude the idea that it can be successfully cultivated by white labor. From these more fertile regions is produced by slave labor in superabundance, the staple commodity, cotton—justly stiled commercial king of Europe and America. From the exportation of this article alone, our people receive annually an influx of capital, which permeates the hill-tops and the valleys of every section and portion of the state. The cotton planter of the South exposed to insolubrious climes, indeed is but the factor for his northern neighbor—inhabiting the mountain region, blessed with health, free trade, and remunerative prices for his grain, fruit, stock, and other articles produced for and sold in a southern market. Who could find a market for the surplus products of North Arkansas, if the more genial soil of the South was deprived of slave labor? God in his omnipotent wisdom, I believe, created the cotton plant—the African slave—and the lower Mississippi valley, to clothe and feed the world, and a gallant race of men and women produced upon its soil to defend it, and execute that decree.

There are two prominent points pressing themselves upon the attention of the people. First—to which portion or fragment of the old Union does Arkansas, by reference to her own interests, owe her allegiance. And in solving this difficulty, I assume that seven states having gone out, there is no Union—no United States government. There being thirty-three states to the compact, if one withdraws, is the compact broken? I think so. If seven withdraw, is it not then broken? That being denied—if thirty withdraw, leaving three behind, do the remaining three constitute *the Union?* Surely no man would answer that in the affirmative. Then the principle is the same from first to last, whether one or thirty states withdraw—the contract—the agreement—the partnership is dissolved. And each partner, whether by his act or the act of his associate, is released, and stands intact as he did before he signed the articles of agreement. If this course of reasoning is correct, the question for Arkansas to determine is, whether she will join her sister states of the South, with whom she has a common interest, and must have a common destiny, or whether she will turn her eyes North, to Missouri, Kentucky, Maryland, and the eighteen abolition states, for sympathy and protection. If the cotton states had formed one government, and the border slave states and the North another, when Arkansas asked for admission, to which government would she have turned her attention, seeking an alliance? Certainly not to the northern government, wherein she must perpetually remain subordinate! but to the southern of which she would have been an equal.

Fifteen southern states have failed in the past to protect slavery—how then can the remaining eight accomplish that object by remaining in the Union? Secondly, the doctrine of coercion announced by Mr. Lincoln, and indorsed recently by the lower house of Congress on the Branch amendment by a vote of 136 to 53, leaves the whole question of secession or no secession a barren field for argument. The doctrine of coercion now stands at the summit of the controversy. Practically with Arkansas the question is, whether she is willing to contribute men and money to subjugate her southern sisters to the condition of conquered colonies. If she withdraws, she is lawfully relieved at once from the performances of this onerous duty. If she stays in, she must perform it, or rebel against proper authority, and this, when pressed to such a necessity, I believe her people will do. Amendments to the federal constitution are urged by some as a panacea for all the ills that beset us. That instrument is amply sufficient as it now stands for the protection of southern rights, it was only enforced. The South wants practical evidence of good faith from the North, not mere paper agreements and compromises. They believe slavery a sin, we do not, and there lies the trouble.

All confidence is lost and it is too late to repair it. The honor and sensibilities of southern men have been trampled upon and wounded until the two sections stand in undisguised antagonism. What house can stand divided against itself? Let us then separate in peace if possible; if it not, then let it be in war, for separation must come sooner or later, and our danger increases in magnitude.

But with the fifteen slave states combined, as must ultimately be the case, having a population of 12,433,508 and comprehending in their area 857,090 square miles—having the exclusive control of the cotton zone of the world, with the necessity on the part of Great Britain, France, and other European governments of securing aliment for their cotton looms and spindles—the southern confederacy could not only soon induce peace at home, but exert an important influence upon the commercial interests of the world.

The shipping, mining, and manufacturing interests of the North could not consent to lose, by incessant war, the advantages to be derived from peaceful and respectful intercourse with the agricultural states of the South.

The burden of taxation necessarily imposed upon the people of the new government, it is said, must be onerous and oppressive. The expenses incident to a government are proportionate to its magnitude. The government of the United States, when first organized, was manifested for years at a cost of less than seven millions of dollars annually. The indirect annual tax paid by the slaveholding states, upon foreign importations, exceed an amount sufficient to maintain and operate a southern confederacy.

Cotton is king, and will open up the channels of commerce to every portion of the civilized world, free of cost, to the country which produces it. Relieved of the fishing bounties now paid by the general government to the northern states exclusively—the tax upon iron now given Pennsylvania as a peace offering and a gratuity—the annual loss of slave property abstracted from the southern by the northern states, it may readily be perceived that the new government would be less expensive to the people than the old one, kept up at an annual expenditure of $60,000,000. Then, as a matter of honor—as a matter of future security, happiness, safety, and independence—or as a question of dollars and cents, I am unable to perceive that the slaveholding states, by adhering to the old Union will consult their own interests, immediate or prospective.

In expressing to you these views, nevertheless, I wish it to be understood by all means, that I offer them in all respect to the sentiments entertained by other citizens, who see the matter in a different light; and I avail myself of this occasion to say to you, and to the people of Arkansas, a majority of whom have chosen me as their governor, that whatever your deliberations may result in, whether to secede or adhere to the Union, shall be executed by all the powers of the government subject to my command. I cannot dismiss the subject, however, without urging the propriety of submitting any ordinance that may be passed to the final action of the people by a direct vote. Their voice is omnipotent and ought to be consulted upon so important an event—the majority must rule, for their decision is the law. And if there is another wish that I may be permitted to express, it is, that the people of Arkansas, my native land, and the land of my fathers, may unite in one common verdict and build up a living rampart of freemen, united in one sentiment, eschewing all geographical distinctions—seeking one common destiny now and forever.

It is not unbecoming, I presume, that I should narrate hastily the recent events connected with the surrender of the United States arsenal at this place. In November last, almost immediately supervening my inauguration, a troop of sixty United States artillery was marched from the borders of Kansas, where their services were more needed, to the Little Rock arsenal. Such a thing was unprecedented, and I believed that they were sent here, contemplating the action of the southern states touching the proprietary and right of secession. I must frankly admit that this movement aroused my suspicions, and met my unqualified disapprobation, for I knew full well that their presence would prove a constant source of irritation, and in this I was not mistaken. The states of Louisiana and Mississippi having declared their independence of the general government early in January, and necessarily putting themselves by armed occupation in defiance of hostile invasion by the Mississippi river—citizens of Arkansas on the border of that stream, became sensible of the imminent peril they were in if a collision ensued. Every device was by them immediately adopted to procure arms at their own cost for their defense. The supply at the North proved to be inadequate to the demand from the southern states—restrictions were laid and imped-iments offered by northern people against the transportation of arms south, and none could be obtained.

In this state of insecurity, a public meeting was held in the town of Helena, expressing the opinion that it was my duty, as governor of the state, to take the arsenal at Little Rock, offering 500 men to join in the enterprise. I responded by telegraph, as I had received the intelligence, that my position was, that the arms in the arsenal should neither be removed nor destroyed, nor would I permit the fort to be reinforced by federal troops. Considering a reinforcement in the heart of the state in time of profound peace as tantamount to a declaration of war, but until one or the other of these events occurred, I should not need the services tendered by the people of Phillips county. Various rumors subsequent to this, seemingly well authenticated, reached me that United States troops were on their way to Little Rock to reinforce the arsenal. Feeling that if I permitted this to be done, without making an effort to prevent it, that I should be lacking in duty and being anxious to avoid the necessity of coming in collision with the federal authorities whilst the state was yet in the Union, I addressed a communication to Captain [James] Totten, commanding the arsenal to the purport that I could not consent that the munitions of war under his command should be removed or destroyed, or that the post should be reinforced by additional troops—adding that any assurances that he might be able to give me, touching the observance of these three points, would greatly tend to quiet the public mind, and prevent a collision between the citizens of the state and the federal authorities.

The response to this communication was, that so far as he could or dare act, to prevent a collision, he would act, but that he owed his allegiance to the federal government, and must necessarily carry out any orders made by superior authority, that he would lay my communication before the secretary of war, at Washington, and if permitted, advise me of his instructions. Ten days elapsed, and no response was communicated to me from the secretary of war. From this I felt apprehensive that reinforcements were to be sent, and was on the lookout night and day for their arrival.

In the midst of this excitement and anxiety, Mr. J. A. Ashford, a highly respectable citizen of this place, a Kentuckian by birth, and a true friend of the South, came to my office and announced that he had learned by current report in Pine Bluff the day previous, that the steamer S. H. Tucker, ascending the river, had on board three or four hundred federal troops, destined for the Little Rock arsenal. This seemed improbable, though possible by all means, and luckily, before I consented to act upon his information, I required him to reduce his statement to writing. This he did without hesitation, and it is now on file in my office. I instantly ordered cannon to be planted on the wharf, to intercept the landing of the troops, and dispatched messengers to ascertain the truth or falsity of the report. On Sunday afternoon, February 3d, they returned, reporting that there were no troops on the Tucker, as had been reported. I immediately ordered the cannon to be returned and the volunteer force commanding them disbanded.

The rumor spread, however, in various directions, and on Tuesday the 4th, volunteer troops came in from the counties of Phillips, Jefferson, Prairie, White, Monroe, Hot Spring, and other counties, numbering some eight hundred men, with the avowed purpose of taking possession of the arsenal. The excitement became intense, the town council of Little Rock assembled and passed resolutions expressing the opinion that the demonstrations made on the part of the volunteers, was disrespectful to the executive, communicating their resolves to me through a committee. In a verbal response, I announced to the committee, that I did not so regard it, that the people were the judges of their own safety, and they deeming it necessary for their own protection, to put the arsenal in the possession of state authority, until the people acted in convention, was not, by me, construed into disrespect for the constituted authorities. I advised the committee, however, that the volunteer forces were neither here by my authority, nor within my knowledge. A meeting of the citizens then took place, requesting me to demand the surrender of the arsenal by authority, tendering me their aid and sympathy if I would consent to do so. To this I assented cheerfully, and after some negotiation, Captain Totten surrendered the post to me, to be kept intact until the people of Arkansas, through their delegates in convention, should absolve me from that trust.

Documents 46–48

Resolutions Presented in the Secession Convention, March 9–12, 1861

Source: *Journal of Both Sessions of the Convention of the State of Arkansas* (Little Rock: Johnson and Verkes, State Printers, 1861), 38–40, 51, 60–61.

As the secession convention began debating the ongoing sectional crisis, the defense of the right to hold slaves and the prevention of racial equality between blacks and whites were a significant part of the discussion. Although none of these resolutions were enacted, they illustrate concern over the power of the "black republican party," which was "highly derogatory to the rights of slave states" and promoted black "social and political equality" with whites.

Resolution of Mr. G. P. Smoote (Columbia County), March 9, 1861

1st *Resolved*, That the platform of the party known as the black republican party, contains unconstitutional dogmas, dangerous in their tendency and highly derogatory to the rights of slave states, and among them the insulting, injurious, and untruthful enunciation of the right of the African race in this country to social and political equality with the whites.

2nd *Resolved*, That it is the sense of this convention, from the past history of the party, known as the black republican party—from the past action of its leaders, and their course in the present crisis, and from the acts, utterances, and conduct of its newly elected president, that said party intends to abide by and carry out, if possible, its insulting and unconstitutional platform.

3rd *Resolved*, That the seceded states have ample justification for having dissolved the ties which bound them to the old Federal Union, in the constant and unconstitutional political warfare made by the party, known as the black republican party, upon the institutions of the slave states, which warfare has culminated in the election of a president by that party, by a purely sectional vote—upon an unconstitutional platform, the principles of which, if carried out, would utterly ruin the South.

4th *Resolved*, That this convention cannot shut its eyes upon the fact that the government of the United States is now under the control of said black republican party, and that said party has power to use every arm of the same, except, perhaps, the judicial.

5th *Resolved*, That in the opinion of this convention it is a conclusion clearly resulting from the foregoing that every feeling of honor, interest, and sympathy demand that the State of Arkansas should discontinue her present political relations with the United States of America, and unite herself with the Confederate States of America. . . .

Mr. Bush[1] offered the following as a substitute:

---

1. J. W. Bush was a delegate from Greene County.

Resolved, That if the republican party should increase in strength, and thereby be able to carry out its purposes in the federal government, Arkansas, acting in concert with her sister border states, has ample means of resistance and is fully able at any time to resist any unconstitutional aggressions, and we have no need, therefore, to adopt, hastily, this last resort.

Mr. Johnson[2] offered the following:

Resolved, That any attempt to reinforce any of the forts now held by the government of [Abraham] Lincoln, in the southern states, the first gun fired, in hostility against the seceding states, will be considered as coercion and will be resisted by all the power of the state government of Arkansas.

Resolution of Mr. S. Robinson (Laurence County), March 11, 1861

Resolved, That it is the deliberate sense of this convention, that African negroes, and the descendants of the African race, denominated slaves by all the constitutions of the southern slaveholding states, is property, to all intents and purposes, and ought of right to be so considered by all the northern states, being expressly implied by the constitution of the United States, and a denial on the part of the people of the northern states, of the right of property in slaves of the southern states, is, and of right ought to be, sufficient cause, if persisted in by northern people, to dissolve the political connection between said states.

Resolution of Mr. Mayo (Monroe County), March 12, 1861

Resolved, 1st. That whereas, the power of the government of the United States has passed into the hands of a strictly sectional majority, who have manifested an intention to render the commerce of the South subservient to the interests of the North; the opinion of this convention is, that it is positively necessary for the security of the South that the aforesaid government be forever prohibited, by a constitutional enactment, from levying an impost beyond a strictly revenue point, not to exceed 25 per cent in any one case.

Resolved, 2d. That whereas, abolition incendiaries are attempting to corrupt the minds of the Indians upon our frontier, and stirring them

---

2. J. P. Johnson was a delegate from Desha County.

up to hatred of the people of the South—there should be an amendment to the constitution making such acts felony.

Resolved, 3d. That having attempted, time and again, to obtain an acknowledgement of our rights in this manner, and having been repulsed as often as attempted, we are determined to make common cause with our sister seceding states to maintain our rights and liberties.

Resolved, 4th. Whereas, certain designing enemies of our country's cause have attempted to poison the minds of the people by charging upon the advocates of southern rights an attempt to build up a government founded upon property qualification, by the abandonment of principle; we denounce to the world our disbelief in any such attempt, as neither being founded in reason or fact.

DOCUMENT 49

Speech of Williamson Oldham, Commissioner from the Confederate States of America, March 18, 1861

Source: *Memphis Daily Appeal*, March 23, 1861.

Williamson Oldham had been active in politics in the late 1830s and early 1840s, representing Washington County in the Arkansas General Assembly and eventually becoming speaker in 1842 before serving on the state supreme court from 1844 to 1848. An anti-Family politician, Oldham lost his bid to represent Arkansas in the US Congress and left the state in 1849 for Texas, where he was appointed to the Provisional Confederate Congress. Texans sent Oldham to Arkansas to support secessionism and represent the new Confederate government. Oldham's speech identified why the seceded states left the Union and created a new nation, specifically arguing that disagreements over issues like banks or tariffs could be solved but stating, "The negro question is different. It has been the cause of all the prejudice and hostility of the North against us. It is impossible to settle it in the old Union." Because the North believed in the "ultimate and complete destruction

of slavery," this was a starting point for Oldham's attempt
to show Arkansans why leaving the Union was crucial to
their future well-being.[3]

It may well be said that we are in the midst of a revolution. That
Government which our fathers constructed has been dissevered and
destroyed. Seven of the sovereign States have dissolved their connection
with the others, and I come as the representative of the Government
which those seven States have formed to the State of Arkansas to confer
with you as to your present position and what your future towards us
will be. That Confederacy contains a population which is united in feeling and sentiment, kindred in blood, and homogeneous—following the
same pursuits, having the same purposes and one common destiny. They
have formed their Constitution (provisionally) and their Government is
fairly in operation in nearly all its departments. I bring with me a copy
of that Constitution.

It is well that I should refer to the causes which brought the Southern
Confederacy into existence. The guarantees offered in their Constitution
when the States united for their protection, mutual defense and interests,
have been violated, disregarded, annulled. The principles enunciated in
the Declaration have been trampled under foot, and our catalogue of
grievances are as weighty as against the northern portion of the late
Union, as were those in that instrument against the mother country.
When a government becomes oppressive it is the highest duty of the
patriot to rise up and overthrow or change it. We are the same people
that we were in 1799, bound together by the same interests, sympathies,
and social ties. The people of the North are taught to hate us from their
cradles. And if the southern people do not hate them, they do most
heartily despise and hate their sentiments. If the issue now distracting
the country were one like a bank or tariff, it could be settled between the
two sections. But the negro question is different. It has been the cause of
all the prejudice and hostility of the North against us. It is impossible to
settle it in the old Union—it cannot be compromised. It is as impossible

---

3. For more information on Oldham, see "Williamson Simpson Oldham," Texas
State Historical Association, http://www.tshaonline.org/handbook/online/articles/
fol02, accessed July 15, 2014.

as it would be to stop the tide of the Mississippi with a dam made of sand. Where is the man in the North that has yielded to compromises on this question, that has not been overwhelmed by the popular condemnation? All who have done so there have been swept one after another from the national councils. And still the fanatical aggressive spirit increases. Politicians have attempted time and again to compromise it. They tried it by the Atherton resolutions, by the act annexing Texas, by the measures of 1850, by the Kansas-Nebraska Act; yet all these have only too palpably demonstrated how utterly impotent are the efforts of statesmen to effect a permanent peace between the two sections.

Five millions of southern freemen have raised their standard of independence and have pledged themselves to maintain their institution of African slavery, and they will do it or they will immolate themselves beneath its folds. {Applause.} Our northern enemies have well matured their plans for the ultimate and complete destruction of slavery. By exciting the prejudices, not only of their own population, but of the world, to make it odious in the minds of all, to war incessantly upon it, in the school room, the pulpit, the lecture room, the press, their legislatures, the halls of Congress, to incite insurrections, enkindle incendiarism—these are some of the means they rely upon for their purpose. The States that have passed personal liberty laws have committed moral perjury by their acts. They threaten to exclude slavery in the Territories and wherever it exists. What have we at stake? They threaten to destroy $4,000,000,000 of property—destroy and revolutionize our whole social system, and make of this fair land another Hayti—with all this we are threatened. They have now taken possession of that place once occupied by Washington and Jackson, and the black piratical flag of abolitionism waves over the Federal Capitol. Are we to surrender? No, never, but we will hold them enemies in war; in peace, friends. {Applause.} The preservation of this Union would result, and that immediately, in the destruction of slavery. Shut out from the public domain slavery must in a few years be crowded upon the Gulf States. Its ultimate extinction would be only a question of time; but as certain as the sun now shines in the heavens, our slaves will be turned loose among us and we made the vassals of northern masters—our States their conquered, despoiled, humiliated province. The Union itself is now an instrument of destruction of the very purposes for which it was constructed. While we have been devoted to the Union, we have not confounded it with those great ends and purposes for which it was intended. The Union was the casket only in which the previous jewel of our liberties and rights was deposited. When the jewel is rifled we care not for the empty casket.

We are willing to make out a balance sheet—we must hold them accountable and have a full settlement of all their delinquencies and obligations. While southern statesmen have asked no gratuities and comities, they have freely contributed to a policy and permitted a legislation which has pampered and enriched the North. While the Federal Government has been but a mere machine for phlebotomizing and depleting the Southern States, the commerce, the cities and all the great interests of the South languished. Millions upon millions of southern treasure are annually poured into the northern lap. Our commerce is entirely tributary to them. A bale of cotton that sells in New Orleans at eleven cents is sold by these northern factors in Liverpool for fifteen cents. There are several dollars per hundred gone from the planter which he should not lose, and yet cannot tell where it goes. Twelve dollars and fifty cents are collected upon every bale of cotton raised in the South, which goes into the pockets of northern speculators. These are some of the commercial disadvantages and losses under which we labor. The advantages of sundering our connection with these tyrants and cormorants are obvious. Our slave property will be absolutely secure, and fields soon opened for that expansion which will be indispensable. When we shall be separated from these very fastidious, virtuous and conscientious people, they will no longer feel responsible for the supposed sin of slavery. And that subject will then no longer be made a lever by which politicians may elevate themselves to office. The great vital interests of the country will then claim the attention, long withheld, which they demand.

The northern people have been taught that there is an irrepressible conflict between white and slave labor. It is the doctrine inculcated by Lincoln. We are to teach them that free labor at the North is dependent upon slave labor at the South. They have many lessons to learn from us yet. And when they are enlightened they will crush the politicians among them who have been misleading them. But you may say these things can best be done in the Union. Never, never! We have thrown off the yoke—you too must do it. . . .

I am sent by the Confederate States of America to the people of Arkansas, between whom are common interests and sympathies. I come to invite you to unite with us, not as vassals or inferiors, but as our peers and equals, whose star shall shine as bright as any upon our unsullied flag. But when the Republicans lay all their plans—when they reorganize the Supreme Court—when every department of the Government shall have been seized upon by men, then your proud State will stand in the same relation to the Black-Republican Government that Ireland does to England.

It is with pleasure I acknowledge the honorable reception you have extended me. I see here men of intelligence, nerve, and resolution. I cannot be mistaken in this matter. You have your property at stake in this contest; your commerce, your honor. The Southern Confederacy, with a population of five millions, capable of raising a revenue of at least fifty millions annually, of their known and approved undaunted courage, never can be coerced. {Applause.} If Arkansas, with her chivalrous sons, remains with the northern section, can we discriminate between her and Massachusetts? No; we shall be compelled to treat all alike. Are you still to remain under that commercial vassalage under which you have groaned ever since you entered the Union? For a little tariff to protect her iron interests, Pennsylvania sold the liberties of this country. How is this Southern Confederacy to be preserved? We expect not to do it by force, but by administering its affairs on principles of justice and equity. But if it comes to blows we can make an effectual use of our bayonets. No abolitionist will be permitted to put his foot in our capital to teach his treason and fanaticism. Our flag is thrown to the breeze, our guns shotted and run out at the ports, and we are determined to fight for it to the last. {Loud applause.}

I hold in my hand the original draft of the Constitution of the Confederate States of America. It is open to your inspection. We have made no alterations from the Constitution of our fathers, except such as experience has demonstrated were expedient and necessary, and adapted to the change of circumstances. I have said what I desired to speak in your presence. I hope you will determine to unite with us, and believe that it will be for the honor, prosperity and future glory of your State. {Applause.}

DOCUMENT 50

Border State Convention Resolution
of William Wirt Watkins, March 20, 1861

Source: *Journal of Both Sessions of the Convention of the
State of Arkansas* (Little Rock: Johnson and Yerkes, State
Printers, 1861), 91–93.

William Wirt Watkins, representing Carroll County,
where slaves made up 3.5 percent of the population, was
an Arkansas state senator and a Unionist. He introduced
this resolution near the end of the convention, calling on
all the remaining southern states in the Union to meet in
Frankfort, Kentucky, at the end of May and asking that
Arkansas elect commissioners to be sent to that meeting
in order to make an "effort to accomplish a satisfactory
adjustment of the sectional differences which threaten
ruin and destruction" to the Union. This had been the
aim of most of the Unionist/cooperationist members of
the convention, to cooperate with the remaining border
states in order to make a peaceful resolution instead of
resorting to secession. On March 21, 1861, five delegates
were elected to be sent to the border state convention.

Whereas, The States of Virginia and Missouri, in conventions
assembled, have called upon the border slave states to wit: Delaware,
Maryland, North Carolina, Tennessee, Kentucky and Arkansas, to unite
with them in an effort to accomplish a satisfactory adjustment of the sectional differences which threaten ruin and destruction to our once happy
and prosperous Union; And *whereas,* the State of Virginia, through her
convention, has named the 27th day of May next, at Frankfort, Kentucky,
as a suitable time and place for holding a conference or convention of
said border slave states, for the purpose, if possible, of determining upon
a plan of adjustment which shall be fair and equitable to all the states.

And whereas, the State of Missouri, animated by a like patriotic
desire to obtain a speedy adjustment of our difficulties, has appointed
commissioners, instructed to represent her in such border state conven-

tion, at such time and place as may be agreed upon by two or more of said border slave states:

Resolved, 1, *by the people of the State of Arkansas in convention assembled,* That we accede to the propositions of the States of Virginia and Missouri, for the holding of the convention of the border slave states, declaring it to be our desire and purpose to co-operate with said border states in an earnest effort to settle the unhappy controversies now distracting our country, in the spirit in which the constitution of our Union was originally framed, and consistently with its principles, and in such a manner, and upon such a basis, as shall secure to the people of the southern or slaveholding states, adequate guarantees of their rights.

Resolved, 2. That in accordance with the suggestion of the State of Virginia, we propose Frankfort, Kentucky and the 27th day of May next, as a suitable place and time for holding said conference or convention of the border slave states.

Resolved, 3. That this convention elect five commissioners, or delegates, whose duty it shall be, when notified by the president of this convention, that a majority of said border slave states have acceded to the proposition of the States of Virginia and Missouri, for holding a border state convention, to repair to the city of Frankfort, or to such other place as may be agreed upon, on the day designated to the foregoing resolution, or on any other day that may be agreed upon, to meet such commissioners, or delegates, as may be appointed by said border slave states, for the purpose of deliberating upon the matters hereinbefore referred to.

Resolved, 4. That if said commissioners or delegates, after full and free conference, shall agree upon any plan of adjustment, or upon any course of action to be pursued by said states, then the commissioners or delegates hereby appointed, shall report the same to an adjourned session of this convention heretofore provided for. . . .

Yea—41 Nay—27

DOCUMENT 51

Resolutions Passed by the Convention of the People of Arkansas, March 20, 1861

Source: Printed Ephemera Collection, portfolio 1, folder 34, Library of Congress, Washington, D.C.

In this resolution, convention delegates clearly delineated the issues that they saw within the federal Union as well as the steps they hoped to take in the future to solve the dissension between North and South over slavery. In the first section, they outlined six key issues, largely focusing on the lack of northern support of slavery. In the next section, they outlined eight proposed amendments to the US Constitution that would solve these problems; all protected slavery. In the final section, they recommended that a convention of all states be called to ratify the proposed amendments. This resolution drew support from Unionists/cooperationists as it clearly outlined the steps needed to solve the constitutional crisis imbedded within the secession movement yet stopped short of immediate secession.

We, the people of the State of Arkansas, in convention assembled, in view of the unfortunate and distracted condition of our once happy and prosperous country, and of the alarming dissentions existing between the northern and southern sections thereof; and desiring that a fair and equitable adjustment of the same may be made; do hereby declare the following to be just causes of complaint on the part of the people of the southern States, against their brethren of the northern, or non-slaveholding States:

1. The people of the northern States have organized a political party, purely sectional in its character; the central and controlling idea of which is hostility to the institution of African slavery, as it exists in the southern States, and that party has elected a President and Vice President of the United States, pledged to administer the government upon principles inconsistent with the rights, and subversive of the interests of the people of the southern States.

2. They have denied to the people of the southern States the right to an equal participation in the benefits of the common territories of the Union by refusing them the same protection to their slave property therein that is afforded to other property, and by declaring that no more slave states shall be admitted into the Union. They have by their prominent men and leaders, declared the doctrine of the irrepressible conflict, or the assertion of the principle that the institution of slavery is incompatible with freedom, and that both cannot exist at once, that this continent must be wholly free or wholly slave. They have, in one or more instances, refused to surrender negro thieves to the constitutional demand of the constituted authority of a sovereign State.

3. They have declared that Congress possesses, under the constitution, and ought to exercise, the power to abolish slavery in the territories, in the District of Columbia, and in the forts, arsenals and dock yards of the United States, within the limits of the slaveholding States.

4. They have, in disregard of their constitutional obligations, obstructed the faithful execution of the fugitive slave laws by enactments of their State legislatures.

5. They have denied the citizens of southern States the right of transit through non-slaveholding States with their slaves, and the right to hold them while temporarily sojourning therein.

6. They have degraded American citizens by placing them upon an equality with negroes at the ballot box.

To redress the grievances herein before complained of, and as a means of restoring harmony and fraternal good will between the people of all the states, the following amendments to the constitution of the United States are proposed:

1. The President and Vice President of the United States shall each be chosen alternately from a slaveholding and non-slaveholding state—but, in no case, shall both be chosen from slaveholding or non-slaveholding states.

2. In all the territory of the United States now held, or which may hereafter be acquired, situate north of latitude 36 deg. 30 min., slavery or involuntary servitude, except as a punishment for crime is prohibited while such territory shall remain under territorial government. In all the territory now held, or which may hereafter be acquired, south of said line of latitude, slavery of the African race is hereby recognized as

existing, and shall not be interfered with by Congress, but shall be protected as property by all the departments of the territorial government during its continuance. And when any territory, north or south of said line, within such boundaries as Congress may prescribe, shall contain the population requisite for a member of Congress, according to the then federal ratio of representation of the people of the United States, it shall, if its form of government be republican, be admitted into the Union on an equal footing with the original states, with or without slavery, as the constitution of such new state may provide.

3. Congress shall have no power to legislate upon the subject of slavery, except to protect the citizen in his right of property of slaves.

4. That in addition of the provisions of third paragraph of the second section of the fourth article of the constitution of the United States, Congress shall have power to provide by law, and it shall be its duty so to provide, that the United States shall pay to the owner who shall apply for it, the full value of his fugitive slave in all cases when the marshal or other officer whose duty it was to arrest said fugitive was prevented from doing so by violence; or when, after arrest, said fugitive was rescued by force, and the owner thereby prevented and obstructed in the pursuit of his remedy for the recovery of his fugitive slave under the said clause of the constitution and the laws made in pursuance thereof. And in all such cases, when the United States shall pay for such fugitive, they shall have the right, in their own name, to sue the county in which said violence, intimidation, or rescue was committed, and to recover from it, with interest and damages, the amount paid by them for said fugitive slave. And the said county, after it has paid said amount to the United States, may, for its indemnity, sue and recover from the wrongdoers or rescuers, by whom the owner was prevented from the recovery of his fugitive slave, in like manner as the owner himself might have sued and recovered.

5. The third paragraph, of the second section of the fourth article of the constitution, shall not be construed to prevent any of the states from having concurrent jurisdiction with the United States, by appropriate legislation, and through the action of their judicial and ministerial officers, from enforcing the delivery of fugitives from labor to the person to whom such service or labor is due.

6. Citizens of slaveholding States when traveling through, or temporarily sojourning with their slaves in non-slaveholding States, shall be protected in their right of property in such slaves.

7. The elective franchise and the right to hold office, whether federal, State, territorial or municipal, shall not be exercised by persons of the African race, in whole or in part.

8. These amendments, and the third paragraph of the second section of the first article of the constitution, and the third paragraph of the second section of the fourth article thereof, shall not be amended or abolished, without consent of all the States.

That the sense of the people of the United States may be taken upon the amendments above proposed:

1. *Resolved by the people of Arkansas in Convention assembled,* That we recommend the calling of a convention of the States of the federal Union, at the earliest practicable day, in accordance with the provisions of the fifth article of the constitution of the United States.

2. *Resolved further,* That the President of this convention transmit to the President and Congress of the United States and to the Governors and legislatures of the several States, a copy of these proceedings.

3. *Resolved further,* That looking to the call of a national convention, as recommended in the first resolution above, this convention elect five delegates to represent the State of Arkansas in such convention.

4. *Resolved further,* That a committee of five delegates of this convention be appointed to prepare an address to the people of the United States urging upon them the importance of a united effort on the part of the patriotic citizens of all sections and parties to save the country from the dangers which impend it, and which threaten its destruction—and especially to arrest the reckless and fanatical spirit of sectionalism, north and south, which, if not arrested, will inevitably involve us in a bloody civil war.

DOCUMENT 52

Resolution to Support the Union, March 21, 1861

Source: *Journal of Both Sessions of the Convention of the State of Arkansas* (Little Rock: Johnson and Verkes, State Printers, 1861), 106–7.

On the last day of the secession convention, delegates debated the following resolution and amendment. The resolution, offered by Rufus Garland of Hempstead County, opposed immediate secession in favor of Arkansas working within the Union as long as a compromise could be made to support "equal rights and privileges to all the states alike." This resolution passed, 40–24. The amendment referred to the sectional animus of the North and not only to the threat of abolitionism in the federal government but also to it supporting abolitionism in Indian Territory. This amendment to the resolution, offered by William Mayo, a planter with fifty-three slaves from Monroe County, passed, 39–24.

Resolved, As the sense of this convention, that the people of Arkansas prefer a perpetuity of this Federal Union to its dismemberment, or disruption—*provided it can be perpetuated upon a basis guaranteeing equal rights and privileges to all the states alike, south as well as north.*

Resolved further, That whenever time shall have proven the Constitution of the United States to be in any particular deficient; or whenever disputes shall arise upon questions touching which the constitution is not explicit; it is more in accordance with the spirit and genius of our government, as understood by its framers, to meet in conventions of the people for the purpose of taking into consideration the causes and nature of our complaints, and of amending the constitution to meet the exigency, than to overthrow or change our present form of government. . . .

Mr. Mayo (Monroe County) offered to amend the resolutions as follows:

But in making this declaration of a mere abstract opinion, truth and justice compels this convention to declare the power of the federal government now being entirely in the hands of a sectional black republican party, who are entirely unfriendly to the domestic institutions of the south, and there is almost a positive certainty that emissaries are now being sent to the Indians on our frontier, to spread the dreadful heresy of abolition among them; Mr. Dale,[4] a notorious abolitionist, being appointed to the head of that department; and who has declared the power of this government shall be used to destroy African slavery whenever the power of the federal government could be brought to bear upon it, and who has announced a policy destructive of southern commerce—all attempts having failed of adjustment, longer delay to dissolve the ties that bind Arkansas to the Federal Union, is fraught with serious danger, both to domestic quietude and prosperity.

Documents 53–58

Newspaper Reports during the Convention

Sources: *Fayetteville Arkansian*, March 8, 1861; *Arkansas True Democrat*, March 9, 11, 12, and 14, 1861; and *Fayetteville Arkansian*, March 15, 1861.

While the convention was in session, Arkansans continued to debate the merits of secession and the potential reasons why the state might want to secede. In this series of articles, the newspaper editorials and letters to the editor reproduced here had a strong secessionist bent, arguing that Abraham Lincoln and the Republican Party believed in "negro equality" and that any attempt at staying in the Union would be met with the destruction of the southern way of life. Several of the authors highlighted that Lincoln's government would support full equality for blacks as well as block returns of fugitive slaves.

---

4. Likely referring to William P. Dole, commissioner of Indian affairs. Dole, however, tried to assure the Indians that the federal government had no interest in limiting slavery in Indian Territory.

Fayetteville Arkansian, March 8, 1861: "The Sober Second Thought"

It has been said that the sober second thought of the American people is always right and it is to be hoped that it may be so in this crisis, with the citizens of our own country, particularly. Now that the election is over, the Southern Rights party defeated by an overwhelming majority and our position and paper crowned over very extensively by the victors we may indulge in a few general reflections as to the causes and means brought to bear to defeat the party to which we belong and to cheat the people of their rights. We have been a close observer of political action for many years but never have we witnessed a contest in which the people have been more completely bamboozled and humbugged than the one just terminated.

Among other things the people were told that if this State seceded and followed the fortunes of her Southern sisters, that they would be ground down and overburdened with taxation; that already the tax levied on negroes in South Carolina was 160 dollars per head, and forced loans were being resorted to in that State. . . . Reader, stop and reflect; have you as yet heard any complaint coming up from South Carolina? Does that gallant people complain of being ground down and their very existence crushed out by onerous taxation. Never. And we charge the truth to be and challenge denial and proof that the tax paid in that state on negores is only $1.60 about fourth the present tax paid in this State per head; and that is no instance has a forced loan been resorted to in that State.

Again, the submissionists urged that if Arkansas seceded, war would inevitably follow; and thus in addition to playing up on the cupidity of the people, excited their fears by depicting in all its horrid forms the consequences of civil war. And thus the people seem to have forgotten the fact that seven states had already gone out and were laying the foundation stones of a permanent Southern Republic, and the very fact of a portion of the Southern States refusing to join those already out, invited coercion and aggression at the hands of the incoming Black Republican administration, and was the only sure means of bringing about the very state of affairs so much dreaded and feared by our peace-loving people. . . .

But above all, and to be regretted more than all, the leaders of the submissionists sought to inaugurate the Helper doctrine, the most pernicious of all others to the South. We know they will start back and hold up their hands in holy horror at this charge, but to the proof, Helper recommends: "Thorough organization and independent political action on the part of nonslaveholding whites of the South."

> In an article headed "King Cotton and President Davis," the Fayetteville Democrat says: The same mob that can make cotton king and Davis President, this same mob can tell you that only he can be trusted at the ballot box who is a slaveholder, that a Republican Government based upon the universal suffrage of white men is a disgraceful failure.

Don't this look something like arraying the non-slaveholding whites in one party against the slaveholder as Helper recommends? We think it does.

Having fastened Black Republican teaching of the most damning character on the organ of our submission friends we next appeal to the people to know if the submission orators during the late canvass did not address the same doctrine. If they did not say they were willing to give up property, negroes, and everything else to remain in the Union. That some of them came here with $2.50 and were willing to surrender all save that amount and start anew, that their negroes were more trouble than they were worth any how. Did they not urge that in some of the seceding States a man had to own at least eight negroes before he was eligible to the office of Governor and did they not reason therefrom that in the Southern confederacy a like law would be enacted and that a negro property qualification would be required to entitle a man to the right of suffrage? All of which we charge to be absolutely false and resorted to only for the purpose of arraying the non-slaveholder against the slaveholder as Helper recommends. And this done too by those who pretend to be the friends of the South! . . . Following blindly these Republican Helper teaching leaders, you have spoken in thunder tones at the ballot box against a Convention, thereby saying that you were willing to submit to the administration of Lincoln and had nothing to demand from the North.

Do you not already begin to see the strong game that has been played on you and that you have been most thoroughly humbugged. We are satisfied that the people are opposed to Lincoln's policy—the Chicago platform. We know they are not yet prepared for negro equality and that whenever they fully understand the deep laid scheme to degrade them to the level of the negro, they will arise in their might and repudiate THE CLIQUE who attempted to fasten this eating sore upon the body politic.

Think for a moment, and we appeal to the non-slaveholder, how would you like to have a buck negro come up to the polls and tell you to stand back and let him vote? How would you like to sit on a jury with a negro and how would you like to have a negro give testimony against you; in a word how would you like to have him associate with you and your family as an equal? Disgusting beyond description! And yet you have been told that you have no interest in this matter.

We submit these reflections to you calmly, and earnestly entreat of you to give them your attention, for they concern you, your wives, and your children.

Arkansas True Democrat, March 9, 1861: "An Earnest Appeal"

The sovereignty of Arkansas is not in convention assembled. Our relations with the federal government are of such character, that the people of the State by an overwhelming vote for a convention, declared that some definite step must be taken to secure the rights of Arkansas in or out of the Union. The overwhelming vote for a convention can mean nothing else than a full adjustment of our rights in the Union or secession from it. Many of the delegates were immediate secessionists, and a majority of them advocated secession in case something was not done by the fourth of March. That time has arrived, but it has brought no peace to the country, and the cloud that gathered above us still looms there in murkier gloom. The peace congress has failed completely. The plan submitted, though not even acceptable to the South, was voted down by black republicans.

The policy of Lincoln as foreshadowed in his inaugural is coercion. In view of these facts, we do not hesitate to say, that the people of Arkansas are overwhelmingly in favor of secession. The vote for convention proves this. The increasing feeling all over the State shows that the people are getting impatient at the degradation of submitting longer to the domineering insolence of Lincoln and his myrmidons. We have seen the feeling in our own town,[5] once so very conservative. Men

---

5. Little Rock.

here have declared for secession, who two weeks ago were the strongest Union men in the State. We understand that the same feeling is going on in Sebastian, in Jefferson, and in all the counties bordering on the Mississippi. In some sections the Union men have come over en masse, and we verily believe that in six weeks a submissionist would not be tolerated in a majority of the counties of this State.

In view of these facts, why does the convention longer hesitate? Are we to be humiliated and disgraced as Tennessee has been? Are we to have revolution and anarchy in our midst by the inaction of the only body that can give us peace and quiet? The State is impatient, the people are satisfied that all hope of compromise is at an end. They will soon begin to murmur at the inaction of the convention, which while it hesitates to act, has no hesitation about consuming four or five hundred dollars per day of the people's money. Something must be done, and why delay longer? There is a point beyond which forbearance ceases to be a virtue. We believe that a large majority of the convention are good and true men, and our only regret is that a few submissionists are allowed to thwart the action of this body, which we are free to say, is the best looking and most intelligent collection of men, we have seen for many a day.

Let us have action. The people are convinced that all hope of compromise is at an end. The convention must be convinced of it by this time. The change of feeling in Tennessee, Virginia, and North Carolina, as we learn by telegraph, will soon make the South a unit. Let us not be the last to join our sister States of the South. Let us take a proud and independent position and not wait till we are driven out of the Union. For God's sake, give us an ordinance of secession. It is our last, but only resort—it is a necessity.

Arkansas True Democrat, March 11, 1861: "Lincoln's Inaugural"

THE UNION DECLARED PERPETUAL!

THE FEDERAL LAWS TO BE EXECUTED IN ALL THE STATES!

The Property of the Government to be Held,
Occupied, and Possessed by the Government!

DUTIES TO BE COLLECTED IN SECEDING STATES!

Majorities to Govern or Government Must Cease!

Secession is Anarchy!

THE SUPREME COURT NO POWER OVER SLAVERY!

NO POWER TO FIX THE TERMS OF A SEPARATION!

The South has taken no Oath to Destroy the Government—
He has taken one to Defend it!

If declaring the Union perpetual means coercion,
then LINCOLN'S INAUGURAL MEANS WAR!

If "Enforcing the laws" is coercion,
then LINCOLN'S INAUGURAL MEANS WAR!

If collecting duties in the seceded States is coercion,
LINCOLN'S INAUGURAL MEANS WAR!

If taking and hold the forts in seceded States is coercion,
then LINCOLN'S INAUGURAL MEANS WAR!

All members of Lincoln's Cabinet must oppose our social system.

Arkansas True Democrat, March 12, 1861:
"A Convention of the States"

The most sanguine Union-saver can think of nothing more practicable, or reasonable, than a general convention of all the States to consider some plan of readjustment. But is this plan either reasonable or practicable? Suppose the convention now sitting in the Hall of Representatives recommends such a convention, does not every sensible and even honest man know that the recommendation would be disregarded, and that it would fall unheeded upon the northern and southern ear? Has not the peace congress submitted a plan of adjustment to the people of the United States, and though that congress assembled under the call of Virginia, and was supported by great names, no section of the Union has adopted or even taken into consideration its suggestions. How impotent then will be the voice of Arkansas, calling for a convention of the States? The haughty monarch commanding the tide of the ocean to recede did not occupy a more ridiculous position. The black republican States, after refusing to repeal their personal liberty bills, would treat with contempt the idea of a convention, which would compel them to do so, if it did anything, and which might oust their President from his seat, and order a new election for the chief magistracy. The republican leaders have too much at stake to entertain such a proposition. On the other hand, the seven seceding States would laugh at the simplicity of such a proposition at this late day. Who will then be the imbecile and shallow suggester of such a remedy to the people of Arkansas? Who will meet the sneers of the people when they learn that this is the cheat practiced upon them, and their just indignation when they witness the want of manliness and nerve in those whom they have trusted and honored?

Arkansas True Democrat, March 14, 1861: "Letter from Fayetteville, March 6, 1861"

Messrs. Editors:—Yesterday was held in this place a meeting expressive of the sense of those there assembled from the country with regard to the infamous negro equality, coercion speech of Lincoln, who has desecrated by his language and person, the highest position within the gift of the people.

While all those honest substantial citizens who have kept themselves posted, have now declared themselves in favor of the cotton confederacy, and for cutting asunder those bonds which connect and degrade us to an equality with negroes and black republicans—but there are a few here yet, who, not having the fear of God before their eyes, but fearing more their earthly master now in your city, undetermined what course to pursue, lest, as in a certain notorious abolition white case, they may have to crawfish—unite only in denouncing Lincoln's inaugural address, but still like the tories of the revolution, cry hold—wait—he, Lincoln, is a liar, and does not mean to coerce—he does not intend to enforce by law, that doctrine of negro equality and citizenship which he there promulgated. They denounce coercion in the strongest terms, and yet do not define coercion, and some say they are totally unable to see coercion in his address.

Sirs, you can have no idea of the base metal of which some of the opposition politicians are composed, their misrepresentations and fabrications are astonishing to men of honesty and decency.

Our citizens were told that in South Carolina, if a man had less than ten negroes he could not vote; if ten he has eleven; if a hundred, a hundred and one votes, one for each negro and one for himself. That the negro tax was $16 per head, and that a poor man had to pay $40 just for permission to live there. That Mississippi's taxes were twenty-two times greater than before. That Jeff. Davis was President *forever;* that we would never get to vote for another; that a monarchy would soon be established in the South, and only a man that owned negroes allowed to vote for anything; that poor men would be taxed to death, and that rich ones, although having to pay $40,000 forced contributions, would speculate upon the poorer, and were told yesterday by one cock-eyed orator of the opposition, that no man or set of men can transfer his allegiance from the United States government (meaning I suppose the foul, filthy abolition administration) to another, that, that act can only be done by "each individual signing away his allegiance under his own sign manual."

This man, who has been denounced by his own party as a hair-brain, fit for a straight-jacket, who himself said he could only see one side of a question, who has declared that he would not go under Jeff Davis, but is willing, wishes and strives to stay under Lincoln, who stated immediately after reading Lincoln's address that *it contained straight out coercion,* yet leads a few honest, but ignorant men by the nose. He said it contained coercion, yet when it was inquiringly asserted in his presence, that, that doctrine was not contained in it did not dare to announce the same there for fear of losing his position with them, or being convicted of falsehood on the other hand.

What think you of another, who upon the reading of the message, said they were ready to meet black republicans and secessionists. How? In what manner? The glorious old democratic party which up to this time has successfully battled against the aggressions of the North, but now in all the hopelessness of despair intends to assert her rights upon her own soil, even if need be by the aid of the God of battles, is now told that we, the opposition, the combinations of odds and ends, the fragment of all parties, that we can baffle the schemes of the northern enemies and control the will and wish of the southern people. 'Tis the varies nonsense.

But the greatest traitorism, is, that of those who say they will raise the standard of rebellion, and if Missouri does not secede and this State does, that they will join to her, unless the ordinance is submitted, and they the great mighty *I am's* can take a "pass" at it, so anxious are they to get under black republican rule. None but traitors to the southern feeling, interest and country, can and will do this. I must confess that I don't believe a word of it. I don't think from my personal knowledge of the men who have uttered those sentiments, that they would even attempt it.—I am with them like they are about Lincoln and coercion. . . .

Fayetteville Arkansian, March 15, 1861: "Lincoln's Message"

We published this document[6] last week without any comment and in as much as some of our Union friends have taken the pains to proclaim it in the streets of this city as well as to ride over the country calling the people that they have been most agreeably disappointed and find it to be a very conservative message, we desire to be heard in reaction to it.

That there are in this as well as in all other communities, political bigots who on account of their ardent attachments to party and old party names and their inveterate hatred of the democratic party could be driven almost to an endorsement of a message from his Satanic Majesty, we will not pretend to deny; and to such we do not even hope by anything we may say to even be able to have them stop and think whither they are drifting. Therefore it is not to these hardened political fossils that we would address ourselves, but to the honest masses, the hardy yeomanry of the country who have no deep seated revenge and malignant fooling to gratify. Then, is Mr. Lincoln's message conservative and should the South be satisfied with it?

The President takes up the fugitive slave law which he touches delicately and as lightly as possible, nowhere asserting that a fugitive slave should be delivered up, but says "if the slave is to be delivered up" and if any law should be passed upon the subject, he is very anxious that "all the safeguards of liberty known to civilized and human jurisprudence be introduced so that no freeman may be surrendered as a slave." Then follows the extraordinary sentence to which we invite your special attention: "And might it not be well at the same time to provide by law for the enforcement of that clause in the Constitution which guarantees that all shall be entitled to all the privileges and immunities of citizens in the several States."

Let us compare the above with the clause in the Constitution to which he refers, which is as follows: "The citizens of each State shall be entitled to all privileges and immunities of citizens in the several States."

---

6. This document was Abraham Lincoln's inaugural address.

Here is an emphatic endorsement on the part of the negro loving President of his favorite doctrine of negro equality. He says the
Constitution guarantees that *all* shall be entitled to *all* the privileges
and immunities of citizens in the several States, while the Constitution
which he hypothetically says he has taken an oath to support says that it
is the citizens of each State that shall be entitled to these privileges and
immunities. Then it is plain to be seen that if this policy of Mr. Lincoln
. . . [in] Ohio for instance, [a slave] would not be delivered up because
in that State a negro is regarded as a citizen, proof of which is given in
the fact that Mr. Lincoln in that State received some 15,000 negro votes.
Here then we have the doctrine of negro equality distinctly enacted and
endorsed for the first time by a President of the United States—Yet he
has his apologists and endorsers in the South! . . .

DOCUMENTS 59–60

Remembrances of the Secession Convention, 1906

Sources: Alfred Holt Carrigan, "Reminiscences of the
Secession Convention: Part I," *Publications of the Arkansas
Historical Association*, Volume I, Book II (1906): 305–13
and Jesse Cypert, "Secession Convention," *Publications
of the Arkansas Historical Association*, Volume I, Book II
(1906): 314-23.

Years after the Civil War, those who lived during the
secession crisis began to record their memories of events.
Of the members of the convention, two recorded their
version of events in 1906 with support from the Arkansas
Historical Association. The first, Alfred Holt Carrigan,
who represented Hempstead County in southwestern
Arkansas, owned twenty-five slaves. Although a planter
from a large, slaveholding county, Carrigan voted with
his fellow delegate, Rufus Garland, in support of the
Unionist/cooperationist position. The second, Jesse
Cypert, a lawyer representing White County, also supported the Union position on March 21, 1861. By the call
of the second convention in May after Fort Sumter, both
had shifted to secessionism. Most of Carrigan's memo-

ries revolve around the men involved in the convention, while Cypert, on the other hand, discussed the role of the Republican Party and slavery in the secession debate. Unlike other veterans of the Civil War at this time who expunged the role slavery played, Cypert claims that Arkansas, like the rest of the South, "was a slave State, and all her relations, both by consanguinity and commercially, were with them" when discussing how Arkansas left the Union.

Alfred Holt Carrigan

. . . The entire State was in a high state of excitement and many that were strong Union men were daily going into the secession ranks, and some members who were elected, it was said, without positive alignment, as soon as they reached the Capital, by outside pressure, fell into the ranks of the secessionists. Little Rock was filled with politicians of excitable natures who were anxious for secession at any cost; adventurers and would-be soldiers, for all conceded that to take the step meant war, and the pressure was intense. The Union men were taunted as submissionists, abolitionists, and all kinds of raillery came from the lobbies. The galleries and lobbies were always crowded and it was constantly feared that violence might occur, and at times it looked as if it were inevitable.

. . . When the convention met, the anti-Union or secessionists were anxious to carry the State to extreme measures at once. . . . On the 8th Judge Floyd introduced an ordinance of secession. Mr. Carrigan moved its rejection. The journal states, on page 35, that Mr. Floyd moved to refer to a committee on ordinances and resolutions, which was, I think, not the case, for on the 11th I withdrew my motion at his request so that it might be referred. The incident excited much interest, and it was the last heard of the ordinance for some time. Floyd was very belligerent in the beginning.

Although comparatively a young man, A. H. Garland of Pulaski County exercised as much or more influence than any other one in the body; still he seldom spoke or made a motion; in fact, the Union men were on the defensive and simply attempted to keep wrong from being done. My colleague, Rufus Garland, was more frequently drawn into debate and had few equals when it came to an impromptu debate. A man of great sprightliness and versatility, Garland of Pulaski did not attempt oratory, but used a colloquial and argumentative style that was attractive and convincing. Garland of Hempstead had an encounter with [William P.] Grace that was interesting and a little strenuous. Grace, secessionist from Jefferson, has no superior in oratory. In debate General [James] Yell, the inimitable, was certainly a very strong man without much cultivation. The convention made him one of the brigadiers of State troops, but he was not in command long and did not gain any laurels. He was on the Mississippi River and suffered reverse in some way and received criticism. He was on the floor of the convention as much as any other member. Yell and Grace were a strong representation from Jefferson County. To further refer to the Garlands, the Governor, or Garland of Pulaski, was elected by the convention to the Provisional Congress by 52 votes, the largest any of the five received. Many, as I did, recognized the high standing and integrity of Hon. R. W. Johnson, United States Senator, and were anxious for him to be one—the Union men more so than the secessionists. The five were: Johnson, Garland, [Hugh F.] Thomasson, W. W. Watkins, and Albert Rust, an ex-congressman and a strong Union man, Senator Johnson alone representing the original secession wing. General Yell was a strong, strenuous aspirant, but found he could not get the place and his name was not put forward.

Judge [Thomas B.] Hanley, a secessionist, was really the ablest and most prominent man on that side. He was an able lawyer and in framing the new constitution was chairman of the judiciary committee and acted well and nobly his part. There was no one but could admire the part he took in attempting to give the State a good constitution. His colleague, C. W. Adams, was an able man, and noted for the frequency of his orations. Nothing delighted him more than to engage [William] Fishback in debate. He was a scholarly man, of fine appearance, wore his hair long and was sometimes called Pike, the Second. Certainly Phillips County was ably represented. My impression is he distinguished himself in the Civil War; still he did inflict on us many long orations to prove the right of secession.

. . . J. M. Smith of Saline and Union Counties, lawyer, a man of considerable ability, loved a controversy. Slow and deliberate, a good man, true as steel. During the war he commanded a regiment; after the war he was circuit judge. W. M. Fishback, presumably about 25 years of age, a strong Union man, a Virginian, a slaveholder, certainly loved the Southland. He was as much on the floor as any member. He stood well intellectually, and while not an orator, never came out second best. Adams and Grace had many debates with him and their closing and best argument with him was the taunt of abolitionist and black Republican. For his age he was certainly a noble exponent of the Union men of that day. He was always ready for the fray, and commanded respect by his mental vigor and moral courage, by adhering to the position he occupied. At the time the ordinance of secession was called the Secession Act. It was intended to dissolve the Union between the State of Arkansas and the other states under the compact entitled "Constitution of the United States of America." The Union men never yielded the principle of secession, simply claiming the right of revolution or separation.

. . . The Tottens—B. C., from Prairie County, an elderly man and lawyer, was considered a man of ability and participated largely in debate. He was an ardent secessionist, and I think, became one of the military board of the State. James L., from Arkansas County, was a planter. No one was more radical and extreme in his views. B. S. Hawkins of Sevier County, a large planter, and, although of the secessionist wing, had no ultra views and looked at the matter very seriously. At one time there was a disposition to confiscate all the property of Northerners in the State and do so indiscriminately. When every one seemed wild over some fire-eater's speech, he came to my seat in the hall and implored me to do all I could to hold the Union men firmly opposed to such a course, as he said his side had gone wild. We were close friends, and he told me he would hold me personally responsible if such a vicious course were pursued. The truth was, he owned interests in the North, and he saw it was a two-edged sword. He was a man, though very silent, of fine intelligence, and served as senator from about 1852 to 1854 from Sevier County, which now forms part of the district which I was then representing. Hawkins of Ashley County, a nice, affable gentleman, as I remember, was scarcely ever on the floor. He is one of the very few now alive. I think he was a very young man. He has since served as circuit judge and chancellor. . . .

Jesse Cypert

The presidential election in November, 1860, resulted in the election of presidential electors pledged to vote for Abraham Lincoln, a candidate of a purely sectional party, the main feature of which was the opposition to the extension of slavery in the territory of the United States. This party was styled the Republican party, and drew to its support the Abolition party and the Free Soilers, all of which tended to irritate the South, and was regarded by the Southern and Slave States as a menace to the institution of slavery and a threat against their constitutional rights as they understood it under the constitution of the United States. Soon after the result of the election was known, on the 20th day of December, 1860, South Carolina passed what was termed an ordinance of secession, after which Mississippi, on January 9, 1861, passed a like ordinance, followed by Florida and Alabama seceding on January 11th. Georgia seceded on the 19th of January, Louisiana on the 26th of January, and Texas on the 1st day of February, 1861.

These states soon formed by their delegates elected for that purpose, what was known as the Confederate States of America, and established the seat of government at Montgomery, Ala.

While these events were taking place, the legislature of Arkansas, being then in session, on the 15th day of January, 1861, passed an act authorizing the State of Arkansas to hold an election for the election of delegates to a convention to be held at such time and place as should be designated by the governor by proclamation, in the event of such a majority of the votes cast being in favor of holding such convention. The election was held on the 18th of February, 1861, and resulted in calling the convention by a majority of the popular vote of 11,586. . . .

The convention met in the old hall of the house of representatives at the State House, which is now used as the senate chamber. The secession and Union men in the organization of the convention each sought to elect a president favorable to their views. Thomas H. Bradley of Crittenden County placed in nomination of David Walker of Washington, and L. D. Hill of Perry County nominated B. C. Totten of Prairie.

With the exception of the candidates themselves, all the members who were opposed to secession at that time voted for David Walker, and those in favor of secession voted for Totten. The vote resulted in Walker receiving 40 votes and Totten 35, a majority of five for the Unionists or anti-secessionists. . . .

Judge Walker and Judge Totten each voted for the other, although their views on the question of secession were different. The personnel of the convention was of the highest order of talent, generally men of prominence at that time, or men who have since become prominent. Judge David Walker, the president, had served for a number of years as associate justice of the supreme court of the State, and Judge James Totten of Arkansas County had served on the circuit bench in Mississippi. B. C. Totten of Prairie, who was voted for for president, had been on the circuit bench in Tennessee. Thomas B. Hanley of Phillips had been on the supreme bench, and for a number of years was circuit judge of the first judicial circuit of Arkansas. His colleague, Charles W. Adams, had served with distinction as circuit judge. [Harris] Flanagin of Clark had been on the supreme bench, and afterwards was one of the war governors of the State. [Augustus] Garland of Pulaski was afterwards governor, United States senator and attorney general of the United States under Cleveland's first administration, besides representing the State in the Confederate Congress during the war.

. . . There was a great deal of interest taken in the deliberations of the convention, the galleries being crowded nearly all the time while the convention was in session. There was also much wrangling, and a great number of the delegates seemed disposed to have their views on the various issues made a part of the record in order that they might "square" themselves with their constituents, or enlighten posterity as to what influenced them in their votes. . . .

After a great deal of debate and consideration of a number of resolutions, Mr. Thomasson of Crawford offered a resolution declaring the many grievances of the South against the actions of the Republican party, and its declarations in relation to the institution of slavery, and looking to an adjustment of these questions by a calling of a convention of all the states, for the purpose of amending the constitution as to prevent the necessity of evil strife, and the coercion of Southern States, which resolution, with some minor amendments, was adopted on the 11th of March. Also the report of the committee on Federal relations through Jesse Turner, chairman, was adopted.

This consisted of a series of resolutions defining the position of the

State of Arkansas, in relation to the Federal Government, in which the declaration was made "that any attempt on the part of the Federal government to coerce a seceding state by an armed force would be resisted by Arkansas to the last extremity."

In the meantime the delegates had, at their own expense, obtained a telegraphic report of a synopsis of President Lincoln's inaugural address, and the pacific utterances contained therein exerted great influence on the delegates in preventing secession at that time.

However, all were agreed that any attempt on the part of the Federal Government to coerce the other Southern States would be, or should be, resisted by the State of Arkansas, however anxious the people were to remain in the Union. . . .

Immediately after the firing on Fort Sumter, or about April 15, 1861, President Lincoln issued his proclamation calling on the several states for volunteers, to suppress what he termed the rebellion in the several states composing at that time the Confederacy and calling upon Governor H. M. Rector of Arkansas for that State's quota of volunteers asked for.

This action on the part of the Federal authorities was deemed sufficient emergency to justify the president of the convention to reconvene that body, which he did by proclamation, calling the convention to meet on the 6th day of May.

In the meantime Virginia had seceded on the 16th of April, the day following President Lincoln's proclamation, and events were culminating and preparations for the great conflict that was to follow were being made all over the country, both north and south; the people of both sections were thoroughly aroused, and the greatest excitement prevailed that has ever been known in the history of the country. Very few seemed to realize what would be the final result.

The convention met on the day appointed by the president, and at four 'o clock on the same day passed the ordinance of secession, reported by Wm. P. Grace, chairman of the committee appointed for that purpose. The ordinance after reciting the various grievances of the State of Arkansas at the hands of the Federal authorities, "declared and ordained" that the "Union now subsisting between the State of Arkansas and the other states under the name United States of America is hereby forever dissolved." It was further "declared and ordained" that "The State of Arkansas hereby resumes to herself all rights and powers heretofore delegated to the government of the United States of America—that her citizens are hereby absolved from all allegiance to said government of the United States, and that she is in full possession and exercise of all the rights and sovereignty which appertain to a free and independent state.

. . . It is enough to say for the whole body that they were as honest and patriotic a body of men as ever assembled in the State; that their final action was indorsed by the people of the State is attested by the fact of the thousands of volunteers from all parts of Arkansas who joined the cause of the Confederacy, and for four years, amid the greatest privations, dangers and hardships, upheld what was conceived to be their constitutional rights. Nine of the members of the convention of 1861 were also returned to the convention of 1874, thirteen years after, and when the people of the State had in part regained control of affairs and when reason had resumed sway, after the reconstruction period.

There are at this date (August, 1906), so far as I can learn, only four survivors of the secession convention, but the above tribute is due to all alike, living and dead, of the body of men who were convened at the most momentous period of the country's history to do that for Arkansas which seemed the best and wisest. After a retrospect of forty-five years, and in the light of subsequent history, I am not yet prepared to say that their action, in the interest of the State, was not right and I still believe that if the people of Arkansas had to take up arms, that it was better to stand by the South and her own interest and kindred, notwithstanding she had been originally in favor of the Union. President Lincoln's proclamation, with reference to the other seceded states, and demand for Arkansas to furnish troops to make war on them, left us no alternative but war on one side or the other. A large majority of the people of the State had come from other Southern States; their kindred were in those states; she, like them, was a slave State, and all her relations, both by consanguinity and commercially, were with them.

By them she stood when the crucial hour came, and her representatives in that convention only voiced the sentiment of the people of the State when they adopted the ordinance of secession.

[CHAPTER 5]

Moving toward Secession

APRIL AND MAY 1861

With the secession convention adjourned, delegates returned home to explain what had gone on in Little Rock to their constituents. Unionist delegates especially were interested in explaining their hopes for what action would be taken in the ensuing months to settle the sectional crisis. However, on April 12, 1861, South Carolinians opened fire on Fort Sumter in Charleston Harbor—the beginning of hostilities changed the dynamic within Arkansas.

This chapter contains letters and documents relating to the move toward secession, mainly after the shelling of Fort Sumter. The battle changed the minds of some of the staunchest Unionists and all the cooperationists, compelling them to support secession, frequently arguing that no other option was left for Arkansas to follow if it wanted to protect its slave property. Abraham Lincoln's call for 75,000 volunteers to put down the southern rebellion, including 780 men from Arkansas, met with further indignation as few Arkansans wanted to take up arms against fellow southerners. By late April, convention president David Walker knew that he had to reassemble the convention, fearing that eastern and southern Arkansas might act independently and leave both the Union and Arkansas. On May 6, the convention reassembled and quickly voted to secede from the Union, with only five delegates voting against secession. Four of them changed their vote in an attempt to ensure unanimity, with only Isaac

Murphy of Madison County remaining steadfast in support of the Union.

DOCUMENT 61

Unionist Manifesto

Source: *Arkansas State Gazette*, April 6, 1861.

> Thirty-nine members of the convention who voted against secession published this shortly after the first convention adjourned to explain the reasoning behind their vote. Important to note is that these Unionists were very much interested in securing slavery and defending against northern coercion of the southern states that had already seceded. In addition, they clarified that the entire North was not against slavery and that southerners should not mistake the actions of a few abolitionists for northern sensibilities in general. In the end, the statement demanded patience instead of brash action and called for further working within the Union to find a solution to the crisis and protect slavery.

To the People of Arkansas—The undersigned, Union members of the Convention, which met on the 4th and adjourned on the 21st of March, deem it their duty, to issue an address, briefly stating the action of the Convention on the subject confided to it and offering some suggestions as to the course to be pursued in the future, in view of the circumstances now surrounding our State.

Upon assembling at the Capital, on the 4th of March, we found a clear majority of Union delegates had been elected, representing a majority of more than five thousand of the votes cast,—though but little over two-thirds of the votes of the State were polled. The path of duty to us was clear, and the ordinance of secession was voted down; but there being a large minority, of delegates, representing a respectable minority of the votes polled, it was deemed most wise, as well as just, in view of the fact that the new administration had but lately been installed, and its policy to a great extent undeveloped, not to place the

State in a condition, that she could not act upon any new exigency that might arise without the expense and delay of an extra session of the Legislature, and a new election for delegates to a Convention; and with a view of obtaining a full and fair expression of the opinion and wishes of the people after the policy of the new administration became known, resolutions in favor of a National Convention, and declaring what in our opinion would be a proper basis of settlement of the differences between the slaveholding and non-slaveholding States. . . .

Other resolutions were adopted, approving the call of Virginia, for a Convention of delegates from the border slaveholding States, at Frankfort, Kentucky, on the 27th of May, in which Arkansas will be represented by delegates elected by the Convention; and providing for the submission to the people at the ballot box on the first Monday in August, of the question, shall Arkansas cooperate with the border or unseceded slave States in efforts to secure a permanent and satis-factory adjustment of the sectional controversies disturbing the coun-try, or immediately secede. To give effect to the wishes of the people thus expressed the Convention will reassemble on the third Monday in August. Other resolutions declaring against coercion of the seceded States, and protesting against the quartering of United States troops in places owned by the United States in the Southern States, to coerce seceding States or prevent secession, were also adopted.

Thus it will be seen, that while Arkansas is not committed to the doc-trine of secession, she condemns coercion by the Federal Government, and recommends the removal of causes that might lead to a collision; and the adoption of Constitutional means to restore peace and fraternal relations between the sections, and happiness and prosperity to our once united but now distracted country. Four months will intervene before the election—affording ample time for reflection and the formation of a just conclusion. None can complain that the people—the source of all power in this country—have not been consulted, or their voice stifled, and it is to be hoped that the expression, thus fairly obtained will be respected, and the decision acquiesced in by all.

Fellow citizens, your destiny is in your own hands. The vote on the first Monday of August, will seal the fate of the State, and in all prob-ability determine whether the Union shall continue to exist and shed its blessings upon millions of people, or cease to occupy a place upon the map of Nations. Whether our National greatness is to be perpetual, affording a bright example—and living evidence that man is capable of self-government, or be destroyed in the morning of its existence, and prove the truth of the theory of those who advocate the diving right of Kings, and the enemies of free government. We cannot doubt the result. Your verdict we shall await, with confidence, that you will not determine to destroy that government, which has bestowed upon us so many blessings, and secured to us so many rights not enjoyed by any other people, without uniting your efforts with those of the people of Virginia, Tennessee, Kentucky, Missouri, and the other slaveholding States still in the Union, to secure our rights, and at the same time preserve that Union.

We make no appeal to your passions. To your patriotism, love of country and reverence for the memory of your fathers, who handled it down to you to be transmitted as a sacred inheritance to your children, none is needed. Everyone should know and understand the dangers that surround us and the interests involved, and determine to act as duty dictates. We know what our government is and its value, what will follow its destruction—what the future will develop, once the work of a disintegration passes to a point beyond control, which it surely will if Arkansas secedes, is beyond the wisdom of man to determine. Secessionists cite the acts of Northern men in and out of Congress to excite our indignation and convince us there is no hope. If we are to take the mad ravings of Phillips, Garrison,[1] and other disunionists at the North, as an index to the sentiment of the Southern people, we would be forced to despair of the Republic. But it is as unjust to judge the great mass of the Northern People, by these men, as it would be to judge the people of the South, by the declarations of our politicians of the ultra school. The politicians are one thing, the people another. The politicians have created the difficulty, and will *never* settle it. They stand between the people of the sections, and stifle their voice. Until the voice of the people of the North, expressed in a Constitutional way can be heard, we should not conclude, that they are blind to their own interest or deaf to the appeals of patriotism and justice. The answers of the present difficulties North and South, unite in opposing all propositions of compromise

---

1. Refers to abolitionists Wendell Phillips and William Lloyd Garrison.

and settlement, for the obvious reason that if such a one as is proposed by your Convention is adopted, the slavery question, that fruitful source of contention, and favorite theme of the demagogue, can never figure as a question of National politics—their vocation will be gone, and they fear, as well they may, their places will be filled by men after the order of the statesmen of the better days of our government.

The secessionists say, the Northern people are aggressive and we have often demanded our rights even implored them to do us justice. True it is, that the conduct of some of the Northern States, and finally the election of a President upon a sectional platform by a sectional vote, evidence, that there is a danger of aggression on their part, and for our future security we demand additional guarantees, and this when made will be the first demand properly made. These we demand, and for the purpose of making such a demand as will be satisfactory to all, and of presenting it to the Northern people, we responded to the call of Virginia for a Convention at Frankfort, and recommended that a National Convention be held. That the Frankfort Convention, composed as it will be, of delegates from the slaveholding States, the most deeply interested in the subject of controversy, will mature a plan of settlement that will be satisfactory to all men in the South, who desire to see the Union preserved, we cannot doubt, notwithstanding it is alluded to as a trick, a sham, and every possible effort made to forestall its action, and prevent its favorable consideration by you.

It may be hardly respectful to you to enquire whether the demand will be acceded to by the Northern people, for we feel assured that you will not despair until the last means provided by the Constitution is exhausted, and every reasonable expectation disappointed, following the example of the citizens of the greatest Republic of the olden time, who awarded a public reception to one of their generals on his return from a disastrous campaign, which had resulted in the destruction of the army under his command, because he did not despair of the Republic. But as it is urged as a reason why Arkansas should secede, that all appeals have been unheeded—all propositions rejected, we trust it is not improper to allude to the condition of things since the secession or disunion movement commenced, events that have transpired. . . .

Previous to the Presidential election, there were very few men in the South who took the ground that the election of Mr. Lincoln would justify a destruction of the Union, though his election was hardly doubted by any for several weeks before the election. But scarcely had the result been announced, when we were startled by the cry raised in every town, village, and hamlet, in the entire South. In but little over one month after the election and but one week after the assembling of Congress, South Carolina called a Convention, and twenty days later adopted an ordinance of secession, and unexampled efforts and appliances were used to precipitate other States after her and several followed in rapid succession. There was no statement of grievances—no demand for redress by the seceding States. Of course there could be no united action. The seceding States defeated it. Virginia called for what is known as the Peace Conference, which unfortunately met at Washington where, being surrounded by the same corrupt influences that had produced the lamentable state of the country, and composed also principally of delegates elected by legislatures or appointed by Governors elected during the summer preceding the Presidential election and representing their views, not the people's, forbade our expecting much from it, though we looked to it with some hope. It reported a plan for settlement which it is not necessary to discuss here. But no matter what its merits or demerits are, the extremists heading the disunion movement North and South, denounced the Convention and predicted its action would prove an abortion in advance, and now with marvelous consistency complain that it did not receive the favorable consideration of Congress. There was still less reason to expect any favorable action from Congress then in session, than to expect the Peace Conference to present a satisfactory plan of adjustment for its action, composed as it was, to a great extent, of extremists from both sections, elected in time of high party excitement, when the existing state of the country was not anticipated, working for a common purpose, making inflammatory speeches to be scattered broadcast over the land, and keep alive sectional excitement. Even if there had been a disposition to act, there was not sufficient time to discuss the amendments proposed to the Constitution.

During the session of Congress petitions signed by thousands of Northern people praying for a settlement were presented. There is still the deepest interest manifested by them. Many of their ablest and best men are engaged in the work. Several State Legislatures have repealed or nullified their offensive legislation. Indiana, Illinois, and Ohio have by resolution requested the calling of a National Convention; the President and many of his leading political friends have expressed themselves in favor of the proposition.

Nor is this all. The Federal troops have been, or very soon will be, withdrawn from Fort Sumter, and thereby the danger of a collision avoided. Moreover, by the withdrawal of Southern Senators and Representatives from Congress the Republicans had a decided majority in both houses and the power to pass any law they chose, notwithstanding, they refused to put in the hands of the President the means of coercing the seceding States, and by a two-thirds vote of both houses passed an amendment to the Constitution declaring that no amendment shall be hereafter made to authorize or give to Congress the power to abolish or interfere within any State, with the domestic institutions thereof, including *persons held to labor or service by the laws of said State*. We do not infer from this that the Republican leaders have abandoned any of their dangerous dogmas, but that they have found that their own people will not sustain them in their ultraism, and are disposed by concession to accommodate and settle the difficulties between them and us.

The question is not plainly presented for your action. Be not deceived by the delusion that it is necessary for Arkansas to secede, in order to secure the united action of the South. Once out of the Union the designs of the disunion leaders are accomplished. By a vote upon resolutions declaring it to be the sense of the people of this State that the Union ought to be preserved if possible, on terms consistent with the rights of all sections, and that it is more in harmony with the spirit of our government, to amend the Constitution in such respect as it may by experience prove deficient, than to overturn and destroy it, the secession members are fully committed against the Union—*twenty-five* of them voted *against* these resolutions, *one* voted *for* them and *eight* were absent or did not vote. By these resolutions disunionism was unmasked and the true object and character of the movement disclosed, and shown to be a total overthrow and entire dismemberment of the Constitution and Union. It is hard to credit that any desire such an end, and we feel confident that there is not one in a hundred of the people of the South, who does not desire the perpetuity of the government and the Union, if the rights and interests of all can be preserved. We believe it can be done and appeal to you to make the effort. If successful your interests are secured and your honor is imperishable, for we shall not only see the people of the States still adhering to the Union, once more united, prosperous and happy, but our brethren, *the people* of the seceded States, will arise in their majesty and decree that they shall resume their places in the sisterhood of States, and under our glorious national flag we will resume our march to national greatness; the star of our destiny will reappear, and its splendor, temporarily obscured illuminate the path and cheer the hearts of all people thirsting after liberty.

Document 62

Letter from C. C. Danley to David Walker, April 15, 1861

Source: David Walker Collection, Center for Arkansas History and Culture, Little Rock, Arkansas.

C. C. Danley, writing from Little Rock to David Walker, the president of the secession convention, describes his fears that the revolutionary elements in the state might take this opportunity to seize power from the more conservative Unionists. Danley, the editor of the *Arkansas Gazette*, had been, along with Walker, a strong Unionist voice, even though he had previously allied with T. C. Hindman in favor of reopening the Atlantic slave trade in the late 1850s. However, Fort Sumter changed the political dynamic for Unionists who had not seen a credible reason to secede in March 1861. Danley urged Walker to call the convention back into session in order for the conservatives to take leadership before the governor, Henry Rector, a pro-secessionist, took charge and pushed Arkansas into war.

Dear Judge,

The news received yesterday and today makes war between [Abraham] Lincoln's administration and the South inevitable if it has not already begun and with the administration of Lincoln rests the inevitability. . . . Mr. Butraud told me he had written you and I thought it better that I should write also. The telegraph has told you already of the existing state of affairs outside of the state. We of this place can here talk of affairs and advice by all . . . that you call the convention together at their earliest possible day. It is necessary to prevent revolutionary movement on the part of the Governor and other powers at this place and in other sections of the state. The existing circumstances make the call necessary. By the time the convention meets developments enough will be made to enable us to shape our course wisely. If we take the initiative, the conservative men of the state will control this movement. If we do not, the revolutionists will take charge and we will have to blame ourselves for the evils which will necessarily follow.

If things remain in their present attitude, I, for one, would not be in favor of <u>secession</u> but for <u>a declaration of Independence</u> . . . the standout of revolt against the government. But our course . . . to this matter will have to be determined by further developments. . . .

Document 63

Leroy Pope Walker to Thomas C. Hindman, April 16, 1861

Source: US War Department, *The War of the Rebellion: A Compilation of the Official Records of the Union and Confederate Armies* (Washington, DC: GPO, 1880), series 1, 1:684–85.

Leroy Pope Walker, the Confederacy's first secretary of war, responded to Thomas C. Hindman's request for information on supplying the Confederacy with military aid even though Arkansas had not yet seceded from the Union. The previous letter from C. C. Danley to David Walker indicated that the governor and other pro-secessionists would push the state into war quickly. This letter from Leroy Walker confirmed Danley's fears that Arkansas secessionists were working to move Arkansas closer to the Confederacy.

SIR: In reply to your inquiries in regard to the policy of this Government on the subject of accepting military aid from Southern States which are not yet members of the Confederacy, and especially as to Arkansas, I beg leave to state that thus far this department has thought proper to decline for the present all tenders from those States, simply because the forces easily and rapidly raised in convenient proximity to the scenes of operation have been ample for all the needs of the country.

Since the forced surrender of Fort Sumter to the forces of the Confederate States, followed by a most warlike proclamation from the Executive of the Washington Government, the probability that serious and perhaps long-continued hostilities will ensue is greatly increased.

If the war shall be commenced with the spirit which seems to animate our enemies, there is every reason to anticipate the operations of both the belligerents will be conducted on a much more imposing scale than this continent has ever witnessed; and I may add that the general opinion preponderates strongly in that direction.

While this Government has an unfaltering confidence in the means and resources, pecuniary, moral and military, of the Confederate States, as they now exist, to defend themselves against all assaults and to repel all their enemies, it yet by no means undervalues the assistance which it is in the power of the border slave States to render; and of these latter there is no one to which the people of this Confederacy have looked with more undoubting confidence for cordial sympathy and support than the State of Arkansas.

It is not possible yet to state absolutely that this Government will be in condition to need forces drawn from any State not in the Confederacy, but it is extremely probable that in the event of war (now, in its widest sense, apparently inevitable), which shall continue through the approaching summer, a brigade organized in conformity to the act of Congress "to provide for the public defense," will be gladly accepted at an early day in the next fall—say about the middle or last of August. Such a military organization, if required, as I think it will be, would be composed of course, as similar organizations will be, from the several Confederate States. It would be expected to elect its own officers, but would be subject to the control of such field officers as the President of the Confederate States might place over it.

All the signs of the times, as I view them, so conclusively favor the belief that war in its sternest phase is upon us, that I have not hesitated to intimate how strongly we rely on your State for active co-operation in what is, after all, a common defense. That she will prove true to herself, and so prove true to this Confederacy, I never for a moment have questioned.

Documents 64–66

Newspaper Responses to Fort Sumter, April 20 and 27, 1861

Source: *Arkansas State Gazette*, April 20 and 27, 1861.

The mood of Arkansans changed quickly after the attacks on Fort Sumter. Newspapers promptly published letters to the editor and editorials critical of Abraham Lincoln and in support of secession. The quick abandonment of Unionism after Sumter matched the position that most Unionists (in reality, cooperationists) had taken—the use of military force to compel seceded states to return to the Union would be cause for immediate departure. These first shots then convinced many in the state to abandon the Union and join the Confederacy.

Arkansas Gazette, April 20, 1861

. . . The recent action of the weak and perfidious Administration of Mr. Lincoln has made the Southern People, a united people.

Its abrupt adoption of a war policy in the midst of protestations of pacific and conciliatory purposes has convinced it of a duplicity and treachery towards the conservative portion of the Southern people, only equaled in degree by the incapacity and stupidity which dictated it.

Without abandoning our opinions upon the original question of the Constitutional right of a State to secede from the Union or retracting our criticisms upon the initiation a year ago of the policy which has so quickly ripened into civil war, we feel it to be our duty to declare to the People of Arkansas, and to the Government of which Mr. Lincoln is the nominal head, that we are ready to embark "our lives, our fortunes, and our sacred honors," in the rebellion or revolution, as the result of the conflict already begun, shall determine its character to be.

The employment by the Federal Government of its military power and material resources which have been supplied alike by all the States of the Union, to compel any of them to submit to its jurisdiction, is utterly opposed to the spirit and theory of our institutions, and in a little while would reduce the States which constitute the weaker section, to the condition of mere appendages or provinces to the dominant and stronger section, to which anarchy itself would be preferable.

The South is "our country"—and while we are satisfied that up to the moment when the Government at Washington committed the folly and wickedness of making war upon the seceded States, the conservative party in Arkansas was largely in the ascendant, we cannot believe that her soil is polluted by a being base and cowardly enough to stop to consider in casting his lot in the unequal struggle in which she is engaged, whether she is "right or wrong."

Our faith in the prudence and patriotism of the people's Convention, not yet dissolved, authorizes the hope and belief on our part, that its President will convene it at the earliest practicable moment, and that it will take such action as duty to our Southern brethren prompts, and the safety and honor of their State and people demand at their hands.

Arkansas Gazette, April 20, 1861

The Work of the Coercion Commenced—Let the People of Arkansas Resist it as one Man—the readers of our paper can testify, if witnesses were necessary, as to the zeal and earnestness of purpose with which we opposed the precipitate secession of Arkansas from the Union. A native of the South, and in every pulsation of our heart devoted to her interests, we took no position in which we thought they could be compromised in the least. We were in favor of a Convention of the border slave states, in the hope that they might propose a plan of adjustment alike honorable and acceptable to the whole country—a plan which would not only induce the border slave States to remain in, but which would also induce the seceded States to return. Opposed to the doctrine of coercion, as a matter of policy, from the first and believing that the Constitution granted no power to Congress to coerce a State, we said when South Carolina seceded—wo to the government or the power that attempts to coerce her into the Union. Denying to a State the Constitutional right to secede, we have always held to the sacred and inalienable right of revolution and resistance of wrong and oppression.

The Union members of the Convention, too, representing the entire

Union sentiment of the State, held views similar to those which we had expressed. . . . The Union members of the Convention, and of the State, relying upon the pacific professions and promises of President Lincoln, after passing the foregoing resolutions, also proposed a plan for the adjustment of our difficulties which would have been just to all sections and satisfactory to the South. But Lincoln has acted in bad faith—he has violated his promises of peace—he has shown himself to be one of those "that palter with us in a double sense; that keep the word of promise to the ear and break it to our hope."

President Lincoln has attempted to coerce seceded States by forces of the Navy and the Army, both at Fort Sumter and Fort Pickens. . . . [H]e has kept troops quartered at the Forts and Arsenals within the seceded States, as developed by his policy, for the purpose of coercing them; and he has kept troops, as shown in like manner, in the Forts and Arsenals in the States which have not seceded, without consent of such States, when the United States is at peace with all foreign nations. . . .

He has blockaded ports in the seceded States, and attempted to recapture the Forts and Arsenals within their borders, by an armed force . . . in violation of the plain letter of the Constitution, which places the war making power solely in Congress, he has issued a proclamation which is tantamount to a declaration of war against the seceding States—this too in the face of the fact that the best Constitutional lawyers in the country hold that the Constitution does not confer even upon Congress the power to coerce a seceding or a refractory State.

In like violation of the Constitution, after assuming the war making power, he has assumed to call upon the States for 75,000 men to carry on his war—when the Constitution is clear that Congress, and Congress alone, has the power even in a legitimate war, to call State troops into the service of the General Government. . . .

Looking at what has been done by President Lincoln, and looking to what he menaces us with, we can see but one course for the State, and for the Union men who compose a majority of the State, to adopt and pursue, and that is, as the Convention recommended, *to resist to best extremity.*

We have no doubt that Judge Walker will call the Convention together at a very early day; and of the further fact, that, when it meets, its action will be harmonious and unanimous. Speaking for ourselves, we are opposed to the doctrine of secession, but the right to rebel against an oppressive government is one upon which all agree. Peaceable secession has proven to be what we thought it from the first—an impossibility. As well expect to pull a stout man's arm from its socket in his shoulder without pain, as to sever the Union without violence. We seek no protection behind any pretense that secession is a Constitutional remedy, and may be exercised without the violation of law or the incurring of its penalties. We fairly and deliberately in the light of day, and in the exercise of our calm and cool judgment, take upon ourself the position of resistance to, and rebellion against the present government of the United States; and if there be any who wish to denounce us for this as treason against Lincoln's government, or war against Lincoln, we are willing and ready to furnish them the testimony, by the commission of an overt act whenever an opportunity offers.

Arkansas State Gazette, April 27, 1861 (from the Van Buren Press)

WAR INEVITABLE—The telegraphic dispatches in today's paper are of startling import. War seems now inevitable unless the outstretched arm of Omnipotence shall preserve our imperiled and distracted country.

Lincoln has proved himself utterly unequal to the great crisis which is upon us, and ought in justice to the cause of humanity and free institutions, to be deposed from power. Under the pretext of executing the laws, and maintaining the integrity of the Union, his measures are calculated to destroy both.

The idea has been held out since the inauguration of Lincoln up to a very recent period, that the forts in the seceded States were to be evacuated, and this was especially true in reference to Fort Sumter. But we have seen, within the last few days, an attempt to reinforce this identical fort, has resulted in a collision between the troops of the seceded States at Charleston and the garrison in command of Maj. Anderson, at Fort Sumter, this inaugurating civil war, with all its untold horrors. This policy of Mr. Lincoln of holding onto, enforcing, and recapturing the forts and arsenals in the seceding States is, under all the surroundings of the case, a most miserable policy. However right and proper it may be under ordinary circumstances, for a President of the United States to see that the laws are faithfully executed, and however delusive and injurious *secession* may be regarded either as a theory or practice, no patriot or statesmen, of enlarged or comprehensive mind can or ought to ignore or trifle with the fact that seven states of the Union have thrown off their allegiance to, and repudiated the authority of, the General Government.

The Legislatures and Conventions of the Border States, have declared against coercion, and none more decidedly so, than the Convention of Arkansas, as will be seen by referring to the Resolutions, reported from the Committee on Federal Relations, and adopted on the 21st of March.

The people of Arkansas of all parties, will stand as a unit against coercion and in defense of Southern rights, and none will be truer in the day of trial, than the Union men of Arkansas. Early and vigorous preparations ought to be made to meet the emergency, come what may and to that end, we take it for granted, that the Convention will be reassembled by the President of that body, at the earliest day possible.

Document 67

Governor Joseph Brown of Georgia to David Walker, April 19, 1861

Source: Willard E. Wight, ed., "The Governor of Georgia Urges the Secession of Arkansas," *Arkansas Historical Quarterly* 16 (Summer 1957): 192–202; reprinted in *I Do Wish This Cruel War Was Over: First-Person Accounts of Civil War Arkansas from the Arkansas Historical Quarterly*, ed. Mark Christ and Patrick Williams (Fayetteville: University of Arkansas Press, 2014), 1–8.

On January 19, 1861, Georgia had seceded from the Union and became one of the founding members of the Confederacy. Despite large numbers of non-slaveholders in Georgia, especially in the Appalachian Mountains of northeastern Georgia, the state's secessionist majority pushed for immediate secession, whereas the conservative Unionists in Arkansas waited for a compromise that would avert war. Pro-secession Georgia governor Joseph Brown wrote to David Walker outlining the reasons why he believed secession was in the best interests of Arkansas. Brown at length discussed the role that slavery played in the sectional crisis and told Walker, "We are an agricultural people; so are you. We are slave-holders; so are you," making clear that the interests of Georgia and Arkansas were aligned, especially after Fort Sumter.

. . . You also do me the honor to say, that you would be pleased to hear from me touching "the political affairs of the Country, and of the proposed remedies for existing evils." In compliance with this request, I have to state that, in the opinion of the Convention of the people of this State, there was but one remedy for existing evils, and that was immediate Secession from the Union when it passed into the hands of a black Republican administration.

The Ordinance of Secession passed by the Convention of the people of the State of Georgia, is an irrevocable decree: and there is not the slightest probability that this State will ever return to the old Union or reunite with New England, or other abolition States. The pro-Slavery and the anti-Slavery States in the Union together, have long presented a spectacle of a house divided against itself. The Bible declares that a house in this condition cannot stand. In this instance, as in all others, the declarations of Divine inspiration as revealed in that book, have proved infallible. The people of the Anti-Slavery States, especially the rising generation of them, have been educated to abhor the institution of Slavery; and to regard it, not only as a political and moral evil, but as a great national sin. From the pulpit and by the politicians, they have been taught that: While they remain in the same government with it, they are morally responsible for it; and that it is their duty to wage a war of extermination against it. In other words, they have been taught that the conflict between the so called free States and the Slave States, is *irrepressible*; and that it is their duty to see that Slavery is abolished in all the States where it exists. They have not been taught to believe that they owed the same duty to Cuba or Brazil, because they were not united with them in the same government.

On the other hand, a great change in favor of Slavery has been wrought upon the public mind of the South, within a short period. A few years ago, many good men in the Southern States regarded the institution as a moral and political evil; and apologized for it on the ground that it was entailed upon us by our ancestors, and that we must make the best we could of an evil which we inherited and of which we were unable to rid ourselves. The constant assaults made upon us on account of the institution, at length awaked in the South a Spirit of investigation upon the subject. In this investigation, our most learned and pious divines of different denominations, have tested it by the Standard of eternal truth, as revealed in the Bible: and have become thoroughly satisfied that it was an institution established and sustained by God himself: that it has existed since the days of Noah, when it was established by Divine decree, as an institution which was to endure forever: that it was fully recognized and regulated by the Jewish Theocracy, which was a law given by God for the government of his people; that our Savior, while on Earth, referred to it as being an existing institution without the slightest disapprobation; that Paul, and other inspired writers, laid down rules for the regulation of conduct between master and servant: and that John, in his Revelations, looking forward to the winding up of all things earthly, still saw the *bond man* and *free man*. These investigations have, therefor, led to the conclusion that, whatever may be the abuses for which individuals may be morally responsible, slavery is an institution which has been established by Divine decree, and declared perpetual and cannot, in itself, be immoral or sinful. These conclusions of the Southern mind, founded upon the truths of the Bible, are the very reverse of those of the Northern mind, above referred to, which have been formed in open conflict with the teachings of the Bible and to sustain which the Bible has been openly repudiated.

While the people of the two sections of the country were embraced in the same political Union, the conflict between them upon this great moral question, was vital and irreconcilable. The agitation was perpetual. The people of the South only asked to be let alone; the people of the North refused to comply with this reasonable request; they had a superiority of numbers; they formed a sectional party, and seized the whole power of the Government in their own hands. New York and Massachusetts with other Northern States, claimed the right to dictate laws to Georgia and Arkansas and other Southern States. By force of numbers they had the power to do it. We denied their right to dictate laws to us; and sooner than submit to its exercise, Georgia and six other Southern States, resumed the powers which they had delegated to the Federal Government, on account of the abuse of those powers by that Government. The house was divided against itself and it fell. The Seven

Seceded States have formed a new government upon the basis of the old constitution; which I trust, will commend itself to the good people of Arkansas. The people of Georgia entertain for the people of Arkansas the most fraternal feelings. Many of them are "bone of our bone, and flesh of our flesh," who went out from among us to seek their fortunes in the far off fields at the west. We have watched their success with constant interest; and doubt not their minds have often reverted with pleasure to the scenes of their youthful enjoyment in our midst. We are an agricultural people; so are you. We are slave-holders; so are you. That which promotes your interests, promotes ours; that which affects you injuriously, affects us injuriously. In a word, we have common interests, common sympathies, common institutions and a common destiny. Abolition fanaticism has made war upon us. We are now invaded by a black republican army because we refuse to submit to black republican rule. If we are subjugated or exterminated, because we are slave-holders, and you stand by and see it done, what can you promise yourselves in future? Think you that the sacrifice of seven gallant Southern States would quiet the morbid sensibilities of abolition fanaticism. Never. The Southern States must all stand together or fall together. They are one people; and it is unnatural that they should fight against each other. The ultimate and perpetual separation of all the pro-slavery States from the anti-slavery States must, therefore, be regarded as fixed fact. The question, then, naturally arises, what is to be the future of the two sections? Can each maintain itself as a separate and independent government, and maintain and perpetuate the republican institutions bequeathed to the country by the fathers of the Republic? I entertain the belief that the Northern Section cannot maintain republican institutions; but that the Southern States can and will maintain and perpetuate the institutions of our fathers, to the latest generation. And I will, at the risk of trespassing upon your patience, briefly give you the reasons for this opinion. So soon as the Southern States no longer act as a balance wheel in the government, the conflict between *Capital* and *labor*, in the Northern Section, is inavoidable. Upon a great portion of that section of the country, the population is already dense, and is rapidly increasing. Large numbers of laborers and paupers are constantly pouring in upon it from all parts of Europe. This immigrant population is a heterogeneous mass, from different nations, speaking different languages, with no common sympathy for each other; and in many instances, with feelings of hostility which have been transmitted from generation to generation. These all congregate in the Northern States, and are soon admitted to equal rights of Citizenship with each other, and with the native born inhabitants. Thus they become voters; and each has a voice in the choice of rulers. They are generally poor; and are, therefore, mostly laborers. They have been accustomed to low prices for labor in Europe; capitalists in the Northern States are aware of this fact, and will naturally seek to turn it to their own advantage. They have no interest in the person of the laborer, and no sympathy for him beyond what is dictated by common humanity. They will, therefore, naturally unite with each other, and by a concentration of the control which all the capital of the Country gives them over its industrial pursuits, they will use all their power to bring down the price of labor to the lowest point at which its wages will sustain life.

The large annual influx of laborers who will be obliged to have immediate employment to sustain life, will be used by them to compel the native born laborer to submit to the reduction of prices. This domination of Capital over Labor, will naturally make the laborer rest less and jealous. This restlessness will finally develop itself in the larger cities and towns, in rebellion and mobs. While capital is thus maintaining its ascendancy over labor, and oppressing the laborers, their feelings will naturally run to the opposite extreme of agrarianism; and they will seek to undermine and prostrate the capital of the country. When their minds are fully prepared for this, they will readily find leaders who, by the aid of their suffrage at the ballot box, will be placed in position to head them in their efforts to prostrate Capitalists and divide the spoils among themselves. The result will be anarchy, and the complete prostration of our present republican form of government.

In this state of things, the Capitalist of the country must naturally look to a stronger government for protection. They will then be ready to unite the whole of their capital as the strong pillar of a throne, to be mounted by some bold leader, who will engage by the aid of the purse, to wield the sword for the restoration of order, the suppression of rebellion, the triumph of capital, and the subjugation of labor.

In this rapid review of the causes, which must, in my opinion, result, at no distant period, in the prostration of republican government in the

Northern States, I have omitted to mention the blind, religious fanaticism of the Puritan Character; the natural excitability of the Northern people; their proneness to worship foreign Princes or Nobles who may travel among them, and their inclination to run wildly after every new ism that is invented or propagated in their midst; none of which are favorable to the perpetuity of republican liberty.

I now proceed to give some of the reasons why, in my opinion, the people of the Southern States, can and will maintain and perpetuate our republican institutions, in their original purity to the latest generation. And I remark in advance, that the Southern Character is very different from the picture which I have just drawn of the Northern character. While our people know how to appreciate intelligence and position, and are always ready to treat every distinguished foreigner whom business or pleasure may bring among them, with consideration and respect naturally due him, or the government to which he may belong; and while they are essentially a religious people, they are neither man worshipers or religious fanatics. They are intelligent and high toned, with noble impulses and chivalrous bearing; and are as prompt at all times to do justice to others as to exact it from them. In a word, they worship God according to the dictates of their own consciences and are content to attend to their own business, and let other people's alone.

We have no heavy influx of foreigners; and those of them who do come among us, are generally an industrious and useful population; while pauperism and poor houses are almost unknown in the South.

The great political point however, to be considered is, that in the South, there is no alarming conflict. There are in the Southern States, over four million of Slaves. These Slaves constitute a very large item in the capital of the South. They generally belong to men of capital. The value of the Estate of each slave-holder, depends, in a great degree, upon the value of this slaves; and the value of the slaves depends upon the price of labor. Each capitalist, who is a slave-holder, is, therefore, directly interested in keeping up the price of labor; because he has property in the person of the laborer. If labor is high, that property is valuable. If labor is so low as to sustain life, that property is worthless—nay, more, it is an absolute burden. Allow me to illustrate: A.B. owns one hundred Negroes. If labor is worth one dollar per day, his Negroes are worth an average of $1,000 each, and has in them an estate of $100,000 for his children. If labor is worth only a half dollar per day, they are worth $500 cash and his estate is worth only $50,000. If labor is so low that it will hardly support the laborer, then his slaves are a burden to him, and his estate is worth nothing. This is not only true of the slaves he now has, but as he is raising more and his estate increases with the increase of their number, he is interested in keeping up the price of the labor; not only of the present, but of the succeeding generations.

Having, I trust, succeeded in showing that is the interest of the capitalist and Slave-holder, to keep up the price of labor, I now remark that, for this very reason, it is the interest of every free white laborer in the South, who is not a Slave-holder, to sustain and defend the institution of Slavery. If the work of the Slave is worth only twenty-five cents per day, the work of the White man will command more; but if the work of the Slave is worth one dollar per day, the work of the white man in the same occupation, is worth as much. Hence, every white laborer is interested in sustaining the institution of slavery; since by so doing, he makes it the interest of every slave-holder to strive to sustain and keep up the price of labor. Here is not only perfect harmony between Capital and labor, but all classes of society are harmonized with each other, and linked together by the chain of interest, which, after all that may be said, is the great motive power in Government.

Not only are the Slave-holders and the free white laborer mutually interested in sustaining each other, but the slave himself is interested in the common welfare of both. If his labor is worth one dollar per day, the master has, in addition to common sympathies of our nature, a strong motive of interest prompting him to treat the slave well; to look well to his health and comfort, and with a view to his long life; to see that he is not overworked or abused. The anecdote of the Negro and the Irishman may better illustrate my meaning; The master ordered Cuffy to go down into the well and clean it out; Cuffy replied: Master, I think you had better hire the Irishman. He will do it for a dollar. If he get killed you lose nothing; but if you send me down and I get killed you lose a thousand dollars. The argument was satisfactory, and the Irishman was employed. If the price of labor is reduced so low that the Negro is no longer valuable, and he is emancipated, the owner loses his property in him, and is greatly damaged. But how does this effect the free, white laborer? Several millions of laborers, who are content with a bare subsistence, are set free in our midst, and at once come in competition with him in the labor market. Then the whole aspect of things is changed. I do not now speak of the social degradation to which our free, white laborers would then be exposed in the necessary contact and competition which would follow between them and the black race. The whole capital of the country would then combine, as it now does in the North, to depress labor to the lowest possible point. The capitalists would then no longer have an interest in the person of the black laborer or his increase, but only an interest in the day's labor, which he would desire to get at the lowest possible price; nor would he any longer have a motive beyond that of common humanity, in looking to the comfort, health or long life of the laborer himself. Nor would he longer be liable for the support of the laborer in case of sickness, old age, or their inability to labor.

It is very evident, therefore, that a complete harmony between capital and labor, and a community of interest between the different classes of society, exist in the Southern States, which does not, and from the very nature of their social and industrial fabric, never can exist, in the Northern. The existence of this harmony, is the strongest guarantee for the perpeutity [*sic*] of republican liberty in the South; while the absence of it, is the most certain evidence pointing to the destruction of Republican institutions in the North.

Here most of the menial labor is done by Negroes, who do not belong to the ruling class, and who are intellectually our inferiors. While they are docile and manageable, they are physically able to perform all the duties required of them in their station. They are generally uneducated, as is the class who do most of the menial service in every government. And while they supply a most important place in society, they feel and acknowledge their incompetency for self government; and they neither claim nor desire to exercise political rights, or in any way to interfere in the government of the State. It is true, they are required to do reasonable labor: but they are well fed and comfortably clad: they aspire to nothing more, and are, therefore, contented and happy. The superior intelligence of the white man directs the physical strength of the Negro; and his pride at the ballot box is stimulated by a consciousness of the fact that he belongs to the ruling race; and that, however poor he may be, there is a menial class below him, who are neither politically, socially nor intellectually his equals. Hence, we have few paupers—no mobs—no riots, and no rebellions. Rulers are obeyed; government is supreme; civil and religious liberty are firmly established; and all the great interests of society, harmonizing with and sustaining each other, are moved forward as one great harmonious whole.

In conclusion, (for I have already occupied too much of your time) permit me to express the ardent hope, that the gallant and glorious young State to which you belong and to which every true son of the South now looks with so much interest—stimulated by the example so recently set by our noble old sister State of Virginia, justly, styled "the Mother of States and of Statesmen"—and soon arise with giant strength, shake off the chains which political fanaticism has forged for her, and assume the proud position to which she is so justly entitled as one of the brightest stars in the splendid galaxy of Southern States.

Document 68

S. R. Cockrell to Leroy Pope Walker, April 21, 1861

Source: US War Department, *The War of the Rebellion: A Compilation of the Official Records of the Union and Confederate Armies* (Washington, DC: GPO, 1880), series 1, 1:686–87.

In his letter to the Confederacy's secretary of war, Leroy Pope Walker, S. R. Cockrell detailed an eyewitness view of the political situation in both Arkansas and Tennessee at the end of April. Interestingly, Cockrell identified both whites and blacks in both states as interested in going to war, though he was clear that free blacks had to be separated from the enslaved in order to protect the institution of slavery. Few blacks fought for the Confederacy. Rather, slaves were impressed for military service, usually as laborers and teamsters, by both the states and Confederate government.

DEAR SIR: I arrived here to-day from the Arkansas River, and it is with pleasure that I report a complete revolution in public sentiment since I left. Tennessee is with the cotton States, and you may now consider the slave States a unit. "Armed neutrality" has no advocates, not even the authors of that card, which was conceived in error. The patriotism which would stand by unmoved and witness the murder of your neighbor's wife and children, because of an imaginary line, is not the growth of Tennessee, nor of any State where the rays of a genial sun shine.

The legislature meets next Thursday, and the plan is to pass the ordnance of secession and let the people ratify it, arm the State, and stand ready to march South or North.

Arkansas will go out 6th May before breakfast. The Indians come next. Companies are forming rapidly, and I expect both my sons to go whenever the insolent invader shall tread a hostile foot upon our soil. The slave States a unit are omnipotent in defense.

Arkansas and Tennessee are wild with indignation at the insolence and usurpation of the buffoon at Washington City. They are ready for the fight, every man, white and black. The blacks in Arkansas would be entirely reliable, if necessary, in defense. I know the fact is so. They are more obedient and loyal than ever before. When the fight is over, a separation of free blacks from the slaves is the true plan to protect and guard the institution. It is one of the domestic relations that I have studied with much care.

I indorse without a proviso every act in the cotton States, done separately or together, by President, Congress, and Cabinet, and am ready to aid in all that may be necessary to accomplish what has been undertaken. . . .

With streamers gay push forward with sanguine cheer. The God of Battles must and will be with you. Success to the arm which strikes for our rights.

DOCUMENTS 69–71

Responses to the Requisition of Federal Troops, April 22 and 23, 1861

Source: US War Department, *The War of the Rebellion: A Compilation of the Official Records of the Union and Confederate Armies* (Washington, DC: GPO, 1880), series 1, 1:687.

In the aftermath of Fort Sumter, President Abraham Lincoln called for 75,000 volunteers to suppress the ongoing rebellion in the South. Each state in the Union was required to furnish a specific number of troops, including the slaveholding states that had not yet seceded. Arkansas was required to send 780 men to muster at Little Rock. Governor Henry Rector responded to this request by Union secretary of war Simon Cameron on April 22, 1861. His response, contrasting free white Arkansans with slaves to the federal government, was particularly interesting given that slavery was the major issue surrounding secession. He received the message from Confederate secretary of war Leroy Pope Walker the same day. However, in Rector's response on April 23, he indicated that nothing at this point could be done to support the Confederacy, in opposition to T. C. Hindman's previous interest in supporting the seceding states; but in other correspondence, the leaders of militia units around the state corresponded with Walker to organize for war before the secession convention met. Undoubtedly, Rector believed that Arkansas would soon leave the Union.

Governor Rector to Secretary Cameron

In answer to your requisition for troops from Arkansas to subjugate the Southern States, I have to say that none will be furnished. The demand is only adding insult to injury. The people of this commonwealth are freemen, not slaves, and will defend to the last extremity their honor, lives, and property against Northern mendacity and usurpation.

Secretary Walker to Governor Rector

SIR: Your patriotic response to the requisition of the President of the United States for troops to coerce the Confederate States justifies the belief that your people are prepared to unite with us in repelling the common enemy of the South. Virginia needs our aid. I therefore request you to furnish one regiment of infantry without delay, to rendezvous at Lynchburg, Va. It must consist of ten companies, of not less than sixty-four men each. . . . The officers, except the staff officers, are to be appointed in the manner prescribed by the law of your State. Staff officers are appointed by the President, the term of service not less than twelve months, unless sooner discharged. They will be mustered into the service at Lynchburg, but transportation and subsistence will be provided from the point of departure. They will furnish their own uniform, but will receive its value in commutation. You have arms and ammunition with which to supply them. Answer and say whether you will comply with this request, and, if so, when.

Governor Rector to Secretary Walker, April 23

You may be assured of the immediate action of Arkansas in joining the Southern Confederacy; but I have no power, I regret, to comply with your request. Our convention assembles on the 6th of May. Then we can and will aid.

DOCUMENTS 72–73

Divisions within Arkansas:
Mass Meeting in Calhoun County, April 22, 1861

Source: *Arkansas True Democrat*, April 18 and May 2, 1861.

After Fort Sumter, citizens across the state rallied to recall the secession convention early and advocated for immediate secession, arguing that the Union had used coercion against the seceded states in calling for 75,000 volunteers. In this meeting in southern Arkansas near Camden, where slaves made up almost 25 percent of the population, citizens argued not only for immediate secession from the Union, but also, if the Unionist northwestern and northern parts of the state continued to vote to stay in the Union, then for the immediate division of the state. This discussion of dividing the state encouraged David Walker to recall the convention as the reality that the state was geographically divided, with the slaveholding eastern and southern counties as hotbeds of secession, was increasingly becoming apparent, as indicated in the letter to the editor from Isaac Henry Hilliard, a secession convention delegate from Chicot County who owned 128 slaves; his letter follows the Calhoun County meeting resolutions.

Calhoun County's Mass Meeting Resolutions

At a public meeting of the citizens of the county of Calhoun, assembled at the courthouse in the town of Hampton on Monday the 22nd day of April, AD 1861 . . . the said committee retired and in a short time returned and presented the following preamble and resolutions:

Whereas, At the election held in and for the United States of America for President thereof—the said election resulted in the elevation of Abraham Lincoln to the chief executorship of the nation, by a party having at heart the absolute annihilation of slavery, our dearest and most endeared institution; and whereas, seven States of the South have seceded from the original Union and here allied their interest with each other and formed a Southern Confederacy and whereas, Lincoln, as we are notified and believe, made a requisition on the States of his government for men, boldly proclaiming war against said Southern Confederacy; and whereas, our sympathy and fortunes are with the Southern Confederacy, and the time fixed by the State convention for the vote on secession or cooperation is to admit of Arkansas taking a position with her interest.

Therefore be it:

1st. Resolved, That the president of the State convention of Arkansas is hereby requested to convene the State convention forthwith, for immediate secession. . . .

2nd. Resolved, That the honor, interest, and safety of Arkansas are with the Southern Confederacy.

3rd. Resolved, That in the event that the convention when convened fails to pass an ordinance of secession, that we are unanimously in favor of dividing the State of Arkansas. . . .

Letter to the Editor from Isaac Henry Hilliard

. . . What we accomplished was far less than the honor and interest of Arkansas demanded. Unfortunately, our State is divided into two sections, whose pursuits are totally dissimilar—the grain and stock raising portion looks with no friendly eye on the cotton planter. Indeed, in the convention, sentiments were uttered which would have fallen more fitly from Massachusetts legislators than from southern gentleman.

The whole proceedings have impressed me with the solemn conviction that slavery itself will pass through a life and death struggle on the first Monday of next August. Our partial failure must now stimulate to new efforts—revolutions go not backwards; we will succeed. The time for action and sacrifice has come: of this our secession brothers are convinced, and will carry into every corner of the State the voice of our wrongs, that we may add another star to the illustrious Seven.

DOCUMENT 74

Letter from C. C. Danley to W. W. Mansfield, April 23, 1861

Source: W. W. Mansfield Collection, Arkansas History Commission, Little Rock; reprinted in *A Documentary History of Arkansas*, ed. C. Fred Williams, S. Charles Bolton, and Carl H. Moneyhon (Fayetteville: University of Arkansas Press, 1984), 95.

Like many Unionists, C. C. Danley believed in reconciliation with the Union as long as Arkansas's slaveholding rights could be sustained. In this letter, Danley shows that although he was a Unionist in the beginning, the "overt act," the attack on Fort Sumter, pushed him, along with many other cooperationists, to support secession.

Steamboat Tahlequah

Dear Sir:

Enclosed I send a slip by which you will see that Judge [David] Walker has called the Convention on the 6th of May. I hope to be at home by that time. I think the conservative men of the Convention should take charge of the affairs of the state and prevent the wild secessionists from sending us to the Devil.

Lincoln's administration has committed the overt Act and I am now for war. We are going to attack Fort Smith, if it will not surrender without an attack. We have a battery of eight pieces of artillery and when our force concentrates, expect to have about 500 men. The party is under the command of Maj [Solon] Borland the only man in the state that I know to be fit to command such an expedition. A reinforcement of 9 companies is expected at Fort Smith. If that happens now, we will have to cut off their supplies and call for more help from the adjoining counties. In that view of the case, our friends at Ozark, who desire to do so, might form a company and await a call for their services. The war has commenced. You know that, from the first, I was for the Union. Now that the "overt act" has been committed we should I think draw the sword, and not sheathe it until we can have a guaranty of all our rights, or such standards as will be honorable to the south.

Let me urge you to go to the Convention. I think it's of vast importance that conservative men should continue to control its action.

C. C. Danley

P.S. The Union men whom I have met are all for war. I think in our parts there is a majority of Union men or those who were Union a few days ago.

DOCUMENT 75

David Walker's Proclamation Reopening the Convention, May 6, 1861

Source: *Journal of Both Sessions of the Convention of the State of Arkansas* (Little Rock: Johnson and Verkes, State Printers, 1861), 113–14.

President Abraham Lincoln's call for seventy-five thousand volunteers and the bombardment of Fort Sumter forced David Walker to call the convention back into session earlier than originally scheduled. In this message, Walker referred to "preparations" that were underway "for a war between the citizens of the free and slave states," which referenced not only Lincoln's call for volunteers but also the preparations by Henry Rector and the Confederate government.

Proclamation of the President of the Convention of the People of the State of Arkansas, Reconvening the Convention

Whereas, By an ordinance of the state convention, passed on the 21st day of March, A.D. 1861, it was ordained that the President of the convention be authorized and empowered to convene the convention at an earlier day than the 19th of August, A.D. 1861, if in his opinion an exigency should arise requiring the same.

And whereas, From reliable information, I am satisfied that preparations are being made for a war between the citizens of the free and slave states, in which the safety, peace, and prosperity of the people of Arkansas are involved, and for the preservation of which we must provide; for which purpose, in my opinion, the convention should be convened at the earliest practicable time.

Now, therefore, David Walker, President of the Convention, under the authority and in accordance with the provisions of said ordinance do declare and make known that a convention will be holden on Monday the sixth day of May A.D. 1861 at the city of Little Rock, when and where the delegates to said convention are notified to attend as required by the second section of the said ordinance.

DOCUMENT 76

Message of Governor Henry Rector to the Convention, May 6, 1861

Source: *Journal of Both Sessions of the Convention of the State of Arkansas* (Little Rock: Johnson and Verkes, State Printers, 1861), 150–57.

Henry Rector outlined much of what had occurred between the secession convention's adjournment in March and the current political and military situation. Rector indicated that Arkansans had seized federal installations across the state, including the garrison at Fort Smith, and that they had begun to cooperate with Tennessee to defend the Mississippi River. Further, Rector indicated the necessity of communicating with the Indians to secure Indian Territory for the Confederacy. In this message, Rector continued to refer to northern efforts in Indian Territory as "the abolition crusade."

In response to the invitation given me by your honorable body to communicate to it any views that I might desire to submit, I avail myself of the opportunity to present the following, touching the military and financial condition of the government, having as its executive officer been intimately connected recently in important movements necessary for its defence and safety.

Unexpectedly by the late proclamation of President Lincoln, a state of war has been provoked, involving each and every state of the old confederacy.

That document I regard as a declaration of hostilities as well against the states seceded as those still lingering in the old Union; each slave-holding or southern state having announced distinctly an utter repugnance to the doctrine of coercion or subjugation of American freemen in or out of the union.

Upon this point at least, we are and have been a unit, for it strikes away the corner-stone from the temple of American liberty.

Immediately following the proclamation issued by the President, I had the honor of receiving from the Hon. Simon Cameron, secretary of war for Mr. Lincoln's government, a requisition for seven hundred and eighty men to be raised from my fellow-citizens of Arkansas, for the very humane and christian purpose of "wiping out" and desolating the south by fire and sword, and other select appliances conceived of by the horde of motley mercenaries now marshaled under and desecrating the flag of the American Union.

To the communication of Mr. Cameron, I returned . . . what I, as the executive of this free people, conceived to be a fitting response to such a piece of presumption and ignorance. For I take it for granted that whatsoever is evolved from so high a political circle as the cabinet at Washington, is put forth at least in a spirit of candor and not in hypocritical pretense and parade. . . .

The purpose declared by President Lincoln of retaking the forts and arsenals being peculiarly pertinent to the attitude assumed by Arkansas, in reference to such properties, I, as precautionary against any movement contemplated for the recapture of the Arsenal at this place, took immediate steps to inform myself if a concentration of troops should be attempted at Fort Smith, assuming that such a movement would be clearly indicative of a present intention to repossess the arsenal here.

On the 19th April, I received intelligence direct from Fort Smith, and from a source that I esteemed reliable, to the effect that a reinforcement of 1,000 United States troops had been ordered to repair promptly to that post. A sense of duty prompted me to take steps to intercept the additional command, and that said fort might not in future become the nucleus of an imposing force, I thought it best to reduce it to statue authority, and convert it into an encampment, fort or barracks, for the accommodation and security of an army of friends instead of a "masked battery," manned by astute and agile enemies. . . .

Very shortly subsequent to Mr. Lincoln's declaration of war, the people of Cincinnati [2] having instinctive proclivities toward public plunder, arrested as it is understood, a portion of arms and equipments contracted for in New York by Messrs. Danley and Churchill, commissioners appointed by the legislature to perform that service; four pieces of artillery, ammunition and fixtures therefor, and some cavalry accou-

---

2. Cincinnati, Ohio.

trements being the articles detained, the residue of the goods bought in New York having been received here previous to the inauguration of the Cincinnati policy. Self-preservation being the first law of nature from which the *lex-talionis* is well established, our citizens very properly, as I think, followed the precedent set by the people of Cincinnati, and captured for detention, not confiscation, several vessels northward bound, and belonging exclusively to the people of that city—and upon inquiry made of me upon this subject, I gave an order to Major General James Yell to take charge of said steamboats, "Mars" and "Ohio Belle"—to secure them and their cargoes against waste or damage until restitution should be made of the property captured in Cincinnati. So far no exchange has been made, and the boats remain under and subject to the proper authorities of Arkansas. . . .

In connection with this subject, I will mention also that the citizens of Napoleon and Pine Bluff, upon their own volition, have recently captured a large amount of government subsistence stores and some cavalry equipments. Which transpiring subsequent to the late proclamation of Mr. Lincoln, I also approbated and consented to receive in the name of the state, and pay the current charges due for freight out of the public treasury. . . .

On the 2d ult., intelligence was received from the authorities and the people of East Arkansas and West Tennessee, that a large force of Mr. Lincoln's troops were assembling rapidly at Cairo,[3] having heavy ordnance, horses, and adjuncts necessary for aggressive warfare. Universal alarm and uneasiness prevailed upon the eastern border, evincing a well grounded apprehension that a descent from Cairo was contemplated down the Mississippi for the avowed purpose of laying waste to all which might perchance be in the way. Believing that even short delay might invite an attack upon our citizens, and knowing their utter destitution of the means of defence if invaded, I dispatched a message to Gov. [Isham] Harris enquiring whether he by authority would co-operate with Arkansas in the defence of the Mississippi. His assent to the proposition was prompt and fully to the point. Gen. Yell was called immediately into service, and orders issued by me to rendezvous such forces as

---

3. Cairo, Illinois, is at the junction of the Mississippi and Ohio Rivers.

in his opinion became necessary, opposite or near the city of Memphis, and to act in conjunction, as far as possible, with that city and the people of Tennessee in the common defence of that portion of the country; confining his operations however to our own limits and not for aggression, but for defensive purposes.

From his verbal report, I learn that he has five hundred men under arms at Mound City,[4] under strict discipline, armed and equipped for the most efficient service. This much, in a military point of view, I deemed it my duty to do; the constitution and laws passed in conformity thereto authorizing and directing me "to protect the state against invasion," in such manner as the exigency may require, and to employ the army thereof for that purpose.

The timely convocation of your honorable body, possessing plenary powers under the scope of its delegated authority, representing the entire people of the state, evades the necessity of assuming further responsibilities on my part touching these important movements until the status of the government shall be authoritatively fixed, and a policy indicated for the future guidance of those who may be charged in future with the maintenance and defence of the state. If left to me, it must not be anticipated else than that the last sinew in the last arm of the last man in Arkansas, myself with the rest, shall be brought in requisition rather than a flag of conquest and dishonor shall be unfurled over our people. For to us, it is a war of successful defence or extermination—one of liberty or death—between which I cannot doubt that Arkansans will hesitate to choose.

War, though no luxury, is nevertheless an expensive indulgence, and requires money to conduct it successfully, or even at all.

Arkansas I regard as being in the most exposed condition of any state in the Union. Her contiguity to the Indian territories west, which countries are regarded by the opposing governments respectively, as important—nay, indispensable adjuncts, will make her western border almost the exclusive theatre of war west of the Mississippi. The germ of present difficulties was found in Kansas, and their solution will be had in a great battle to be fought upon the same soil, I predict.

Nor are we less, but more exposed on the shores of the Mississippi.

---

4. Mound City is in Crittenden County on the Mississippi River.

The topography of the country there is inauspicious for defence, insalubrious for troops, and presenting formidable obstacles for their transportation or necessary local movements or evolutions.

With the co-operation of Tennessee, however, our security is much increased, and successful defence made practicable.

Amongst others to the state, there is a serious difficulty in the lack of arms. The supply consists in 10,000 stand of infantry, cavalry service for one regiment, with thirty pieces of artillery, all told—the latter generally of small caliber, and many pieces unfit for service.

A moiety of these given to the eastern and western borders, would afford each section or locality, arms for 5,000 men. This force, though formidable under ordinary circumstances, might nevertheless be confronted by an army of six times their number, making an unequal contest or precipitate retreat inevitable.

I would suggest, therefore, that renewed efforts be made for the acquisition of additional guns, to the extent at least of the unexpended balance appropriated by the legislature for arming the state . . . and offering some suggestions pertinent to the defence of the western frontier, which I commend to your attention.

If I may venture to suggest any definite mode of operations for the defence of Arkansas, it is that from the volunteer forces now organized in different portions of the state—commissioned, uniformed, and in many instances equipped and well drilled in company discipline—there be called into immediate service, and rendezvous at the arsenal at this place; a number sufficient to form five regiments, having proper regard to the necessary proportions of cavalry, artillery and infantry. This force to be organized under existing laws into battalions and regiments; and after complete organization and discipline to be equipped and marched to the point where danger seems most to threaten. And so again, if circumstances require it, others be called to undergo the same training and preparation to make them effective soldiers. Without training and preparation of this kind at some point previous to entering the field, the most disastrous consequences must be entailed upon our troops if an engagement ensues. . . .

Our present and future relations with the two sections of the original Union having been determined upon, it will become at once important that we should pay due regard to our red neighbors of the west. By securing their sympathy and co-operation, we will acquire valuable allies and be able to reciprocate favors by affording them protection against the abolition crusade, that is held in store for them by the northern government. The country occupied by the Indians immediately west of Arkansas, is regarded with intense solicitude by the government at Washington and that of the Confederate States. Fertile, salubrious and most inviting in character and topography, in its geographical position indispensably requisite to the southern government, it ought not and cannot be abandoned to the North if it is in the power of the South to retain it. And I regard it now as being in the most precarious condition; demanding from Arkansas, as matter of security to herself, immediate and prompt action.

I earnestly recommend, therefore, the appointment of commissioners familiar with Indian character, and such as will command the respect and confidence of that people, delegated with authority to enter into preliminary arrangements preparatory to definite treaty stipulations hereafter to be ratified and solemnized with the Confederate States.

I regard this as of pressing importance, because of the utter incapacity on the part of the Indians to resist alone the occupation of their country by federal troops or federal agents.

As the only means of attaining definite information as to the feelings and purposes of these people touching the southern movement, I sent in January last, Maj. J. J. Gaines to confer in person with the chief men of the Cherokees, Creeks and Choctaws. The result of which was, that the two latter nations were found to be the fast and enduring friends of the South; though by no means, in the unsettled condition of their monetary affairs, and the lack of means and preparation of defence courting difficulty with the federal government—yet declaring their sympathies and attachments for the South and southern institutions, with the announcement that when it become necessary to make a choice, that they would share a common destiny with the people of Arkansas, their natural friends and allies. The Cherokees, however, then, and still do occupy a more dubious attitude; and encouragement and assurances of the most explicit character will be required by them from the South to secure their support. With their assent, these nations ought to be admitted as states in the southern government. . . .

DOCUMENT 77

S. H. Hempstead to the Convention, May 6, 1861

Source: *Journal of Both Sessions of the Convention of the State of Arkansas* (Little Rock: Johnson and Verkes, State Printers, 1861), 117–20.

When the convention adjourned in March of 1861, delegates had selected five representatives to send to a border states convention in late May. This convention would, as Unionists hoped, negotiate a settlement to the sectional crisis and prevent war. After Fort Sumter, most states that had appointed representatives withdrew from the Union, making the convention moot. In this message, S. H. Hempstead withdrew himself from the delegation and, like most Unionists, indicated that reconciliation was no longer an option.

SIR—During my absence I was chosen by the convention, of which you are president, as one of the five delegates from Arkansas to a border states convention, proposed by Virginia, to be held this spring at Frankfort, Kentucky.

I avail myself of the occasion, to express to the members of your body, through you, my grateful thanks for this unsolicited mark of confidence, and the honor thus conferred, for so it ought to be considered. And surely, if I could be of any use to Arkansas, in that position, I would most cheerfully and zealously devote whatever ability I possess to her service. For Arkansas is my own, and the home of my family; I neither look to, have, nor desire any other. A continuous residence here of twenty-five years duration, has indissolubly attached me to her soil, and taught me to appreciate and admire the worth, patriotism, hospitality and chivalry of her people. Arkansas is endeared to me by affection toward the living, and regretful memories for the dead; some of whom, near and dear to me, sleep peacefully in her soil. All my interests, hopes and feelings are, from voluntary choice, inseparably identified with Arkansas, and wherever she may lead, I will follow cheerfully, contentedly and with no grudging or measured loyalty. I sincerely say of her: may she always be right, but right or wrong, I am for her, and with her.

Recent and startling events, occurring since my election render it proper, in my opinion, that I should yield back to the convention the trust with which I was honored. I do not stop to speculate upon the probabilities of the border states convention being held; but, if I understand the original purpose of it, it would now fail to accomplish it; recent events having entirely changed the position of the border states, and of Arkansas also.

When I was chosen, I was a Union man, and opposed to a disruption of the Federal Union, as long as there remained a hope or prospect of preserving it, and of securing our just rights, and privileges, and of maintaining our honor under, and in it. And I fondly believed that prudence, patriotism, peace, justice, and concession prevailing, that result might ultimately be accomplished.

But that hope has now vanished. The war cloud has risen, and is fast spreading over our country north and south, east and west. Preparations for civil war, are witnessed everywhere, and hostile squadrons are ready to meet each other in deadly conflict. President Lincoln, the nominal head, and urged on and sustained by at least the most violent of the black republican party, has, without authority and without necessity, committed himself to the criminal folly of prosecuting a coercive and warlike policy towards the seceded states, and the people thereof. In point of authority, it is a palpable violation of the constitution he professes to respect. In point of policy, it is unwise and short-sighted; because, if persevered in, must eventually result in forcing every border state out of the Union; and pitiless and cruel, because it must inevitably bring an unnatural civil war upon the country—the most dreadful and desolating of all wars, recorded in history. And it is contrary to the implied, if not express, pledges, repeatedly and solemnly given to the American people, to the effect that his administration would be peaceful and conciliatory towards the seceded states. It is a fatal error, on his part, if he supposes that he can coerce or subdue the southern states, or find men in them to aid him, or sympathise with him, in such a criminal and unholy work. The very hills and valleys will swarm with multiplied thousands of brave hearts and valiant arms, eager to resist him, and his marshalled hosts, in the defence of their own and their sister states.

It was only under a peaceful, prudent and conciliatory course towards the seceded states—the policy of leaving them undisturbed and unmolested—avoiding the use of force—that Arkansas was willing to remain in the Union; and this, with the hope that, in due time, there might be a reconstruction of the Union on fair, just and honorable terms; or that the present difficulties and troubles—perhaps not just now, but at no distant period—might be satisfactorily and honorably adjusted. And such, in my opinion, would have been the result of a peaceful policy, and of just and statesmanlike measures on the part of the administration. But unfortunately the war policy—the coercive policy has prevailed; and on the heads of the black republicans be the bloody consequences. Being in the possession of the government, and all its departments, the supreme court excepted—they held the power to save the Union, but would not do it. They had the power to prevent the effusion of blood but would not do it; and now the responsibility rests with them.

By such means the Union sentiment in Arkansas has been completely changed. The honest differences of opinion that have existed among us, in reference to immediate secession—arising from expediency rather than principle, have passed away. The South has become a unit; all of us standing pledged to resist force; well knowing that no free government can live if force is required to keep it together.

I am a southerner by choice and by adoption. I have lived in a slave state nearly all my life. All my interests and feelings and hopes are bound up with the South. For weal or for woe, I am with her, and for her. Not having been heretofore, I never expect to be, unmindful of her rights, true interests, or honor.

The black republican policy of war being now clearly indicated, Arkansas cannot see it with unconcern, nor submit to it without resistance. Every one must now take sides for or against coercion. There can be but one voice in our state on that proposition. We shall all stand by the South; nor do I believe there are any who would think of acting otherwise. We are now a unit, and ready now, and at all times, to defend the people of the South, their homes, firesides, property and rights to the last extremity, if need be, and against all foes.

DOCUMENT 78

Arkansas Ordinance of Secession, May 6, 1861

Source: US War Department, *The War of the Rebellion: A Compilation of the Official Records of the Union and Confederate Armies* (Washington, DC: GPO, 1900), series 4, 1:287–88.

The delegates to the convention voted on May 6, 1861, for the state to leave the Union by a vote of 65–5. A subsequent revote left only Isaac Murphy of Madison County, who by 1864 would be elected Arkansas's pro-Union governor, voting against disunion. For the Unionists/ cooperationists who had initially opposed secession in March, the political situation had so dramatically changed that by May any hope of compromise and reconciliation had severely diminished.

AN ORDINANCE to dissolve the union now existing between the State of Arkansas and the other States united with her under the compact entitled "The Constitution of the United States of America."

Whereas, in addition to the well-founded causes of complaint set forth by this convention, in resolutions adopted on the 11th of March, A.D. 1861, against the sectional party now in power at Washington City, headed by Abraham Lincoln, he has, in the face of resolutions passed by this convention pledging the State of Arkansas to resist to the last extremity any attempt on the part of such power to coerce any State that had seceded from the old Union, proclaimed to the world that war should be waged against such States until they should be compelled to submit to their rule, and large forces to accomplish this have by this same power been called out, and are now being marshaled to carry out this inhuman design; and to longer submit to such rule, or remain in the old Union of the United States, would be disgraceful and ruinous to the State of Arkansas:

Therefore we, the people of the State of Arkansas, in convention assembled, do hereby declare and ordain, and it is hereby declared and ordained, That the "ordinance and acceptance of compact" passed and approved by the General Assembly of the State of Arkansas on the 18th day of October, A.D. 1836, whereby it was by said General Assembly ordained that by virtue of the authority vested in said General Assembly by the provisions of the ordinance adopted by the convention of delegates assembled at Little Rock for the purpose of forming a constitution and system of government for said State, the propositions set forth in "An act supplementary to an act entitled 'An act for the admission of the State of Arkansas into the Union, and to provide for the due execution of the laws of the United States within the same, and for other purposes,'" were freely accepted, ratified, and irrevocably confirmed, articles of compact and union between the State of Arkansas and the United States, and all other laws and every other law and ordinance, whereby the State of Arkansas became a member of the Federal Union, be, and the same are hereby, in all respects and for every purpose herewith consistent, repealed, abrogated, and fully set aside; and the union now subsisting between the State of Arkansas and the other States, under the name of the United States of America, is hereby forever dissolved.

And we do further hereby declare and ordain, That the State of Arkansas hereby resumes to herself all rights and powers heretofore delegated to the Government of the United States of America; that her citizens are absolved from all allegiance to said Government of the United States, and that she is in full possession and exercise of all the rights and sovereignty which appertain to a free and independent State.

We do further ordain and declare, That all rights acquired and vested under the Constitution of the United States of America, or of any act or acts of Congress, or treaty, or under any law of this State, and not incompatible with this ordinance, shall remain in full force and effect, in nowise altered or impaired, and have the same effect as if this ordinance had not been passed.

DOCUMENT 79

Letter from Creed Taylor to Samuel Taylor, May 29, 1861

Source: Small Manuscript Collection, 18.8A, Arkansas
History Commission, Little Rock, Arkansas.

Creed Taylor, a resident of Pine Bluff in Jefferson County,
served as Jefferson County sheriff, county judge, and
commissioner of swamp lands during his political career.
In this letter, written after the convention, Taylor outlined his support of secession, arguing to his brother that
a united South was necessary in order to battle against
northern collusion at the federal level and to ensure property rights for southerners. Taylor's conviction that staying in the Union would diminish southern power was
critical to many in supporting secession.

. . . I would be much better pleased to see you and talk with you
for a day or two, but that privilege is denied me and therefore I take
my pen to give you a few of the reasons that have impelled me to take
a position antagonistic to the government at Washington. It is a serious
thing my dear brother for me [to] be in opposition to every brother
and sister that I have in the world but conscious of my own rectitude
of intention at least, I embark in the cause with my whole mind, soul,
and strength. I have adhered to the government, as long as there was
hope of a compromise or reconstruction. I even adhered to it when I
knew that all fraternal feelings and union of sentiment had been dissolved and banished from . . . a northern majority but when I saw all
peace offerings presented in the Congress of the United States and in the
. . . Congress voted down I became satisfied that a united South was our
only hope and I still think that if all the slave states could have gone out
together that the chance for an amicable adjustment would have been
greatly increased.

But don't understand me now to hope for or desire a reconstruction
or compromise otherwise than our perfect independence and recognition as such by all the powers of the Earth. Why? Because we have
become entirely alienated by abuse heaped upon us by the northern

press, pulpit, and forum. . . . With this take into consideration that all
. . . starving mutinys they were advocating the doctrine of disunion as
the only remedy to crush the slave power, until finally they elected a
man who had declared that this Government could not stand half slave
and half free that his Cabinet was chosen from among the most rabid
abolitionists in the United States and all hope cut off of ever getting
justice. Thus what was to be done? Wait and let them get the Army and
Navy in their hands before we pretended to move in the cause. To have
done so would have been to wait until shackles were on our hands. We
took some public property to defend ourselves with, had we have taken
more, we would have done better, and had we at once commenced revolution and Civil War, we would have been justified by every impartial
man and nation in the world. But no gallant South Carolina set the
example of peaceable secession. Had she the power to do so, I think she
had and I think we have an illustrious example in the thirteen colonies
that composed the first union. The union that fought the battles of
the revolution and won our independence . . . each of the colonies as
sovereign states. They did elect delegates and sent them to communion
and declared to the world that to form a more perfect union, established
justice, ensure domestic tranquility, provide for the common defense,
promote the general welfare, and to secure the blessings of liberty . . .
that Constitution was not above its enactor and therefore the convention
that ratified could withdraw those powers delegated or repeal the act as
our legislature can repeal the act of a previous one. As all government are
made for the good of the governed, wherever that government became
subversive of the ends for which it had been made and entered into it
is the right of the people to secede and I don't think it is a cause of war,
when we look at our origin and think how grievous was that apprehension or attempted coercion of our Fathers we should forbear shedding
blood, the blood of our brothers but alas that has been done and war
with all its horrors are upon us, and to that war there is and can be but
two powers, the slave and free states. . . .

If this government that we have both been taught to love so dearly
had never done but the one act of wrong, the violation of the provisions
of the treaty with France, it alone is cause sufficient to break it down. In
that treaty you know the government negotiated by and with Napoleon
the first, that every citizen of Louisiana should be citizen of the United

States and that they should enjoy all the rights of property and conscious that they did under the Emperor that they might carry their property and their religion any where within the Louisiana Territory and be protected there. . . . [F]our free states have already been made out of the Louisiana Territory and every remaining foot of it is a fair way to become antislavery Territory. . . .

Now my dear brother, all those old Frenchman had negroes and many of them added to the number by purchase from your northern free states and the title guaranteed of course to them and their children after them, but that guarantee turns out to be as worthless as the guarantee of the US in the treaty aforesaid of the whole of Louisiana Territory for the exercise of the right they enjoyed under Napoleon. But this is only a part of a systematic opposition that have been inaugurated for our distinction, the impressible conflict was invented for our subjugation. . . .

DOCUMENT 80

Letter from John Campbell to Neal Walters, June 10, 1861

Source: Small Manuscript Collection, 5.4, Arkansas
History Commission, Little Rock, Arkansas; reprinted in
James Johnson, ed., "Letter of John Campbell, Unionist,"
Arkansas Historical Quarterly 29, no. 2 (Summer 1970):
176–82.

John Campbell represented Searcy County in northern Arkansas, which had less than a 2 percent enslaved population, in the convention. A farmer who owned 240 acres and no slaves, Campbell was a former Whig and had served as both a county judge and member of the Arkansas General Assembly for two terms before he was elected as a Unionist to the convention. In the final secession vote in May, Campbell voted with four other delegates against Arkansas's secession ordinance. After David Walker appealed for a unanimous decision, Campbell, along with three others, changed his vote. In this letter to Neal Walters in Eureka Springs, Campbell explained his vote, claiming that he steadfastly supported the Union cause and tried to get the decision for secession to be referred to voters. In the end, he did not sign the ordinance of secession and hoped that the Union would be restored, even though he himself later served in the Confederate army.

Upon arrival home from the Convention I understand that there is some dissatisfaction relative to my course when at Little Rock in consequence of a report that I had voted for secession turned secessionist, turned traitor and played the Devil generally; if these reports were true it is or would be Just cause of compliant. All I have to say for the present is that I hope my fellow Citizens will wait until they see how I did vote (as the Journals of the Convention will soon be published) before they pass sentence against me. I have made a record upon the Journals in the face of as violent opposition to the views of my constituency (as well as my individual opinion) as any man ever had to vote against, a record that will give satisfaction to all reasonable minds; when that is done I think I should be acquitted; that of course is not for me; but for those who elected me to decide.

When the Convention first met they counted their respective numbers. The Union side was four the strongest and some two or three wavering. We voted Down their ordinances of Secession in every form they was presented. The Secessionists would not submit; we found out their next plan was to get the State out through the Governor and Legislature. To prevent that course we made a compromise with them and agreed to refer it to the people for them to vote in August, Secession or Cooperation, in order to find whether a majority was willing to cooperate with the border States or Secede without them; before that time arrived circumstances not expected took place and changed the minds of whole States; Virginia the Mother of States & Statesmen had changed from a majority of three to one to Secession. North Carolina and Tennessee followed as quick as they could do so.

The Convention of Arkansas was convened again. When we met the news was that everybody had changed from Union to Disunion except Searcy County. The Deligates from Independence County said that out of 2600 votes 2000 were for Secession. The Deligate from Izzard said he would be run over and out of the County if he did not go for Secession. From Newton and Marion (and) Pope and in fact all the Counties that had elected union deligates but this; the sentiment had change; or the Deligates lied. Something had changed their minds before they got back for they took the State out on Monday the day of meeting. There was no changes took place at the Rock because they voted before they told each other Howdy. There was some fifteen of us that voted to refere the action of the convention relative to the Secession ordainances back for affirmance or rejection by the people. This was the first vote, then on the final passage of the ordainance cutting our ties from the Old Government all voted for it but for a five. My vote was one of the five. After the die was cast and the State out of the union, at the earliest request of many prominent Statesmen that has been and still was union men at heart among whom I will mention that the Hon. David Walker, President of the Convention, Albert Rust—and others; four out of five admitted their votes changed in order that the announcement could be made on the wires to the Northern States that Arkansas was a unit against being subjugated or that her love for the union would not make her submit to be the instrument in the hands of abolitionists to coerse the Seceded States back. All hands had agreed at the first meeting of the Convention that Coersion would be resisted. I was the very last delegate that consented to make or suffer the change made. I did not wish to make Searcy County the pillage ground for the Desperadoes both North and South; there is a qualification or protest written upon the Journal showing that we protested against the Constitution right to secede that we surrendered no principle whatever. I never signed the devlish instrument. And after the ordinance had passed if it had not been signed by a quorum it would have been null and void. I then voted to refer the Provincial Constitution to the people which was lost. I then voted against its adoption.[5] I voted also in favor of referring the perma-nent Constitution to the people that was voted down. I voted against its adoption.[6] I voted against the Confiscation ordinance and against the ordinance relative to the Collection of debts. . . . My love for the Constitution and old union glows in my Bosome with as much ferver as ever; and I still have a lingering prospect that we will get back; when

---

5. Ratification of the provisional Confederate Constitution.
6. Ratification of the permanent Confederate Constitution: Campbell and other former Unionists hoped that the people would be able to vote on ratification.

the storm fury and when the passions of men are subdued. I understand that some say that the union men who was elected on the union ticket purgered themselves when they voted for Secession or to destroy the Constitution; this is a mistake for they was none of them under oath. They assembled in a sovereign capacity and was above Constitutions; that was their business to abolish and make organic laws and I suppose that there was a large majority of the people in favor of cutting loose from the old Government, at least that was the report of the Deligates from the respective Counties. I must in Justice say that I do not think any of the Union Deligates acted from anything; but of sense of representative duty.

INDEX

A

abolition/abolitionists: congressional legislation, 35; Hindman's perspective, 9–10; Indian Territory, 104–5, 162–63, 174–75, 228; Republican Party, xvii–xviii, 57–62, 188; slaveholding rights, 171

Adams, Charles W., 186, 189

Adams, C. W., 187

Adams, John, 4, 7

Alabama: Confederate government, 112; secession, xix, 61, 88, 95, 104, 141, 188; secession convention, xxi, 39, 122; secession debates, 49, 64; slaveholding rights, 129

amalgamation. *See* black equality

American Colonization Society, xviii

anti-slavery sentiment: 1860 election, 41–45, 55–62; Hindman's perspective, 7–8, 15–27; newspaper editorials, 35–39; northern states, 10–11, 142–43, 163–67, 208–10. *See also* abolition/abolitionists; Black Republicans; fugitive slave law

anti-union rebellion, xix–xx, xxii, 146–50

Arizona, 19

Arkansas County, 73–74, 187

Arkansas River, economic importance of, xv

Arkansas State Gazette: on anti-slavery sentiment, 34–36; on the Fort Sumter attack, 203–7

Arkansas Toothpick, xiii

Arkansas True Democrat, 178–83

Articles of Confederation, 130–31

Ashford, J. A., 159

Ashley County, 187

B

Badger Proviso, 35

Bean, Mark, 106–7

Bell, John, xvii, xix, 40

Benton County: secession debates, 69–73, 119–23; slave population, 69

Bentonville, 73

black equality: Black Republican platform, 58, 161–62; Johnson address, 112; newspaper editorials, 177–78, 181, 183–84; Republican Party, xvii–xviii; secession debates, xiv, xxi; voting rights, 171, 173

Black Republicans: black equality platform, 58, 161–62; compromise proposals, 116; definition, xvii; Hindman's perspective, 7–8, 18–21, 26; legislative petitions, 55–56; newspaper editorials, 37–39, 176–77; report on perceived abuses, 57–62. *See also* Lincoln, Abraham; secessionists

Bleeding Kansas, xviii, 66

Border States: balance of power, 105; doctrine of coercion, 112; secession convention, 168–69, 229–30; secession debates, 89–90, 116–19, 122–23, 125, 146–48, 162; slaveholding rights, 66–67

Borland, Solon, 221

Bradley, Thomas H., 188

Breckenridge, John C., xvii, xix, 40

Brown, John, 9, 15, 59, 73

Brown, Joseph, xxii, 207–15

Bush, J. W., 161–62

C

Cairo, Illinois, 225

Calhoun County, 219

Nebraska, 59. *See also* Kansas-Nebraska Act (1854)

negrophobia, 100

New Hampshire, 58

New Jersey: free labor system, 19; fugitive slave law, 58

New Mexico, 58

newspapers: on anti-slavery sentiment, 33–39; Fort Sumter attack, 203–7; secession debates, xxi, 175–84, 205–7

Newton County, xv, 93–94, 237

New York: anti-slavery sentiment, 10–11; constitutional amendments, 127; free labor system, 19; fugitive slave law, 58

North Carolina: abolition laws, 35; secession debates, 168; secessionist movement, 104; state convention petition, 102

Northern Democratic Party, xvii

northern states: anti-slavery sentiment, 7–8, 10–11, 15–27, 35–39, 41–45, 55–62, 142–43, 163–67, 208–10; free labor system, 9–14, 19, 166, 210–14; fugitive slave law, xvii–xviii, 10–11, 22, 37, 43–44, 57–59, 171; report on perceived abuses, 57–62; states' rights, xviii. *See also* abolition/abolitionists

Northwestern Territory, 35

O

Ohio: defensive operations, 224–25; fugitive slave law, 37–38, 58; secessionist movement, 198

Oldham, Williamson, xxi, 163–67

Old Line Democrat, xvi

ordinance of secession, 232–33

Oregon Territory, 35

P

Peace Conference, 198

Pemberton Spinning Operatives and Strikers, 11–14

Pennsylvania: free labor system, 19; fugitive slave law, 58

perceived injustices, 43–44, 57–62, 87–88, 140–41, 164–65, 170–71

Perry County, 188

personal liberty laws, xviii, 11, 36, 100, 165

Phillips County, 9, 41–42, 159–60, 186

Phillips, Wendell, 196

Pierce, Franklin, 35

Pike, Albert: anti-union rebellion, xix–xx, 146–50; on the right of secession, 124–50

Pine Bluff, 225, 234

Pittsburg, 105

plantation agriculture, xv

Polk, James K., 35

Pope County, 237

popular sovereignty doctrine, xvii, xix–xx, 130

Prairie County, 160, 188

property rights, xvii, xix, 120–22, 165, 170–73

Provisional Confederate Congress, 163

Pulaski County, 185

R

railroads, xv

Rector, Henry: on abolition agitation, 104–5, 228; call for volunteer troops, xxii, 190, 217–18, 224; on defensive operations, 224–27; 1860 election, xvii; on the extension of slavery, 154–56; federal arsenal crisis, xx, 158–60, 224; message to secession convention, 223–28; military preparations, 65–66; militia code speech, 30–32; on the right of secession, 152–58; secession debates, 62–65, 81; western border security, 66–67

report on perceived abuses, 57–62

Republican Party: anti-slavery sentiment, 10, 15–27, 35–39, 55–62, 142–43, 163–67; 1860 election, xvii–xix, 29, 34, 188; Hindman's perspective, 9–10, 15–27; report on perceived abuses, 57–62. *See also* Black Republicans

Reussell, J. B., 107
Rhode Island, 58
Robinson, S., 162
Ross, John, 104–5
Rothman, Adam, xiv
Rust, Albert, 186, 238

S

Saline County, 91–93, 186
Searcy County, 93–94, 236, 237
Sebastian County: delegate campaigns,
98–101; secession debates, 78–80;
slave population, 42, 94; state
convention petition, 94–95
secession convention: border state
convention, 168–69, 229–31; call to
reconvene, 218–21, 222; key issues,
170–71; message from Rector,
223–28; newspaper editorials,
175–84; opposition resolution,
174–75; ordinance of secession,
232–33; proposed constitutional
amendments, 171–73; remembrances, 184–91; slaveholding rights,
160–67; Unionist manifesto,
194–200; Unionists/cooperationists,
151, 168–73, 184–90, 200–201,
219–21, 229–32, 234–39
secessionists: Faulkner correspondence,
39–41; federal arsenal crisis, xx,
46–47, 158–60, 224; General
Assembly Resolution, 32–33, 43–47;
historical perspective, xiii–xiv, xviii–
xxii; military aid, 201–3; platform
comparisons, 119–23; political
debates, xxi–xxiii, 33–39, 60–62;
on the right of secession, 124–50,
152–58; Robert Ward Johnson,
47–54, 112–19; slaveholding rights,
76–78, 142–45, 160–67, 207–15; state
convention campaigns, 97–103; state
convention delegates, xx–xxiii;
Taylor correspondence, 234–36
sectionalism: Confederate government,
113; 1860 election, 68, 74, 75, 77, 79,
85, 91, 197; fugitive slave law, xviii;
Indian Territory, 90; newspaper

editorials, 35, 36; northern states,
207, 209; Republican Party, 10, 16,
21, 170, 188, 232; secession convention, 160–62, 168, 174, 195, 229;
state convention petition, 92, 173.
See also Black Republicans
Sedition Act (1798), 5–6
Sevier County, 187
Sevier family, xvi
Seward, William, 15, 18–19, 116, 126
Sherman, John, 9, 10, 17, 18, 21–25, 59
S. H. Tucker (steamship), 159
slavery: abolition laws, 35; anti-slavery
sentiment, 7–8, 10–11, 15–27, 35–39,
41–45, 55–62, 142–43, 163–67,
208–10; Crittenden Compromise,
103; economic importance, xiv–xv;
military service, 216; political
debates, xvi–xxi; population
percentages, xv, 41–42; slaveholding
rights, 66–67, 76–78, 142–45,
160–67, 170–73, 207–15; slave
stealing, 17–18, 22–24; Unionist
manifesto, 194–200; westward
expansion, xvii. See also fugitive
slave law; secessionists; states' rights
Smith, J. M., 186–87
Smoote, G. P., 161–62
Sons of Confederate Veterans (SCV),
xiii
South Carolina secession: committee
report, 61; doctrine of coercion,
204; Faulkner correspondence,
39–40; historical perspective, xix,
41, 75, 95, 141, 154, 188; Johnson's
perspective, 49, 51; justifications, 86;
legislative petitions, 42, 45;
newspaper editorials, 34; ordinance
of secession, 122, 198; Rector's
perspective, 64, 104; state convention impact, 67, 69, 80, 88, 95, 107
Southern Democratic Party, xvii
southern states: anti-union rebellion,
xix–xx, xxii, 146–50; perceived
injustices, 57–62, 164–65, 170–71;
property rights, xvii, xix, 120–22,
165, 170–73; secessionist movement,